Henrie Stewart Duke of
Albanye and Marie
Quem of Scotland
1566

THE MEMOIRS OF SIR JAMES MELVILLE OF HALHILL

Containing an impartial Account of the most remarkable AFFAIRS of STATE during the Sixteenth Century, not mentioned by other Historians: more particularly relating to the Kingdoms of ENGLAND and SCOTLAND, under the Reigns of Queen ELIZABETH, MARY, Queen of Scots, and King JAMES. In most of which TRANSACTIONS the AUTHOR was Personally and Publicly concerned.

Edited and with an introduction by
GORDON DONALDSON

THE FOLIO SOCIETY
LONDON 1969

PRINTED IN GREAT BRITAIN
Printed and bound by W & J Mackay & Co Ltd, Chatham
Set in Van Dijck 12 point
Illustrations printed by Jarrold & Sons Ltd, Norwich

Contents

The arms used for the binding design are taken from a sixteenth-century manuscript Scotland's Nobility *in* The College of Arms, London, *and show the arms of Mary, Queen of Scots, impaled with those of her second husband Lord Darnley.*

Illustrations

Introduction

I

Sir James Melville of Halhill was a courtier not only in his native Scotland but also in England and on the Continent, in the era of the Reformation and in the time of Mary, Queen of Scots, Elizabeth Tudor and Catherine de' Medici. For many countries the period was one of crisis and decision, and for Scotland in particular the question was whether she should cast off the papacy, break her ancient alliance with France, embrace the Reformation and come to terms with England.

For more than two centuries Scotland's history had very largely been shaped by her relations with England and France. England was the 'old enemy', whose repeated attempts to conquer Scotland had inflicted on the Scots many heavy defeats but had in the end been successfully resisted. France, if only because she also was England's enemy and, like Scotland, a target for English attempts at conquest, was Scotland's 'old ally', tied to Scotland by a treaty made so early as 1295 and many times renewed. On paper, the Franco-Scottish alliance committed the two countries to mutual assistance against English aggression, and in practice many Scots frequently gave military service in France, while French forces occasionally came to Scotland; but on the whole the French tended to invoke the treaty when it suited them to stimulate the Scots into making attacks on England which would divert English attention from the Continent. The latest occasion on which the Scots were prevailed on to serve as a French tool had been in 1513, when James IV, in Melville's words, 'without purpose passed with his army at the pleasure of France against his own brother-in-law the king of England,★ where he lost his life at the field of Flodden and imperilled his whole country.' After Flodden, the Scots, or some of them, began to reflect that the old alliance had been a one-sided affair, and never again could the Scottish nobles be prevailed on to cross that fatal frontier and risk a repetition of the disaster of 1513. This was one reason behind the emergence in Scotland of a pro-English party, or at any rate a party which thought that

★ James was married to Margaret Tudor, sister of Henry VIII.

the orientation of Scotland's foreign policy should be reconsidered.

The growth of a definitely pro-English faction in Scotland was soon encouraged by the onset of the Reformation. Already in the 1520s, the teachings of Luther were reaching Scotland, and within a decade, as Melville shows, many prominent Scots were committed to the reforming cause. After Henry VIII repudiated papal supremacy, those Scots who favoured the Reformation saw in England an example, and some of them, at odds with the authorities in their own country, found in England a refuge. On the other hand, those whose ecclesiastical opinions were conservative tended to favour the old alliance with France, and by the late 1530s there had taken shape two distinct parties – a conservative or Roman Catholic party, looking to France and willing to see Scotland used in a crusade against the schismatic Henry VIII, and a reforming party which thought that Scotland should follow English example in ecclesiastical affairs and should stand with England against the papalist powers of the Continent. In the divisions among the Scots lies the explanation of the disaster which brought the reign of James V to an end in 1542.

James V, although he was not unaware of the moral shortcomings of the Scottish clergy and of the unrest caused by the financial exactions of a corrupt church, was by upbringing and policy inclined to orthodoxy and to the French alliance, and by 1537 was under the domination of the clerical and francophile faction. He contracted two successive French marriages, the second of them to Mary of Guise-Lorraine, and committed his country to the cause of France and the papacy. Henry VIII, anxious to avoid encirclement, resorted to various persuasive tactics, and in 1542 brought James to the point of agreeing to meet him at York.

James, however, was exposed at home to both bids and counter-bids. The friends of the Reformation pointed out the financial advantages which would accrue to him if he followed Henry's example. 'Did not one of your predecessors', they asked, 'give the most part of the patrimony of the crown to the kirk, erecting the same into bishoprics and rich abbacies, whereby your Majesty is presently so poor, and the prelates so rich, so prodigal, so proud, that they will suffer nothing to be done without them?' They urged the King to 'take home again to the profit of the crown all vacant benefices as they may fall by decease of every prelate'. James was stimulated into rounding on the churchmen: 'Wherefore gave my predecessors so many lands and rents to the kirk? Was it to maintain hawks, dogs and whores to a number of idle priests? The King of England burns, the King of Denmark beheads you; I shall stick you with this whinger.' Whereupon he 'drew out his dagger upon them, and they fled from his presence in great fear'.

But the Scottish clergy, fearing the possible consequences to themselves should the two kings meet, used all their influence to prevail on
James to break his appointment. They too could offer financial inducements. They told him that if he prosecuted the many nobles and barons
who favoured reform he would augment his revenues by the escheats
of their goods, and Melville is one of the writers who tells us that the
churchmen gave the king the names of the heretical noblemen and
gentlemen 'in a roll of paper, which the king put in his pocket, thinking it a meet proposition and profitable to put into execution'. They
also offered to pay James 50,000 crowns yearly out of the ecclesiastical
revenues to hire soldiers in case the King of England should make war
on him for not keeping his appointment at York.

James yielded to the prelates, and war with England followed. But
the King of Scots was unable to carry the nation with him in the line he
had chosen. 'The king could not but raise an army to defend his
country and subjects, who went to that war to show their obedience,
against their hearts. But when they perceived Oliver Sinclair [the
king's favourite] raised up upon men's shoulders and proclaimed lieutenant over the whole army beside Solway Moss, Lord Maxwell and
the rest of the lords, who misliked that the court and country should be
governed by such men, would not fight under such a lieutenant, but
suffered themselves all to be taken prisoners.' The engagement at
Solway Moss (24 November 1542) was a complete rout for the Scots.
James died in the following month, 'a worn out, desperate man at the
age of thirty years'* leaving as his heir a week-old daughter, Mary.

The office of governor of the realm fell to the Earl of Arran, head of
the house of Hamilton and, as senior descendant of a daughter of James
II, heir-presumptive to the throne. For a brief space, ascendancy over
the governor was gained by the pro-English and reforming faction,
who imprisoned Cardinal David Beaton, head of the Scottish hierarchy,
authorized the circulation of the scriptures in the vernacular, and
arranged for the marriage of Mary to Prince Edward of England, a boy
of six. But within a few months, Beaton, again at large, prevailed on
Arran to change his policy and to withdraw from the marriage treaty.
Henry, in his fury, launched on Scotland two devastating invasions,
in 1544 and 1545, which were in effect actions for breach of promise and
are known as the Rough Wooing. A similar policy was continued after
Henry's death, for the Duke of Somerset, Protector under the young
Edward VI, defeated the Scots at Pinkie (1547) and planted English
garrisons in a number of strong points in south-eastern Scotland. As
Scotland was distracted by the defection to the English side of those
who were committed to the reforming cause, it could not from its own

---

* F. W. Maitland, in *Cambridge Modern History*, ii, 555.

resources eject the occupying armies, and had to appeal to France for help. The help was given, but only on condition that Queen Mary, who had at one time been destined to be the bride of the heir to the throne of England, should be sent to France as the prospective bride of the Dauphin, the heir to the throne of France. She went to France in 1548.

But Scotland had escaped from an English occupation only to be threatened by a French occupation. Especially after 1554, when Arran was superseded as governor by Mary of Guise, the queen mother, Frenchmen were appointed to high offices in Scotland and French soldiers were introduced to garrison Scottish fortresses. In French eyes, Scotland was a base from which an attack could be mounted against Berwick-on-Tweed, the last relic of English attempts at the conquest of Scotland, at the same time as an attack was also made on Calais, the last relic of English attempts to conquer France. In 1558 Mary, Queen of Scots, married the Dauphin Francis, who in the following year became King of France, and her mother's family, the house of Guise, directed French affairs. The French view was that the sovereignty of Scotland had been transferred to the French royal house, and the prospect for Scotland was rule by the French king and his descendants, under whom Scotland could not fail to be absorbed into France.

Although financial inducements were held out to influence prominent Scots to acquiesce in French policy, and although Mary of Guise displayed considerable tactical skill in conciliating some sections of Scottish opinion, the Scottish reaction against the display of French imperialism was sharp. It was also predictable, for, despite the long history of the old alliance, the Scots had never cared much for the French at close quarters, and French troops had never been welcome visitors to Scotland. At this juncture, national resentment against the threat of French domination reinforced the other motives which had led to the growth of an anti-French and pro-English party. And it was probably this new factor which was decisive in determining that the pro-English party should prevail. The Scottish protestants had indeed been growing in numbers in the late 1550s, until, as Melville says, 'the most part of the country became professors of the reformed religion'. They were also showing considerable audacity, and they could now appeal to patriotism as well as religion. Even so, it is doubtful if a revolution could ever have been carried through against the queen dowager and her standing army of trained French troops had a situation not developed in which an English government was ready to intervene in Scotland.

Mary Tudor, the English queen who had pursued a papalist policy, died in November 1558 and was succeeded by her sister, Elizabeth.

The latter was regarded as the hope of the protestants who had been persecuted under Mary, and she soon began to move towards a church settlement which would satisfy at least the moderate reformers. But Elizabeth was the last surviving child of Henry VIII, and her heir presumptive, by right of blood if not by the will of Henry, was her cousin Mary Stewart, Queen of Scots and of France. Not only so, but in the eyes of Roman Catholics, Elizabeth, born to Anne Boleyn while Catherine of Aragon still lived, was illegitimate, and Mary was the rightful possessor of the English crown. After the death of Mary Tudor, Mary Stewart and her husband assumed the style of 'King and Queen of Scotland, England and Ireland, Dauphin and Dauphiness of Viennois'; and, Melville says, the Cardinal of Lorraine, Mary's uncle, 'shortly after caused to be renewed all the Queen of Scotland's silver vessels, and engraved thereon the arms of England'. It was clearly to Elizabeth's interest if not to oust Mary from the Scottish throne at least to weaken her position in Scotland and, above all, to have the French ejected from that country.

Elizabeth's opportunity came when a revolt broke out in Scotland in 1559. In the spring, Mary of Guise had suddenly turned fiercely on the protestants: 'she began to persecute, and they to rebel and take the fields, binding themselves together under the name of the congregation. Thereafter they broke down images, kirks and cloisters'. Among the leaders of 'the lords of the congregation' who directed the revolt were Lord James Stewart, Commendator of the priory of St Andrews, an illegitimate half-brother of Queen Mary, and the Duke of Châtelherault (formerly Earl of Arran), heir presumptive to the Scottish throne. Either of them could have been a candidate for the throne should Mary be deposed, but Scottish opinion was on the whole against the formal supersession of the lawful sovereign, and authority was assumed by a 'great council of the realm', with Châtelherault as its figurehead. Elizabeth sent help, first by sea, then by land, and in July 1559, after the situation had been simplified by the death of Mary of Guise (11 June), it was arranged that both French and English forces should be withdrawn from Scotland, leaving the Scots free to settle their own affairs. In August a parliament in Edinburgh repudiated papal authority and adopted a reformed Confession of Faith.

It now seemed possible that Mary, who had been in France for twelve years and whose husband had become King of France in 1559, might remain there and never return to a Scotland which had so decisively repudiated France and much that France stood for. But in December 1560 Francis II died. Contemporaries were agreed that this event completely changed the situation. Melville's comment is, 'The king's death made a great change'; and John Knox remarked 'The death of this king made great alteration in France, England and Scotland.' In France Mary was now nothing more than a widowed queen, and power passed from her family, the house of Guise, to the queen mother, Catherine de' Medici, as regent for the young Charles IX, brother of Francis. 'The queen mother was content to be quit of the government of the house of Guise; and for this cause she had a great misliking for our queen [Mary] . . . for she was in effect a deadly enemy to all of them who had either guided her husband or her eldest son . . . Our queen also, seeing her friends in disgrace and knowing herself not to be well liked, left the court.' Thus Mary's better prospects now lay in Scotland, if only as a possible avenue to the throne of England on which her heart was set. Her friends 'advised her to return to Scotland, rather than to endure the queen mother's disdain in France'.

In Scotland she clearly faced a delicate situation, but skilful preparations were made for her return. Her French advisers counselled her 'to serve the time, to accommodate herself discreetly and gently to her own subjects; to be most familiar with my Lord James, Prior of St Andrews, her natural brother, . . . and in effect, to repose most upon those of the reformed religion'. Lord James himself came to France to request Mary to come home, 'promising to serve her faithfully to the utmost of his power', and he returned again to Scotland before her, 'to prepare the hearts of her subjects against her home-coming'.

When Mary returned to Scotland, in August 1561, she 'was gladly welcomed by the whole subjects; for, following the counsel of her friends, she behaved herself humanely to them all, but committed the chief handling of her affairs unto her brother the Prior of St Andrews, whom afterwards she made Earl of Moray, and to the secretary, Lethington, as meetest both to hold the country at her devotion and also to beget a strict friendship between Her Majesty and the Queen of England. For my Lord Moray had great credit with my Lord Robert Dudley, who was afterwards made Earl of Leicester, and the secretary, Lethington, had great credit with the [English] secretary, Cecil. So these four made a strict and sisterly friendship between the two queens and their countries.' The policy of the Earl of Moray and William Maitland of Lethington was to work for mutual recognition between Mary and Elizabeth – recognition by Mary of Elizabeth's right to the English throne as long as she lived and recognition by Elizabeth of Mary's right to succeed. Mary co-operated in this policy and showed considerable skill in conciliating the reformers in Scotland but at the same time reassuring the Roman Catholic interest in England and on the Continent. Relations with Elizabeth were for a time so good 'that letters and intelligence passed weekly by post between them, and nothing more desired for the first than that they might see one another, by a meeting at a convenient place, whereby they might also declare their hearty and loving minds each to other'. Elizabeth, however, would not be brought either to a conference with Mary or to recognition of her right to the English succession.

The English queen's attitude to proposals for Mary's marriage also proved, for a time, to be mainly negative, and in particular she was critical of the negotiations for a marriage to the Archduke Charles of Austria. At length she made the barely credible suggestion that Mary should marry her own favourite, Lord Robert Dudley, whom she created Earl of Leicester. Melville relates that when he was at the English court in 1564 Queen Elizabeth 'entered with me very familiarly, showing me the sisterly love that was betwixt her and the queen my sovereign, how careful she was of her welfare, how desirous to see her well settled in her own country with her subjects, and also well married'. She also declared that 'she had in her head two persons to propose, any one of the two, for fittest husbands unto her, whereby their amity might best stand and increase'. One of the candidates, it emerged, was Dudley, and Elizabeth's ambassador to Scotland had instructions to sound Moray and Lethington on the subject. But the other candidate, of whom more was to be heard, was Mary's first cousin, Henry Stewart, Lord Darnley, son of the Earl of Lennox. Melville's account is that when it became evident that the Dudley proposal was not likely to be welcome in Scotland, 'occasion was taken to grant leave to Matthew, Earl of Lennox, who dwelt then in England, to go to Scotland, as desirous to see the queen and take order with some of his own affairs. His eldest son, my Lord Darnley, was a lusty young prince, and apparently was one of the two that the Queen of England had told me that she had in her head to offer unto our queen, as born within the realm of England.'

Elizabeth's unco-operative attitude, in refusing to acknowledge Mary as her successor, had gone far to render bankrupt the policy which Moray and Maitland had commended to their queen. It is impossible to say what other course might have proved more politic as a substitute, but Mary's actions suddenly ceased to be guided by politicians. At the beginning of 1565 Lord Darnley arrived in Scotland, and Mary took an immediate liking to him. His father, Lennox, stood next to the Hamilton line in the Scottish succession and, by marrying Margaret Douglas, daughter of Margaret Tudor (sister of Henry VIII), he had put his family next after Mary in the English succession. Lennox had committed himself so deeply to Henry VIII's interest in the 1540s that he had been forfeited for treason and had spent the greater part of twenty years in England, where his son, Darnley, was born and brought up.

Mary's troubles can be dated from her marriage to Darnley (29 July 1565), which made enemies for her on all sides. Elizabeth, although she had permitted Darnley's return from England and knew its possible sequel, expressed indignation; Moray and Maitland lost their influence on policy; the powerful Hamilton interest was alienated by the elevation of the rival family of Lennox; and, although Darnley was not at this time a committed or practising Roman Catholic, the fact that the marriage was by Roman Catholic rites roused apprehensions among the protestants. There was even a rather aimless rebellion, led by Moray and energetically suppressed by Mary. If the queen had thus lost many friends, she had gained nothing in compensation, for Darnley was so worthless, both intellectually and morally, that, although the government was carried on in the names of King Henry and Queen Mary, she could not allow him to share political power, and the two were soon estranged from each other.

Darnley, disappointed and petulant, was prepared to come to terms with the recently defeated rebels and with the politicians who had lost influence through his marriage. It was an unnatural alliance, for men who had objected to Darnley's marriage to the queen now plotted with him to give him power, but their common interest extended at least as far as the elimination of Mary's musician and secretary, David Riccio, who was believed to have supplanted both the politicians and Darnley in the queen's favour. The murder of Riccio, carried out with unnecessary brutality almost in the queen's presence on 9 March 1566, was obviously designed to endanger the life of Mary and the life of the child of which she was six months pregnant. Had its most sinister object been achieved, Darnley would have been sole sovereign of Scotland and heir presumptive to England. Mary, however, not only survived the ordeal, but outwitted her enemies by detaching Darnley from his allies, and they, far from regaining power, had to go into exile. The queen's reconciliation with Darnley endured after a fashion until the birth of Prince James on 19 June 1566, but not much longer, and by the autumn it was evident that there was an irreparable breach between them, while James Hepburn, Earl of Bothwell, rose in the queen's favour.

Darnley had made many enemies. His fellow conspirators against Riccio felt that he had betrayed them; there were loyal subjects of Mary who felt that she should be released from a bond which had become intolerable; there were those who calculated that if both Mary and Darnley were out of the way they might dominate an infant king; the evidence about the Earl of Bothwell's aims at this point is dubious, but if he was already planning to marry the queen then the removal of Darnley was essential. On the other hand, as his share in the Riccio murder had shown, Darnley was no innocent, and the possibility cannot be excluded that he was seeking once more to encompass the death of his wife and his own elevation to power in Scotland as guardian of his son and to the first place in the succession to the throne of England.

Amid a complexity of plotting, the truth about the events at Kirk o' Field on the night of 9–10 February 1567 cannot be determined. The house in which Darnley resided – and in which Mary had sometimes spent the night – was blown up; but Darnley was found dead in the garden nearby, with no marks on his body. Many recent investigators see the coincidental outcome of two plots, one by Darnley against Mary, one by Bothwell or others against Darnley. The common view at the time, shared by Sir James Melville, was that Bothwell was the chief criminal, but Melville did not agree with those who blamed the queen as a partner in the crime.

At any rate, Darnley's death was followed by Mary's marriage to Bothwell and by a rebellion which led to her deposition and her imprisonment in Lochleven Castle, while the infant James was crowned king and Moray became regent. Many, including Melville, felt that Mary had not merited such harsh treatment and that Moray, content with the support of a faction, made insufficient efforts to bring about general agreement among the nobles. The weight of opinion in favour of Mary and against Moray became evident when Mary escaped from Lochleven in May 1568 and rapidly mustered an army, but after her defeat at Langside she fled to England and Moray remained in control in Scotland.

Not for the first time, the future of Scotland and the stability of its government now depended largely on the attitude of Elizabeth. It was open to her either to restore Mary or to recognize James, but she was reluctant to do either, and more than her constitutional irresolution lay behind her prolonged hesitation. On the one hand, Mary as a refugee was an embarrassment because she was a potential focus for disaffection in England; many of Mary's supporters in Scotland were old friends to the cause of Anglo-Scottish amity; and to recognize James involved countenancing revolt against a lawful sovereign. On the other hand, Moray's party had no choice but to maintain the Reformation and could in no conceivable circumstances be a danger to England. It was so difficult for Elizabeth to make up her mind that she could not even bring to a decisive conclusion the investigation which was held in 1568, at York, Westminster and Hampton Court, into the charges brought by Moray against his sister as an adulteress and a murderess. Years more passed before she came down definitely on the side of King James's supporters against Mary. Her vacillation, by helping to keep Mary's cause alive in Scotland, contributed to instability and even civil war in that country, and it is hardly surprising that Melville saw in English policy nothing more than a desire to foster divisions in his country.

Moray was murdered in January 1570, and was followed as regent by Darnley's father, Lennox, who was killed in an affray in September 1571. John, Earl of Mar, the third regent, died, so it is said, because he loved peace and could not have it. Then came James, Earl of Morton, a man with the vigour that the office demanded and a consistent friend to England and the Reformation. In 1573 Elizabeth at last sent an artillery train to enable Morton to capture Edinburgh Castle, Mary's last stronghold, and bring the Scottish civil war between 'Queen's Men' and 'King's Men' to an end.

Morton, although he showed much statesmanship in his administration, seems to have done nothing to try to win the attachment of the young king and little to counter the designs of those who opposed him from either personal or political motives. In the spring of 1578, by the first of a series of palace revolutions which punctuated Scottish history for seven years, Morton was displaced as regent, and power was seized by a group of notables who declared that authority was now vested in the person of the king, although James was as yet barely twelve years old. Within a few months, however, Morton regained his ascendancy and was again at the head of the administration, though without the title of regent. His position was next undermined with the appearance at the Scottish court of Esmé Stewart, seigneur d'Aubigny, who arrived from France in September 1579.

Esmé was a cousin of the king's father, Darnley. Darnley's younger brother, Charles, Earl of Lennox, had died in 1576, leaving only an infant daughter, Arabella. Next in the Lennox line was Robert, Bishop of Caithness, uncle of Darnley and of Esmé, a man over sixty years of age. Thus Esmé was, after his uncle Robert, the male heir of the house of Lennox, the king's nearest kinsman on his father's side, and, failing Arabella, the inheritor of the Lennox interest in the Scottish succession. James, in his early adolescence, was captivated by his cousin, a man in his late thirties, and on the basis of this personal attachment Esmé established an ascendancy in Scottish affairs. The devoted king created him first Earl, later Duke, of Lennox. It seems on the whole unlikely that Esmé had any other intention than to push his own fortunes, but he became entangled in the strife of Scottish factions. Morton had been faithful to the English alliance and to protestantism, though he had no sympathy with the presbyterian party which, under Andrew Melville, was gaining power in the church. But there was a more conservative faction, associated with the cause of the captive Queen Mary, prepared to negotiate with papal agents and interested in maintaining links with

THE SIEGE OF LEITH, 1560

France and Spain. Morton's opponents, whether on personal or political grounds, found a focus in Esmé Stewart, and at the end of 1580 the
ex-regent was arrested on a charge of complicity in Darnley's murder
and was executed. His accuser was James Stewart, who had also become
a favourite of the king and who was made Earl of Arran.

Lennox and Arran found colleagues in some former supporters of
Mary who had been excluded from office while Morton was in power,
like John Maitland of Thirlestane (Lethington's brother). Their
administration can perhaps be characterized as 'right-wing', for it was
based on general conservative preferences, to some extent on the
Marian and Roman Catholic interests, and on the maintenance of
episcopacy against the attacks of the presbyterians. Esmé himself
made no difficulty about professing the reformed faith; it would have
been contrary to his own interest to further the restoration of Mary,
since his influence depended on James; and, while he represented
continental influence in a general way, there is no reason to believe
that he would have supported a Spanish attempt to conquer Britain.
Yet he attracted the attention of those who thought that they could use
him in various fanciful schemes on behalf of Spain and the counter-
Reformation, and the appearance in Scotland of Jesuit priests led to a
kind of 'popish scare' which reaffirmed the hostility of the presbyterians and ultra-protestants to a régime which maintained episcopacy.

Opposed to the interests which were countenanced under Lennox
there was an ultra-protestant faction, militant in both its political and
its ecclesiastical outlook, anxious for complete alignment with England
against the threat of Roman Catholicism at home and abroad. This
party was the heir of the revolutions of 1560 and 1567, and just as those
revolutions had had the support of reforming ministers, so the ultra-
protestant party now had the support of the presbyterians. Lennox's
ascendancy was brought to an end by a palace revolution known as the
Ruthven Raid, involving the seizure of the king's person, in August
1582. This coup was led by the Earl of Gowrie, head of the house of
Ruthven, and his supporters represented the tradition of adherence to
the Reformation and the English alliance. The general assembly of the
reformed church, which found the ultra-protestant and anglophile
character of the new government congenial, gave the coup its blessing
and in return received a measure of countenance for the presbyterian
programme. Here, clearly, the pendulum had swung hard over, and we
have a left-wing administration.

James escaped from the Ruthven Raiders in June 1583. Lennox had
been forced to leave the country, and had died in France, but the
government was soon headed by his old colleague, James Stewart, Earl
of Arran, who became chancellor. This was a right-wing government

once more, though in some ways more moderate than that of Lennox and free from serious involvement in Mary's cause or continental intrigues. The office of secretary went to Maitland of Thirlestane, who resembled his brother, Lethington, in his enthusiasm for amity with England. The conservative character of the régime was shown most markedly in its ecclesiastical legislation, for episcopal government was reaffirmed and the presbyteries condemned. Arran was so feared and hated that his critics had to flee to England, and the leaders of the Ruthven party were followed across the Border by about a score of the leading presbyterian ministers.

The attitude of the English government to this series of palace revolutions was often ambiguous. There were English politicians who were deeply committed to the ultra-protestant and puritan cause, and they constantly strove to secure English support for Scottish governments of whose policy they approved. However, Elizabeth, who on the whole adhered to a policy of detachment, had declined to intervene to save her good friend Morton, to give serious support to the opposition to Lennox or to subsidize the Ruthven Raiders on what they considered to be an adequate scale. When James escaped from the pro-English Ruthven Raiders and took refuge with the friends of Arran, reports that he was in the hands of 'favourers of the French and of the King's mother' caused such alarm in England that Walsingham himself, the secretary of state, was sent to Scotland. With his ultra-protestant prejudices and his presbyterian sympathies he formed a very unfavourable impression of the situation, and refused to have any dealings with Arran. But other English politicians, and the queen herself, saw things differently, and it was with Arran's administration that England finally agreed to formulate a definite league, in July of 1585.

Arran fell from power at the end of 1585, when the exiled lords returned from England and brought about yet another bloodless revolution by making a demonstration in force at Stirling. But the government which emerged was in the nature of a coalition and not a mere replacement of one extreme wing by another. The leading man in the new administration was soon Maitland of Thirlestane, of whom it was said that 'he held the king on two grounds sure, never to cast out with the kirk or with England'. At what precise point real power passed from Maitland to James himself, who was twenty-one in 1587, it is impossible to determine, but it has been neatly said that Maitland 'trained a successor. His successor was the king himself.'*

At any rate, from about 1586 interest centres on the king and his government rather than on the strife of factions. James still had many difficulties to overcome, but the rival factions which had dominated

* Maurice Lee, *John Maitland of Thirlestane*, 291.

Scottish politics in past years had now lost much of their force: the league with England meant that the ultra-protestants could no longer look for encouragement from south of the Border, while the execution of Mary, in 1587, took some of the purpose out of the Roman Catholic faction's intrigues. The conservative northern earls, led by Huntly, engaged in some rather aimless plotting and sometimes set the king at defiance, and one of the notable events of the period was the murder by Huntly of 'the Bonnie Earl o' Moray' (son-in-law of the regent), who was a favourite of the protestants. But after 1586 there were no more palace revolutions, and, despite some startling adventures resulting from the wild escapades of Francis Stewart, Earl of Bothwell, the king steadily increased his authority throughout the country. By 1596 he had established complete ascendancy over both the extreme factions – the northern earls who intrigued with Spain and the fanatical presbyterians who wanted in effect to subordinate the state to the prevailing party in the church. It is approximately at this point – the year of James's triumph – that Melville concludes his Memoirs.

II

Melville's career, as a soldier, a courtier and a diplomat, gave him first-hand acquaintance with the chief events of the reigns of Mary and James VI. His autobiography, as he relates it in his *Memoirs*, begins in 1550 when he was fourteen. It happened that the Bishop of Valence, who had been on a diplomatic mission in Scotland, was returning to France, and Mary of Guise, the queen mother, sent Melville with him 'to be placed page of honour to the queen, her daughter'. Melville's account of his journey to Paris illustrates the manifold hazards of sixteenth-century travel and contains episodes which recall the *Decameron*. Sailing from Irvine, in Ayrshire, in January 1550, their vessel was storm-stayed for seventeen days off the island of Sanda before crossing the North Channel, and then had to put into one of the Ulster loughs after 'the skipper and mariners had lost all hopes of safety'. They were welcomed by a local chieftain, O'Dogherty.

'The next morning O'Dogherty came there, and conveyed us to his house, which was a great dark tower, where we had cold cheer, as herring and biscuit; for it was Lent. There finding two English grey friars who had fled out of England (for King Edward VI was yet alive), the said friars perceiving the bishop to look very kindly to O'Dogherty's daughter, who fled from him continually, they brought to him a woman who spoke English, to lie with him. Which harlot being kept quietly in his chamber, found a little glass within a case standing in a window; for the coffers were all wet with the sea-waves that fell into the ship during the storm. She believing it had been ordained to be eaten, because it had an odoriferous smell, therefore she licked it clean out; which put the bishop into such a rage that he cried out for impatience, discovering his harlotry and his choler in such sort as the friars fled, and the woman followed. But the Irishman and his own servants did laugh at the matter; for it was a vial of the most precious balm that grew in Egypt, which Solyman the Great Turk had given in a present to the said Bishop, after he had been two years ambassador for the King of France in Turkey, and was esteemed worth 2,000 crowns. In the time that we remained at O'Dogherty's house, his young daughter who fled from the bishop, came and sought me wherever I was, and brought a priest with her who could speak English, and offered, if I would marry her, to go with me wherever I pleased. I gave her thanks; but told her that I was yet young, and had no estate, and was bound for France.'

After some weeks in Ireland, the party was carried not on to France but back to Scotland, possibly because the ship in which they had crossed to Ireland was no longer seaworthy. On the crossing, they 'rested a night in the isle of Jura, and the next night in the isle of Bute. But by the way we lost our rudder, and were in great danger of drowning'. They landed at Dumbarton and rode to Stirling, 'where, after eight days, the ambassador took leave of the queen and rode again to Dumbarton, where there were two French ships ready to receive us. So, sailing by the Isle of Man and along the south coast of Ireland, we landed at Conquet in Brittany eight days after our embarking, not without some danger by the way, both from English ships and a great storm; so that once at midnight the mariners cried that we were all lost.' The bishop at once hastened on to Paris, leaving Melville to follow more slowly, with two other Scots. More picaresque adventures awaited him.

'Now we three enquired, and found out two young men, the one a Frenchman, the other a Breton, who were to ride the same way, as also a young gentleman of Spain who was passing also to the college at Paris. Our first day's journey from Brest was to a town called Laderny,★ where we were all six lodged in a chamber with three beds; the two Frenchmen had one bed, the two Scots another, the Spaniard and myself the third. I overheard the two Scotsmen discoursing together, that they were directed by the bishop to let me want for nothing; "therefore", said they, "we will pay for his ordinary all the way, and shall account twice as much to his master as we disburse, when we come to Paris, and so shall gain our own expense." The two Frenchmen, not thinking that any of us understood French, were saying to themselves, "these strangers are all young, and know not the fashion of the hostel-

★ ? Landerneau.

ries; therefore we shall reckon with the host at every repast, and shall cause the strangers to pay more than the custom is, and that way we shall save our own charges." Accordingly the next day they went to put it in execution. But I could not forbear laughing in my mind, and told the young Spaniard, for I understood French, and so we were upon our guard: yet the two Scotsmen would not consent that I should pay for my self, hoping that way to beguile the bishop; but the Spaniard and I wrote up every day's account. On the way, riding through a wood, the two Frenchmen had appointed other two to ride with us, which two, in the midst of the wood, lighted off their horses, and drew out their swords. But the two Frenchmen, beholding our countenance, and seeing that we were making for our defence, they too drew out their swords, then they made a sport of it, and would but see, as they alleged, who would be afraid and who would be stout in case we might be set upon by brigands between that and Paris. But these two rogues that met us left us at the next lodging. And the two Scots scholars never obtained payment of the bishop for that they had disbursed, because of their intended fraud.'

At last in Paris, in April 1550, Melville was presented to the young queen. After three years (of which he tells us nothing) he was prevailed on to enter the service of the Duke of Montmorency, the constable of France. He then saw a good deal of military service, in the wars between the king of France and the Spanish and imperial forces. This phase of Melville's life came to an end in 1557, when the French were heavily defeated at the battle of St Quentin and the constable was taken prisoner. Melville gives a spirited account of how the constable failed to rally the French army: 'no man would tarry with him for any command, nor crying, "Tarry, tarry, return, return". Their heads were homewards and their hearts hence'. Melville himself was 'evil hurt by a stroke of a mace upon the head'. He was again mounted by his servant upon a Scots gelding, 'which carried me through the enemies, who were all betwixt me and home'. He continues, 'So I came safe to La Fer, where I did meet with Mr Harry Killigrew, an English gentleman, my old friend, who held my horse till I sat down in a barber's booth to be treated for the hurt in my head.'

Peace was made between France and her enemies in the spring of 1559, but shortly afterwards the Scottish revolt against Mary of Guise broke out. The constable advised the king of France to send Melville to Scotland to report on the situation and in particular to discover whether the Lord James 'pretends to usurp the crown of Scotland for himself, or if he be moved to take arms only for conscience sake, in defence of his religion, himself, his dependants and associates'. Melville had an interview with Lord James, and returned to France with a reassuring offer by Lord James to accept banishment from Scotland if he could not clear himself of suspicion.

During Melville's brief absence from France, King Henry II had died and his son, Mary Stewart's husband, was now King Francis II. Rather ironically, this elevation of his queen meant that there were poorer, and not better, prospects for Melville in France, because the new king was dominated by his wife's kinsmen, the Guise family, who ousted Melville's patron, the constable, from court favour. The constable therefore recommended Melville to the Elector Palatine, partly so that he could learn the 'Dutch' [i.e., German] tongue, and he remained in the Elector's service for more than three years. During this period, however, he visited France briefly on the Elector's behalf after the death of Francis II in December 1560. This brought him again into close touch with French and Scottish affairs, and when Queen Mary retired from court he happened to be in Lorraine with the Elector's eldest son, Hans Casimir, and was able to visit her and offer his service. Although he was not recalled to Scotland for another two years, he seems for a time to have been employed as a Scottish agent on the continent, but there was a period when he was sufficiently free from employment to be able to go sightseeing in Italy and Switzerland. When he was in France again, after his tour, he received 'writings to come to Scotland, directed by my Lords Moray and Lethington, at the Queen's Majesty's command, to be employed in some of Her Highness's affairs of consequence, which I understood to be concerning her marriage. Whereupon I took deliberation, after my return to Germany, to make a voyage to Scotland, far against the opinion of the constable, the admiral and the Prince Palatine.'

On his arrival in Scotland, Melville found Queen Mary at Perth and was received by her on 5 May 1564. He came at a time when the friction between Mary and Elizabeth had reached a point at which even professions of friendship had ceased. There had, he said, 'ensued so great a coldness that they left off from writing each other, as they had formerly done weekly by the posts that passed between the courts and Berwick, letting two months pass before the queen my mistress took purpose to send me unto the Queen of England to renew their outward friendship; for in their hearts from that time forth there was nothing but jealousies and suspicions'. Melville was not yet fully resolved to settle in Scotland, but Mary's charm captivated him. 'She was so affable, so gracious and discreet, that she won great estimation and the hearts of many both in England and Scotland, and mine among the rest; so that I thought her more worthy to be served for little profit than any other prince in Europe for great advantage.' Thus, he continued, 'I was vanquished and won to tarry with her, and to lay aside

all other profits or preferment in France and other countries, albeit for
the time I had no heritage but my service. So about two or three
months after my home-coming I was sent to the Queen of England, with
instructions out of the queen's own mouth'. It is with this mission that
the most entertaining part of Melville's *Memoirs* begins, for his narrative of his exchanges with a very feminine Queen Elizabeth would of
itself make his work immortal.

The main part of Melville's public life, from his embassy to England
in 1564 onwards, is described in his own words in the text of the present edition, but can be briefly summarized here. In 1566 he carried to
Elizabeth the news of the birth of Mary's son, and again her reaction,
according to Melville, was surprisingly human. On Mary's deposition,
in 1567, Melville had various dealings with the regents who ruled on
behalf of James VI, and when James personally assumed the government
Melville was once more in favour and employment. According to his
own account, he could have gone on many more embassies, to England,
Denmark and Spain, in the 1580s, but declined. However, he continued to be in close touch with affairs, and his comments on events
like the execution of Queen Mary, the Spanish Armada and the marriage
of James VI are of considerable interest. By the time James became
King of England, in 1603, Melville thought it was time for him to
retire from public life, but he did pay one visit to the court in London.

Hardly less important than Sir James's personal experience were his
family relationships, both by blood and by marriage, for they brought
him into immediate contact with several of the men who played notable
parts in Scottish affairs. His father, Sir John Melville of Raith, was one
of those Fife lairds who, like lairds in other parts of Scotland, found
their way into the main stream of Scottish politics for the first time in
the sixteenth century. Sir John played an important part in affairs
before the death of James V in 1542, he committed himself to the pro-
English and reforming cause, as so many of the lairds did, and in 1548
he suffered the penalty of execution for treason through being on what
was for the time the losing side. Sir James's elder brother, Sir Robert,
of Murdocairny, adhered to the cause of Queen Mary after she was
deposed, but he later came to terms with the government of James VI
and held the office of Treasurer Depute from 1582 to 1596. A younger
brother, Sir Andrew, of Garvock, was Queen Mary's master of the
household during her captivity in England. Sir James's mother, Helen
Napier, was the great-aunt of Sir John Napier of Merchiston, the
inventor of logarithms, and her nephew, the mathematician's father,
married a sister of Adam Bothwell, Bishop of Orkney, the prelate who
celebrated the marriage of Queen Mary to James Hepburn, Earl of

Bothwell, and who subsequently crowned and anointed the Queen's son and supplanter, the infant James VI. Sir James's sister, Janet, married James Kirkcaldy of Grange, who was Treasurer of Scotland in the later years of James V and the beginning of Mary's reign. This made Sir James the uncle by marriage of William Kirkcaldy of Grange, who had a renowned career as a soldier on the Continent and who, at the end of his life, was captain of Edinburgh Castle when it was Queen Mary's last stronghold in Scotland. Among Kirkcaldy's garrison in Edinburgh were three of Sir James Melville's brothers – Sir Robert, Sir Andrew and David. Loyalty to the crown, as well as their personal relationship with Kirkcaldy and their admiration for his leadership, explain their presence in the castle. Indeed, the family as a whole have been called 'the loyal Melvilles'.

Sir James lived to a very old age, for he was born in 1535 and did not die until 1617. The latest events mentioned in his *Memoirs* are those contemporaneous with the baptism of Prince Henry, first-born son of James VI, in 1594, but the letter of advice to the King which he inserts near the end of his work cannot have been completed before 1597, and it seems therefore that the volume was not put together until the later 1590s. Melville does tell us that he was making use of existing papers which he had kept by him – 'old written memorials that were lying beside me', as he calls them – and he reproduced the text of some original letters which he had evidently preserved. Yet the general character of the work is that of the recollections in advanced years of events in which the writer had taken part long before. Melville's ostensible purpose in committing his *Memoirs* to paper was, as he explained in a preface not printed in this edition, the instruction of his son, who, he hoped, would be guided by his father's experience in his own career as a politician and courtier: 'no man,' he remarked, 'can show the right way better than he that has oft-times chanced upon by-roads', and he claimed that nothing had stood him 'in more stead than the early embracing of unbought experience, by observing the stumbling errors of others'.

A reader feels that the whole tone of the *Memoirs* is coloured by Melville's self-importance, as well as perhaps by defective memory. It may be that his trustworthiness is especially suspect when he relates the advice he had given to kings and queens – very often advice which, if given, must have been extremely unpalatable. Although, according to his own account, Queen Mary and James VI gave him a free hand to 'admonish, advertise and reprove' them as he wished, it is very hard to believe that he really spoke to Mary about her relations with Riccio in the language which he records. It is not easy, either, to believe that he told Queen Elizabeth, in so many words, 'I know your stately stomach. You think, if you were married, you would be but Queen of England; and now you are King and Queen both. You cannot suffer a commander.' We have all met boastful characters who are ready to declare, 'I just told him so-and-so', and one always suspects that what they are relating is not what they actually said but what they thought afterwards that they might have said. One such character gave himself away by correcting himself: 'And I just said–I mean I might have said'. So it may have been with Melville; he tells us what, on reflection, he thought he might have said, or ought to have said. In his prefatory epistle to his son, he takes credit to himself for 'standing by honesty and virtue' to his own disadvantage, out of 'over great fervency towards the prince's service and over great forgetfulness of my own particular advancement and profit'. But the old man may have been guilty of self-deception, and have persuaded himself that he had really given the advice he sets down in his *Memoirs*.

Melville emerges as a courtier rather than a statesman or even a politician, and when he was engaged on diplomatic missions he does not impress one as particularly able. His narrative shows that he liked a good story for its own sake, but the combination of self-importance and ineffectiveness may have led some to see him as nothing more than a solemn bore. His humourless quality comes out in his account of an exchange with the Earl of Bothwell. Bothwell 'called for a cup of wine and drank to me. . . . He bade me drink it out to grow fatter, for, he said, "The zeal of the commonwealth has eaten you up and made you so lean". I answered that every little member should serve to some use, but the care of the commonwealth appertained most to him and the rest of the nobility, who should be as fathers to the same. Then he said, "I knew well he would find a pin for every bore."'

Melville's interest lay, above all, in schemes for royal marriages, and he was never happier than when he was carrying a portrait of some prince or princess from one court to a potential bride or bridegroom in another. After Mary was widowed by the death of Francis, one of the candidates for her hand was the Archduke Charles of Austria, son of the Emperor Ferdinand and brother of his heir, Maximilian. While Melville was still on the Continent, he received instructions from Scotland to make the acquaintance of the archduke, to inform himself 'concerning his religion, his rents and his qualities, his age and stature, and to send home word to the queen, and therewith to send his picture, if it could be done; which was thought that I might easily know and obtain by means of the Elector Palatine, my master'. Shortly afterwards, Catherine de' Medici sought the hand of Maximilian's daughter for her son, Charles IX, and sent an envoy to the Elector Palatine, in the hope that he would use his influence to further this match. This envoy was instructed to ask for a picture of the princess, and when it was obtained Melville was sent to France with it. He tells us that when he reached the French court, after the delivery of his letters of credence, 'which the king was very glad to hear, being thereby put in hope that the marriage would take effect, he was so desirous to see the picture of that lusty young princess that he cut the threads himself that bound on the wax-cloth about the said picture'. Again, when Melville finally left the Continent for Scotland, the Elector Palatine's son, Duke Casimir, 'took occasion to desire me to present his picture to Queen Elizabeth', and Melville agreed to do so. On reaching the English court, Melville ingeniously introduced the subject obliquely. He explained that he had been most loth to leave the Elector's service, and 'to have the better remembrance of him, I desired to carry home with me his picture, and the pictures of his wife and his sons and daughters. So soon as she heard me mention the pictures, she inquired if I had the picture of the Duke Casimir, desiring very earnestly to see it. And when I alleged I had left the pictures in London, she being then at Hampton Court, and that I was ready to go forward on my journey, she said I should not part till she had seen all the pictures. So the next day I delivered them all to Her Majesty, and she desired to keep them all night, but she called upon my Lord Robert Dudley to be judge of Duke Casimir's picture, and appointed me to meet her the next morning in her garden, where she caused to deliver them all unto me, giving me thanks for the sight of them. I again offered unto Her Majesty any of the pictures so she would permit me to retain the old elector's and his lady's; but she would have none of them. I had also sure information, that first and last she despised the said Duke Casimir. Therefore I did write back from London to his father and him in cypher, dissuading them to meddle any more in that marriage; and received great many thanks afterward from the said young duke, who immediately married the Duke Augustus, Elector of Saxony's eldest daughter.' Melville had thus served a considerable apprenticeship in matchmaking and the conveyance of royal portraits before he became involved in his famous conversation with Queen Elizabeth about Dudley and Darnley.

His preoccupation was with men rather than movements, and he saw politics as the interplay of personal rivalries and as competition between factions rather than as any conflict of principles. He was certainly no zealot and perhaps not even a strong partisan. Consequently, he was not the man to appreciate some of the more profound history of his time, and his *Memoirs* have little to say about some of the matters which occupy the attention of most historians. It was almost out of character that he threw in some pages of prefatory matter describing the situation in Scotland in the later years of James V. But this was a period of which he was far too young to have first-hand knowledge, though no doubt he derived reliable second-hand information because his brother-in-law, James Kirkcaldy of Grange, had been Treasurer of Scotland at the time. At any rate, when Melville's personal knowledge comes in the serious history is apt to go out. He says modestly, 'I only touch such things as I myself was employed in, or where I was present and saw with my eyes and heard with my ears, which may serve for little parentheses to the history-makers'. It is significant of his lack of interest in movements that, although he never wavered in his support of the Reformation, he shows little appreciation of the zeal of the reformers and that he never mentions by name either John Knox or any other Scottish protestant minister. Later, he saw no principle at issue between the supporters of Queen Mary, after she was deposed in 1567, and those of her son: to him it was all a matter of 'ambition, greediness and vengeance'. The one cause which captured his imagination, as it dominated the thinking of most politically-minded Scots of the time, was that of Anglo-Scottish union and the right of the Scottish dynasty to succeed to the English crown. This made him unsympathetic to the procrastination and vacillation of Queen Elizabeth and some English statesmen, and he accused the English government of endeavouring to prevent King James from marrying.

Melville's undoubted patriotism explains some of his assessments, but most of his judgments of men seem to be based on instinctive admiration or distaste for personalities rather than on political or other principles. In his laudatory epitaph on William Kirkcaldy of Grange he is, perhaps, at one with most observers. But some of his judgments on his contemporaries are at variance with those of most historians. He was uncommonly charitable to Darnley, a 'good young prince' who 'failed rather for lack of good counsel and experience than of evil will'. He saw weaknesses as well as strength in the character of the Regent Moray, and in a picturesque assessment of him he drew his simile from tennis: 'like an unskilful player in a tennis-court, running ever after the ball; whereas an expert player would see and discern where the ball will light'. Of the Regent Morton he was intensely critical, and caustically depicts him as 'making the alleys of the garden even, his mind occupied in the mean time upon crooked paths'. Another politician for whom he had the most profound distaste was James Stewart, Earl of Arran, 'a scorner of religion, presumptuous, needy and careless of the commonwealth, a despiser of the nobility and of all honest men'. Esmé Stewart, on the other hand, 'had been tolerable, if he had happened upon as honest counsellors as he was well inclined himself; he loved both the king and common weal, but he wanted experience and was no ways versed in the affairs of state'.

There is no title in Melville's MS., and his work was first published under the title *The Memoirs of Sir James Melville* at London in 1683, by George Scott of Pitlochie, whose mother was a daughter of Sir James. Scott related how Melville's MS. had been discovered in Edinburgh Castle in 1660 and had been given to the Sir James Melville of Halhill of that day, who was the grandson in the male line of the writer of the *Memoirs*. He handed the MS. over to Scott. In preparing his edition for publication, Scott took considerable liberties with the text. His general intention was to modernize the language and make his narrative read smoothly, but in those days, 'it was held to be within the sound discretion, if not the bounden duty, of a careful editor, to retrench the prolixity and expand the careless brevity of his author; to new-model the text into a better or more tasteful form, and to do whatever else he might deem requisite to render the work more acceptable to his readers'. A second edition of Scott's version was published in 1735 at Edinburgh, and it was reprinted at Glasgow in 1751. A third edition was published at London in 1752. A translation into French had appeared at the Hague in 1694, and it was reprinted at Lyons in 1695 and at Amsterdam in 1704. A fresh French translation was published in 1745.

No original MS. was known to exist while those successive editions based on Scott's version were issued, but in 1827, when the original MS. had at last been rediscovered, a transcript of it was prepared for the Bannatyne Club. The MS. revealed the extent to which the printed versions had deviated from the original, and in the Introduction to the Bannatyne Club edition it was remarked with truth that Scott, as editor, had 'made a liberal use of the customary privileges of his office; at the same time, it does not appear that any intention or systematic plan to falsify the meaning and the sentiments of the author had been entertained or acted on'. The one point where Scott does seem to have made an attempt to misrepresent the original lies in his suppression of the most sinister features in the English government's dealings with Mary before her condemnation. Elsewhere, he paraphrases and expands; he sometimes misunderstands or mis-reads an unusual or archaic word or phrase; a word difficult of interpretation he sometimes omits altogether; occasionally he has carelessly left a passage out because his eye had skipped from one occurrence of a word to its next occurrence.

The Bannatyne Club edition, reproducing the precise wording and spelling of Melville's MS., has naturally become the edition which historians of the period now use, but it contains many words, phrases and spellings which are not at once intelligible to the modern reader.

On the other hand, the number of editions of Scott's version, defective though it may be from the scholarly point of view, demonstrate that it became something of a minor classic in its own right, and it is much more easily understood. Consequently the present edition is based on Scott's version. Many modifications have, however, been made to bring the substance and meaning into exact conformity with those of the Bannatyne Club text, to correct errors in words and phraseology, to restore Scott's omissions and, in general, to modernize the spelling of personal and place names.

The value and interest of Melville's work lie in the passages where he adheres to his intention of relating only 'such things as I myself was employed in, or where I was present and heard with my ears'. Consequently it has been thought right to make certain omissions in the present edition. Thus, the earlier part of the *Memoirs*, concerned as it is mainly with the intricacies of continental diplomacy and of military operations in which Melville was not himself involved, is not included in the text, but extracts illustrating Melville's own adventures on the Continent have been quoted in this introduction. Official letters and state papers which Melville inserted but which he had not himself composed are likewise omitted. An attempt has been made to present the clearest possible rendering of Melville's account of Scottish affairs, and to do this a sacrifice has been made of some complexities, especially in the period of the civil war of 1571–3, and of accounts of some intrigues in which Melville was not involved and which did not affect the course of history.

GORDON DONALDSON

THE MEMOIRS OF
SIR JAMES MELVILLE
OF HALHILL

I

Melville at the Court of Queen Elizabeth

BEING arrived at London, I lodged near the court, which was at Westminster. My host immediately gave advertisement of my coming, and that same night Her Majesty sent Mr Latton, now governor of the Isle of Wight, in her name to welcome me and to show me that the next morning she would give me audience in her garden at eight hours. She had been advertised by the Earl of Bedford, governor of Berwick, that I was upon the way. That same night I was visited by Sir Nicholas Throckmorton, one of my old and dearest friends by long acquaintance; first during his banishment in France, in the reign of Queen Mary, and afterward while he was ambassador in France for this queen, where I was for the time (yet very young) pensioner to King Henry II and servant to the constable, his chief councillor. This Sir Nicholas was my dear friend, and had procured a pension for me from my mistress, to help to entertain me when I had willingly banished myself the court of France, so long as there were civil wars between France and Scotland, during the which I remained in Germany. The said Sir Nicholas, being for the time at court, came and supped with me that same night. He was also a devoted friend to the queen my mistress, and to her right and title to the succession to the crown of England. From him I had ample and familiar information and sure intelligence, and friendly advice how to proceed with the queen and every courtier in particular; for he was a great instrument to help my Lord of Moray and secretary Lethington to pack up the first friendship and correspondence betwixt the two queens, and betwixt the Earl of Moray and Lord Robert [Dudley], and betwixt the two secretaries.* Albeit he had no liking for the time either of my Lord Robert or of

---

* The two secretaries were William Maitland of Lethington and William Cecil. There was also a very close friendship between Dudley and Maitland, for twenty years after this Dudley wrote to John Maitland, Lethington's brother: 'I call to mind the good and assured affection that sometime was between your brother the laird of Lethington and me, whom I protest, I loved as dearly as ever I loved man not born in England, and not many in England better' (*Warrender Papers* [Scot. Hist. Soc.], i, 188).

Master Cecil, yet he knew that then nothing could be done without them. Among other things, he gave me advice to use great familiarity with the ambassador of Spain, in case I found the queen his mistress over hard and difficult, alleging that it would be a great spur to move the Queen of England to give our queen a greater contentment in her desires than yet she had done.

The next morning Mr Latton and Mr Randolph, late agent for the Queen of England in Scotland, came to my lodging, to convoy me to Her Majesty, who was, as they said, already in the garden. With them came a servant of my Lord Robert's, with a horse and footmantle of velvet laced with gold for me to ride upon. Which servant, with the said horse, waited upon me all the time that I remained there. I found Her Majesty walking in an alley. After I had kissed her hand, and presented my letter of credence, I told Her Majesty in French the effect of my commission . . .; and sometimes being interrupted by her demands, I answered accordingly. The reason why I spoke French was that, being but lately come home, I could not as yet speak my own language so readily. Her first demand was concerning the letter that the queen had written to her with such despiteful language that she believed all friendship and familiarity to have been given up; which had made her resolve never to write again except another as despiteful, which she took out of her pouch, for she had it already written to show it me. She told me she had delayed to send it, because she thought it too gentle, till she had written another more vehement, for answer to the queen's angry bill. For my part, I appeared to find such hard interpretation to be made upon the queen's loving and frank dealing very strange. I told Her Majesty that the queen could not call to mind what words they were which had given her such offence. Whereupon she showed me also the queen's letter, which she had ready in her hand to let me see. Which when I had seen I said I could find therein no offensive word, when I considered the familiarity formerly betwixt them; alleging that albeit Her Majesty could speak as good French as any who had not been out of the country, that yet she lacked the use of the French court language, which was frank and short, and had frequently two significations, which discreet and familiar friends took always in the best part; praying her to tear the angry letter, which she thought to have sent in answer, and in revenge of the queen's. I protested that I should never let Her Majesty know that her true plain meaning had been so misconstrued. Always at length, she being desirous of an honest colour or pretext, she was the more readily satisfied in that point, for the fear she had that friendship and correspondence should break off; our queen being the first seeker to renew and continue the same, by sending me thither, and could not stand upon ceremonies with her elder sister. In my presence then she did tear all the angry writings and answers, with promise of such friendly and frank dealing in times coming, as all her good sister's dealings and proceedings should be interpreted to the best. . . .

Thus the old friendship being renewed, she enquired if the queen had sent any answer to the proposition of marriage made to her by Mr Randolph. I answered, as I had been instructed, that my mistress thought little or nothing thereof, but expected the meeting of some commissioners upon the Borders, with my Lord of Moray and the secretary Lethington, to confer and treat upon all such matters of greatest importance as might concern the quiet of both the countries and contentment of both their Majesties' minds. 'So seeing your Majesties cannot so soon find the opportunity of meeting, so much desired betwixt yourselves, which is not expedient until all other doubts and desires be first made clear by your most trusty and familiar counsellors, the queen my mistress, as I have said, is minded to send for her part my Lord of Moray and the secretary Lethington, and hopes that Your Majesty will send my Lord of Bedford and my Lord Robert Dudley.' She answered that it appeared that I made but small account of my Lord Robert, seeing that I named the Earl of Bedford before him; but ere long she would make him a far greater earl, and that I should see it done before my returning home. For she esteemed him as her brother and best friend, whom she would have herself married, had she ever minded to have taken a husband. But being determined to end her life in virginity, she wished that the queen her sister should marry him, as meetest of all other and with whom she could find in her heart to declare the queen second person rather than any other. For being matched with him, it would best remove out of her mind all fear and suspicion, to be offended by usurpation before her death; being assured that he was so loving and trusty that he would never give his consent nor suffer such thing to be attempted during her time.

And to cause the queen my mistress to think the more of him, I was required to stay till I should see him made Earl of Leicester and Baron of Denbigh; which was done at Westminster with great solemnity, the queen herself helping to put on his ceremonial, he sitting upon his knees before her, keeping a great gravity and discreet behaviour. But she could not refrain from putting her hand in his neck to tickle him smilingly, the French ambassador and I standing by. Then she asked at me how I liked him. I answered that as he was a worthy subject, so he was happy who had a princess who could discern and reward good service. 'Yet', she said, 'you like better of yonder long lad', pointing towards my Lord Darnley, who, as nearest prince of the blood, did bear the sword of honour that day before her. My answer was that no woman of spirit would make choice of such a man, that was more like a woman than a man; for he was very lusty, beardless and lady-faced. And I had no will that she should think that I liked him, or had any eye or dealing that way, albeit I had a secret charge to deal with his mother, my Lady Lennox, to procure liberty for him to go to Scotland (where his father was already) that he might see the country and convoy the earl, his father, back again to England.

Now I found the Queen of England was determined to treat with my sovereign, first concerning her marriage with the Earl of Leicester, and for that effect she promised to send commissioners unto the Borders. In the mean time I was favourably and familiarly used. For during nine days that I remained at the court, it pleased Her Majesty to confer with me every day, and sometimes thrice in a day, to wit, before noon, after noon and after supper. Sometimes she would say that, seeing she could not meet with the queen her good sister to confer with her familiarly, she should open a good part of her inward mind to me, that I might show it again unto the queen. She told me she was not so offended at the queen's angry letter, as that she seemed so far to disdain the marriage of my Lord of Leicester, which she had caused Mr Randolph to propose to her. I answered that it might be he had touched something thereof to my Lord of Moray and Lethington, but that he had not proposed the matter directly to herself, and that as well Her Majesty as those who were her most familiar counsellors could conjecture nothing thereupon, but delays and driving of time concerning the declaring of her to be second person, which would be tried at the meeting of the commissioners above specified. She replied that the trial and declaration thereof would be hasted forward according to the queen's good behaviour and applying herself to her pleasure and advice in her marriage. And seeing the matter concerning the said declaration was so weighty, she had ordained some of the best lawyers in England diligently to search out who had the best right; and she would wish it should be her dear sister, rather than any other. I said I was assured that Her Majesty was both out of doubt thereof and would rather Queen Mary should be declared than any other; but I lamented that even the wisest princes will not sufficiently pry into the partialities and pretences of their familiar counsellors and servants, except it were such a notable and rare prince as Henry VIII, Her Majesty's father of happy memory, who of his own head was determined to declare his sister's son, King James V (what time Her Majesty was not yet born, but only her sister Queen Mary) heir apparent to the crown of England, failing heirs gotten of his own body, for the earnest desire he had to unite this whole island. She said she was glad he did it not. I said that then he had but one daughter, and was in doubt to have any more children, and yet he had not so many suspicions in his head; and that Her Majesty was out of all doubt ever to have any children, as being resolved to die a virgin. She said that she was never minded to marry, except she was compelled by the queen her sister's hard behaviour towards her in acting against her advice, as said is. I said, 'Madam, you need not tell me that. I know your stately stomach. You think, if you were married, you would be but Queen of England; and now you are King and Queen both. You may not endure a commander.'

She appeared to be so affectionate to the queen her good sister that she had a great desire to see her. And because their desired meeting could not be so hastily brought to pass, she delighted to look upon Her Majesty's picture. She took me to her bed-chamber and opened a little desk, wherein were divers little pictures wrapt within paper, and their names written with her own hand upon the papers. Upon the first that she took up was written, 'My Lord's picture'. I held the candle, and pressed to see that picture so named. She was loath to let me see it; at length my importunity prevailed for a sight thereof [and found it to be the Earl of Leicester's picture]. I desired that I might have it to carry home to my queen; which she refused, alleging that she had but that one picture of his. I said again that she had the original; for he was at the farthest part of the chamber, speaking with secretary Cecil. Then she took out the queen's picture, and kissed it; and I kissed her hand, for the great love I saw she bore to my mistress. She showed me also a fair ruby, as great as a tennis-ball. I desired that she would either send it, or else my Lord of Leicester's picture, as a token unto the queen. She said, if the queen would follow her counsel, that she would in process of time get them both, and all she had; but in the mean time she was resolved for a token to send her with me a diamond. It was at this time late after supper; she appointed me to be with her the next morning by eight hours, at which time she used to walk in her garden. She enquired several things of me relating to this kingdom, and other countries wherein I had lately travelled. She caused me to eat with her dame of honour, my Lady Stafford (an honourable and godly lady, who had been at Geneva banished during the reign of Queen Mary), that I might be always near Her Majesty, that she might confer with me. My Lady Stafford's daughter was my mistress, for I was of their acquaintance when they passed through France. I had good intelligence from her and my Lady Throckmorton.

At divers meetings there would be divers purposes. The queen my sovereign had instructed me to leave matters of gravity sometimes, and cast in merry purposes, lest otherwise I should be tired upon, she being well informed of her sister's natural temper. Therefore, in declaring the customs of Dutchland,* Poland and Italy, the busking and clothing of the women was not forgot, and what country weed I thought best becoming gentlewomen. The Queen of England said she had clothes of every sort; which every day, so long as I was there, she changed. One day she had the English weed, another the French, and another the Italian, and so forth. She asked me which of them became her best. I said, the Italian dress; which pleased her well, for she delighted to shew her golden coloured hair, wearing a caul and bonnet as they do in Italy. Her hair was more reddish than yellow, curled in appearance naturally. Then she entered to discern what colour of hair was reputed best; and whether my queen's hair or her's was best; and which of them two was fairest. I answered that the fairness of them both was not their worst faults. But she was earnest with me to declare which of them I thought fairest. I said she was the fairest queen in England and ours the fairest queen in Scotland. Yet she was earnest. I answered they were both the fairest ladies of their courts and that Her Majesty was whiter, but our queen was very lovely. She enquired which of them was of highest stature. I said, our queen. Then, saith she, she is too high and that herself was neither too high nor too low. Then she asked what kind of exercises she used. I answered that [when] I was despatched out of Scotland, the queen was lately come from the Highland hunting; that when she had leisure from the affairs of her country she read upon good books, the histories of diverse countries, and sometimes would play upon the lute and virginals. She asked if she played well. I said, reasonably for a queen.

That same day after dinner my Lord of Hunsdon drew me up to a quiet gallery, that I might hear some music (but he said that he durst not avow it), where I might hear the queen play upon the virginals. After I had hearkened a while, I took by the tapestry that hung before the door of the chamber, and, seeing her back was towards the door, I entered within the chamber, and stood still at the door cheek and heard her play excellently well. But she left off as soon as she turned her about and saw me and came forward, seeming to strike me with her left hand and alleging that she used not to play before men, but when she was solitary, to shun melancholy. She asked how I came there. I said, 'As I was walking with my Lord of Hunsdon, as we passed by the chamber-door, I heard such melody as ravished me and drew me within the chamber, I knew not how'; excusing my fault of homeliness, as being brought up in the court of France, and was now willing to endure what kind of punishment Her Majesty should be pleased to lay upon me for my offence. Then she sat down low upon a cushion, and I upon my knees beside her; but she gave me a cushion with her own hand, to

* Germany.

lay under my knee; which at first I refused, but she compelled me to take it. She then called for my Lady Stafford out of the next chamber; for the queen was alone. Then she asked whether my queen or she played best. In that I gave her the praise. She said my French was good, and asked if I could speak Italian, which she spoke reasonably well. I said I tarried not above two months in Italy and had brought with me some books to read upon, but had no time to learn the language perfectly. Then she spoke to me in Dutch,* which was not good; and would know what kind of books I liked best, whether of theology, history, or love matters. I said, I liked well of all the sorts.

I was earnest to be despatched, but she said I was weary sooner of her company than she was of mine. I told Her Majesty that though I had no reason of being weary, it was time to return. But I was stayed two days longer, till I might see her dance, as I was informed. Which being done, she enquired of me whether she or my queen danced best. I answered that the queen danced not so high and disposedly as she did. Then again she wished that she might see the queen at some convenient place of meeting. I offered to convoy her secretly to Scotland by post, clothed like a page, disguised, that she might see the queen, as James V had gone in disguise to France with his own ambassador, to see the Duke of Vendôme's sister, who should have been his wife;† telling her that her chamber might be kept in her absence as though she were sick, and in the meantime none to be privy thereto, except my Lady Stafford and one of the grooms of her chamber. She appeared to like that kind of language, and said, 'Alas! if I might do it.' She used all the means she could to cause me to persuade the queen of the great love she did bear unto her, and that she was minded to put away all jealousies and suspicions, and in times coming to entertain a straiter friendship to stand between them than ever had been of before. She promised that my dispatch should be delivered to me very shortly at London, by Mr Cecil; for now she had gone to Hampton Court, where she gave me my answer by mouth herself, and her secretary by writing.

The next day my Lord of Leicester desired me to sail in his barge down the water of Thames to London, which was ten miles from Hampton Court. He had in his company his brother-in-law, Sir Henry Sidney, deputy of Ireland. By the way my lord entered familiarly into discourse with me, alleging that he was well acquainted with my Lord of Moray, Lethington and my brother Sir Robert; and that he was also by report so well acquainted with me that he durst be so homely as to require that I would show him what the queen my mistress thought of

* German.   † James V did go to France in the expectation of marrying Marie de Vendôme (though he actually married Princess Madeleine); but there was no secrecy about the visit.

him and the marriage that Mr Randolph had proposed. Whereunto I answered very coldly, as I was by my queen commanded. Then he began to purge himself of so proud a pretence as to marry so great a queen, esteeming himself not worthy to wipe her shoes; declaring that the invention of that proposition of marriage proceeded from Mr Cecil, his secret enemy. 'For if I', says he, 'should have appeared desirous of that marriage, I should have lost the favour of both the queens.' He prayed me to excuse him unto the queen, that it would please Her Majesty not to impute unto him that clumsy fault, but unto the malice of his enemies.

Being landed at London, our dinner was prepared by the Earl of Pembroke; who, being great master, yet humbled himself so far as to serve the said table, as master of the household himself, and show himself a devoted friend to my queen's title [of succeeding to the crown of England].

After dinner, I took leave of the French ambassador and the Spanish, having received divers advertisements from them. My Lord of Leicester sent also writings with me to my Lord of Moray to excuse him at the queen's hands. The day appointed I received my dispatch from secretary Cecil together with a letter of credit and a more ample declaration of the queen's mind touching the same answers that she had made me herself. He gave me also a letter to secretary Lethington. For, as I have said, my Lord of Leicester and he, my Lord of Moray and secretary Lethington, ruled both queens, and as yet kept correspondence together. When I took my leave, secretary Cecil convoyed me through the close to the outer gate of his palace, as I may call it, after he had himself put a fair chain about my neck. My Lady Lennox and Sir Nicholas Throckmorton sent many good advices to the queen, to be followed forth according to the time and occasions. My Lady Lennox sent also tokens to the queen, a ring with a fair diamond, an emerald to my lord her husband, who was yet in Scotland, a diamond to my Lord of Moray, a watch set with diamonds and rubies to the secretary Lethington, a ring with a ruby to my brother Sir Robert. For she was still in good hope that her son my Lord Darnley would come better speed than the Earl of Leicester concerning the marriage of our queen. She was a very wise and discreet matron and had many favourers in England for the time.

II

Mary, Darnley and Riccio

AT my home-coming, I found the Queen's Majesty still at Edinburgh; to whom I declared my manner of proceeding with the
Queen of England, and her answer to the special heads of my instructions in writing.

Her Majesty answered to the first that whereas the queen thought
the time very long since she received either word or writ from her,
whereby she might understand of her good estate, and had sent me
thither to visit her in her behalf; that she thought the time as long,
albeit she had conceived some grief concerning the angry letter; which
was the greater, in respect it appeared that she [Mary] disdained the
offer of the best good she [Elizabeth] had to give, to wit, the man whom
she esteemed as her brother. And whereas she [Mary] had sent me to
visit her [Elizabeth], she [Elizabeth] was more content with my coming
than she would have been with any other, being of her acquaintance,
with whom she might familiarly declare her inward mind to the queen
my mistress, seeing she could not meet with her so soon as she desired:
as I might declare how familiarly she [Elizabeth] had conferred with
me all her inward griefs and desires, and how well she was satisfied,
and how willing to continue all good offices of amity; and that she
would for that effect send shortly down to the Border commissioners
who were named by herself, to meet with my Lord of Moray and
Lethington. As for the parliament, it was yet in doubt whether it held
or not. If it held, the queen should get no hurt in her right, neither
directly nor indirectly, but she should be fore-warned in due time.

Then I showed Her Majesty at length of all other purposes that fell
out by occasion betwixt the queen and me, together with the opinions
and advertisements of divers of her friends in England, as well catholics
as protestants; I gave her, from the Spanish ambassador, the intimation
of his king's good-will toward her, and likewise of Don Carlos, the
prince, albeit he was for the time in some suspicion with his father,
whereby the purpose of marriage would apparently take some delay
until matters might frame better between the father and the son;
assuring Her Majesty of his own particular service and furtherance

at his power and should from time to time make her intelligence.

Her Majesty was very glad that matters were brought again in so good terms that familiar dealing might continue between her and the Queen of England, having thereby access to get intelligence from a great number of noblemen and others her friends and factioners in England. For she was also afraid to get the blame of this discord, if it had continued.

After that Her Majesty had at great length understood all my management and proceedings in England, she enquired whether I thought that queen meant truly toward her as well inwardly in her heart as she appeared to do outwardly by her speech. I said that in my judgment there was neither plain dealing nor upright meaning, but great dissimulation, emulation, and fear that her princely qualities should over soon chase her out and displace her from the kingdom, as having already hindered her marriage with the Archduke Charles of Austria, and now offering unto her my Lord of Leicester, whom at that time she would be loath to want. Then the queen gave me her hand, that she should never marry the said new-made earl.

Yet shortly after my Lords of Moray and Bedford met near Berwick, to treat concerning the marriage with Leicester, with slenderer offers and less effectual dealing than was expected. But the said Earl of Leicester had written so discreet and wise letters unto my Lord of Moray for his excuses, that the queen appeared to have so good liking of him that the Queen of England began to fear and suspect that the said marriage might perchance take effect. Therefore my Lord Darnley obtained more readily licence to come to Scotland, who was a lusty youth, in hope that he should prevail, being present, before Leicester, who was absent. Which licence was procured by the means of the secretary Cecil, not that he was minded that any of the marriages should take effect, but with such shifts and practices to hold the queen unmarried so long as he could. For he persuaded himself that my Lord Darnley durst not pass forward without consent of the Queen of England to the said marriage, his land lying in England and his mother remaining there. So he thought it lay in the queen his mistress's own hand to let that marriage go forward or to stay the same at her pleasure. And in case my Lord Darnley should disobey the Queen of England's command to return upon her call, he intended to have him forfeited, whereby he should lose all his lands, rights and titles that he had in England.

The Queen's Majesty, as I have said, after her returning out of France to Scotland, behaved herself so princely, honourably and discreetly, that her reputation spread in all countries. She was determined and also inclined to continue in that kind of comeliness unto the end of her life, desiring to hold none in her company but such as were of the best qualities and conversation, abhorring all vices and vicious persons, whether they were men or women. In this her resolution she desired me to assist her, by affording her my good counsel how she might use the meetest means to advance her honest intention in case she (being yet young) might forget herself by any unseemly gesture or misbehaviour, that I would warn her thereof, by admonishing her to forbear and reform the same. Which commission I did at first altogether refuse, saying that her virtuous actions, her natural judgment and great experience she had learned in the company of so many notable princes in the court of France, had instructed her so well and made her so able as to be an example to all her subjects and servants. But she would not leave it so, but said she knew she had committed divers errors, upon no ill meaning, only for want of the admonition of loving friends; because that the greatest part of courtiers commonly flatter princes to win their favour, and will not tell them the truth, fearing to lose their favour. Therefore she adjured and commanded me to accept that charge; which I said was a ruinous commission, begging her to lay that burden upon her brother my Lord of Moray, and the secretary Lethington. She answered, she would not take it in so good part from them, as from me. I said, I was afraid that through process of time it would cause me to lose her favour. She said, it appeared I had an ill opinion of her constancy and discretion; which opinion she doubted not but I would alter, after I had essayed the occupation of that friendly and familiar charge. In the mean time she made me privy to all her most urgent affairs, but chiefly to her dealings with any foreign nation. She showed unto me all her letters, and those which she received from other princes. She desired me to write in her favour to such princes as I had acquaintance of, and to some of their counsellors. In which letters I did not omit to set out her virtues. I used to show to her their answers, and such occurrences as posted for the time between countries, to her great contentment; for she was of a quick spirit, curious to know and get intelligence of the state of other countries. She was sometimes sad when solitary, and was glad of the company of such as had travelled in other parts.

Now there came here, in company with the ambassador of Savoy, one David Riccio, of the country of Piedmont, who was a merry fellow and a good musician. Her Majesty had three varlets of her chamber who sang three parts, and wanted a bass to sing the fourth part. Therefore they told Her Majesty of this man, as one fit to make the fourth partner. Thus he was drawn in to sing sometimes with the rest; and afterwards when the ambassador, his master, returned, he stayed in this country and was retained in Her Majesty's service as a varlet of her chamber, and afterwards, when her French secretary retired himself to France, this David obtained the said office. He thereby entered in greater credit, and occupied Her Majesty's ear frequently in preference to the nobility and when there was greatest conventions of the estates. Which made him to be much envied and hated, especially when he became so great that he presented all signatures to be subscribed by Her Majesty: so that some of the nobility would frown upon him, others would shoulder and shoot him by, when they entered the queen's chamber and found him always speaking with her, and some again that had hard turns to be helped, new infeftments★ to be taken, or who desired to prevail against their enemies at court, or [in law suits before the Court of] Session,† addressed themselves to him, and depended upon him, whereby in short time he became very rich. Yet he was not without fear, and therefore he lamented his estate to me, asking my counsel how to behave himself. I told him that strangers were commonly envied when they meddled too much in the affairs of other countries. He said he, being secretary to Her Majesty in the French tongue, had occasion thereby to occupy Her Majesty's ear, as her former secretary used to do. I answered again that it was thought that the greatest part of the affairs of the country passed through his hands, and advised him, when the nobility were present, to give them place, and pray the Queen's Majesty to be content therewith; and I showed him, for an example, how I had been in so great favour with the Elector Palatine that he caused me to sit at his own table, and, the board being drawn, he used to confer with me in presence of his whole court, whereat divers of them took great indignation against me; which so soon as I perceived, I requested him to permit me to sit from his own table with the rest of his gentlemen, and no more to confer with me in their presence, but to send a page for me any time that he had leisure, to come to him in his chamber; which I obtained, and that way made my master not to be hated, nor myself to be envied. I advised him to do the like. Which he did, and said unto me afterwards that the queen would not suffer him, but would needs have him to use himself in the old manner. I answered that I was sorry for the inconveniences that might follow thereupon.

Afterwards, seeing the envy against the said David to increase, and that by his ruin Her Majesty might incur displeasure, I remembered upon Her Majesty's commandment to forewarn and admonish her of all apparent circumstances that might chance to fall out, as I had done divers times before (which was graciously reformed and redressed by Her Majesty). Now I took occasion likewise to enter with Her Majesty and in most humble manner showed her what advice I had given to

★ Titles to land.   † The central court for civil cases.

Signor David, as is above specified. Her Majesty said that he meddled no further than in her French writings and affairs, as her other French secretary had done of before, and said that, whoever found fault therewith, she would not leave to do her ordinary directions. I remembered Her Majesty what displeasure she had taken of before for the rash misbehaviour of a French gentleman called Châtelard, transported by her affability;* and likewise of the Earl of Arran for the same cause;† not doubting but Her Majesty's grave and comely behaviour towards such strangers and transported light persons would bring them to a more dutiful reverence to her honour and the contentment of her subjects. She thanked me for my continual care, and engaged to take such order therein as the cause required.

I have already told how that my Lord Darnley was advised to ask licence to come into Scotland. At his first coming he found the queen at Wemyss, making her progress through Fife. Her Majesty took well with him, and said that he was the lustiest and best proportioned long man that she had seen; for he was of a high stature, long and small,‡ even and erect, from his youth well instructed in all honest and comely exercises. After he had haunted court some time, he proposed marriage to Her Majesty, which she took in an evil part at first, as that same day she herself told me, and that she had refused a ring which he then offered unto her. I took occasion, as I had begun, to speak in his favour, that their marriage would put out of doubt their title to the succession [to the crown of England]. I know not how he fell in acquaintance with Riccio, but he also was his great friend at the queen's hand, so that she took ever the longer the better liking of him, and at length determined to marry him. This being made known to the Queen of England, she sent and charged him to return. She also sent her ambassador Sir Nicholas Throckmorton to Scotland, to dissuade the queen from marrying him, and, in case the queen would not follow her advice in her marriage, to persuade the lords and so many as were of the reformed religion, to withstand the said marriage unless the said Lord Darnley would promise and subscribe a bond to abide at the reformed religion, which he had plainly professed in England.

The queen, again perceiving the Queen of England's earnest opposition to all the marriages that were offered unto her, thought not meet

* Châtelard had been executed after he had been found secreting himself in the queen's private apartments.

† The third Earl of Arran, son of Châtelherault, was several times a suitor for Mary's hand and his hopes of marrying her, acting on a weak intellect, led to madness in which he plotted the seizure of the queen's person. In 1562 he was placed in confinement.

‡ Finely-built.

to delay her marriage any longer. But my lord Duke of Châtelherault, my Lords of Argyll, Rothes, Moray, Glencairn and divers other lords and barons withstood the said marriage: they made an attempt to take the Lord Darnley in the queen's company at the raid of Baith, and, as they alleged, to have sent him to England. I knew not what was in their mind, but it was an ill-favoured enterprise, wherein the queen was in danger either of keeping* or heart-breaking; and as they that had failed of their foolish enterprise took on plainly the arms of rebellion, Her Majesty again convened forces to pursue them, and chased them here and there,† until at length they were compelled to flee to England for refuge, to her who by her ambassadors had promised to hazard her crown in their defence in case they were driven to any strait for their opposition to the said marriage; though this was all denied at their coming to seek help.

When they sent up my Lord of Moray to that queen, the rest abiding at Newcastle, he could obtain nothing but disdain and scorn; till at length he and the Abbot of Kilwinning, his companion in that message, were persuaded to come and confess unto the queen upon their knees, and that in presence of the ambassadors of France and Spain, that Her Majesty had never moved them to that opposition and resistance against their queen's marriage. For this she had desired, to satisfy the said ambassadors, who both alleged in their masters' names that she had been the cause of the said rebellion and that her only delight was to stir up dissension among all her neighbours, not without cause. Yet in this allegation she overcame them: for she handled the matter so subtly, and the other two so timidly, in granting her desire, upon her fair promise contrary to what was truth, that she triumphed over the said ambassadors for their allegation. But unto my Lord of Moray and his partner she said, 'Now you have told the truth; for neither did I, nor any in my name, stir you up against your queen: for your abominable treason might serve for example to move my own subjects to rebel against me. Therefore pack you out of my presence; you are but unworthy traitors.' This was all their meritorious reward; and had not the more influence been used by some in England that pitied them, they would not have been permitted, during their banishment, to remain within her dominions; although she had promised of new again to assist and help them to the uttermost of her power, upon condition that they would please her so far as to sit down upon their knees in presence of the said ambassadors and make the foresaid false confession. And as for secret help, she gave them none; only they obtained a small contribution of £3000 Scots among some of their own religion there, who had borne them goodwill of before, which was

* i.e., subjection to restraint.   † This affair was called the Chaseabout Raid.

distributed among the rest of the banished lords where they remained together at Newcastle, comfortless and in great misery.

I have declared that the council of England's courtly dealing, shifting and drifting, by staying the queen so far as they might from marrying with any man, far or near, great or small, caused the queen to haste forward her marriage with my Lord Darnley; which was solemnized in the palace of Holyroodhouse, within the queen's chapel, at the mass; wherein Riccio was no small instrument, as said is. Scotland being almost wholly of the reformed religion took a dislike of the king because, as was alleged, he had plainly professed the reformed religion in England.* Then inventions and rumours were raised that Riccio was a pensioner of the Pope, and, having both the king and queen of his opinion, might the rather and more easily attempt with time to plant again in Scotland the Roman Catholic religion. And even in these days the Pope sent 8000 crowns to be delivered to the queen. But the ship wherein the said gold was, did shipwreck upon the coast of England, within the Earl of Northumberland's bounds; who alleged the whole to appertain to him by just law, which he caused his advocate to read unto me (when I was directed to him to demand restitution of the said sum) in the old Norman language; which neither he nor I understood well, it was so corrupt. But he would give no part thereof to the queen, albeit he was himself a catholic and otherwise professed secretly to be her friend.

After that the Queen's Majesty had married my Lord Darnley, she did him great honour herself, and desired every one who would deserve her favour to do the like, and to wait upon him; so that he was well accompanied, and such as sought favour by him for a while sped best in their suits. But because he had married without advice of the Queen of England, my Lady Lennox, his mother, was committed to be warded in the Tower of London, where she remained a long time.

All this time I attended still upon the queen, but with less familiarity than I had of before, and likewise the said Lethington was in suspicion as a favourer of my Lord of Moray. I, seeing my service for the time no more needful, humbly begged liberty of the queen to return to France and other places, where I had spent the half of my life. But Her Majesty refused to grant that I should leave her, marvelling what might move me. I said that the time was full of suspicions, and that I was confident I could do her more service abroad than at home, as matters had fallen out. She said that I could do her as good service at home as any servant she had, if I pleased, but that I had left off to tell her my opinion of her proceedings. I told Her Majesty I feared that my

* The meaning is that Riccio had been instrumental in having the marriage celebrated by Roman Catholic rites and that Darnley's consent to this caused surprise and alarm, because he had conformed to Anglicanism in England.

opinions would be unpleasant to her. But she affirmed the contrary, telling me that I had enemies, who did what they could to put me in suspicion with the king, as a favourer of the Earl of Moray; which she had put out of the king's head, as being better acquainted with my nature and conditions, saying that she knew well that I had a liking to the Earl of Moray, but not of his manner of doing, and that she was assured that I loved her ten times better than him. She said moreover that if as much evil was spoken of her to me as was of me to her, that she would wish that I should give them no more credit against her, than she did or should do against me. She advised me to wait upon the king, who was but young, and gave him and her my good advice, as I was wont to do, which might help her to shun all apparent inconveniences. And she gave me her hand that she would take all in good part whatever I did speak, as proceeding from a loving and faithful servant; desiring me also to be a friend unto Riccio, who was hated without cause. The king also told me who they were who had spoken to him in my prejudice, and said they were known to be such common liars, as their tongue was no slander. By this means, the Queen's Majesty obliged me ever more and more to be careful for the weal of her service, and to take occasion of new to give Her Majesty my opinion, to make her profit by the mishandling of the Earl of Moray and his associates in England, by that queen's uncourteous dealing with them before the French and Spanish ambassadors, she having broken all her fair promises unto them.

First I told Her Majesty that, ever since her return to her own country, she had sundry times endeavoured to get her nobility and whole subjects entirely and soundly affected to take plain part with her in all actions whatsoever, and chiefly against England, in case she might have occasion of employing them; which she could not as yet obtain, because of the secret bond and promise was made among them, when the English army was at the siege of Leith, helping to put the Frenchmen out of Scotland.* 'Now,' said I, 'the occasion is offered, whereby Your Majesty may bring your desired intention to pass, if you could find in your heart either to pardon the Earl of Moray and his associates, or else to prolong† the parliament wherein they are to be forfeited until Your Majesty may advise and see whether it will be more your interest to forfeit them or give them ground of hope of obtaining your pardon, according as they make cause in following and observing such rules and

---

* In the spring of 1560 an English army had come to collaborate with the Scottish insurgents against the French forces of Mary of Guise in Leith. This intervention was preceded by the treaty of Berwick and followed by the treaty of Edinburgh, both of which were bonds between the Scottish reformers and England.

† Defer or postpone.

directions as shall be set down unto them by Your Majesty.' To this she answered that now, when they could do no better, they sought her; but when she sought their concurrence, as subjects to their native prince, they would not hear her: no more would she now hear their suits. I said, 'Whensoever they should make their suits, it should not be by me; but this I propose of myself to Your Majesty, who can choose the best and leave the worst in all accidents; since it is no little matter to gain the whole hearts of all your subjects, and also of a good number in England who favour them and their religion, who would admire such princely virtues, as to see Your Majesty to master your own passions and affections, and thereby think you most worthy to reign over king-doms; finding you ready to forgive, and loath to use vengeance, especially against subjects already vanquished, and not worthy of your wrath, and who are now so willing to be revenged upon your greatest adversary. So that clemency at such a time will be found most con-venient, and that part of justice called equity more profitable than rigour: for extremity frequently brings on desperate enterprises.'

At this Her Majesty entered into choler, saying, 'I defy them; what can they do, and what dare they do?' 'Madam', said I, 'with Your Majesty's pardon, my proposition is, in obedience to your own com-mandment, to show you my opinion and appearances at all times for the weal of your service.' Then she said she thanked me, granting that it was a good advice, and necessary to be done, and that yet she could not find in her heart to have to do with any of them, upon divers con-siderations; entreating me nevertheless to continue giving her my advice at all such occasions, for albeit she might not follow this, she might perchance do better another time. I answered, many noblemen being banished, and so near as Newcastle, having many other noble-men at home of their kindred and friends, so malcontent as I knew them to be for the time, with such unhappy rumours, whereof she was not ignorant, made me fear some attempt towards an alteration. For I told her I had heard threatening speeches that we should hear news ere the parliament was ended. Her Majesty answered that she had also some advertisements of the like rumours; but that our countrymen were talkative. After that I had been this way in hand with Her Majesty, I entered with Signor David in the same manner, for then he and I were under great friendship. But he disdained all danger, and despised counsel; so that I was compelled to say I feared over late repentance.

You have heard that Sir Nicholas Throckmorton was one of the two English ambassadors who were sent hither to stay the marriage, and to make many promises in his mistress's name to so many as would resist the same; which promises were afterwards denied by the Queen of England and by Mr Randolph. But Sir Nicholas Throckmorton stood neither in awe of queen or council, to declare the verity that he had made such promises to them in her name: which the council and craftiest courtiers thought strange, and were minded to punish him for avowing the same promise to be made in his mistress's name, had not he wisely and circumspectly obtained an act of council to produce for his warrant. And the said Sir Nicholas was so angry that he had been made an instrument to deceive the Scots banished lords, that he advised them to sue humbly for pardon at their own queen, and never again to offend her for any prince alive; and because they had no interest or prospects, he penned a persuasive proposition and sent in here to Her Majesty. . . .

When Her Majesty had pondered this discourse, it had great influence to move her, as well for the good opinion she had of him who sent it as being of her own nature more inclined to mercy than rigour; she was also wise, and was convinced that it tended to the advancement of her affairs in England. She therefore resolved to follow this advice and to prolong★ the parliament which she had called to forfeit the lords who had fled. Riccio appeared also to be won to the same effect. My Lord of Moray had sued to him very earnestly, and more humbly than could have been believed, with the present of a fair diamond enclosed within a letter, full of repentance and fair promises from that time forth to be his friend and protector. Which the said Riccio granted to do with the better will, that he perceived the king to bear him little good-will and to frown upon him.

Following this advice and advertisement given by Sir Nicholas Throckmorton, the Queen's Majesty sent my brother Sir Robert Melville to remain her ambassador in ordinary at the court of England, to be ready at all occasions in case any thing were treated at the parliament concerning the succession, and to pursue the design laid down by Sir Nicholas and her other friends in England.

In this mean time, there was a French gentleman sent home here, called Monsieur de Villamonte, with a commission to stay the queen in no ways to agree with the protestant banished lords, because that all catholic princes were banded to root them out of all Europe; which was a device of the Cardinal of Lorraine, lately returned from the council of Trent. He had caused the King of France to write earnestly to that effect. Which unhappy message hasted forward divers tragical accidents. For the queen was loath to offend her friends in France of the house of Guise, albeit she would have done little at that time by her inclination for the King of France, who was yet young and only guided by his mother,† whom she had no good cause to like well of. But Riccio was thought also of opinion not to offend so many confederate catholic

★ i.e. defer.   † Catherine de' Medici.

princes, and especially the Pope, with whom, as was alleged, he had secret intelligence. Hereby the queen was moved to hold forward the parliament and to forfeit the banished lords, against her own intention and her former deliberation.

Now there were a number of lords at home that appeared to be friends to the lords who were banished, as the Earl of Morton, the Lord Ruthven, the Lord Lindsay and divers other gentlemen who favoured them only for their religion. Some of them were discontent that their friends should be forfeited; others had other special reasons. Especially the Earl of Morton and his dependers feared a revocation that was alleged to be made at the said parliament, to bring back again to the crown divers great dispositions given out during the queen's minority, and some benefices which had been taken by noblemen at their own hands during the civil wars, under pretext of religion. These and other considerations moved them to consult together how to get the parliament stayed, and to make a change at court. The Earl of Morton had a crafty head, and had a cousin called George Douglas, natural son to the Earl of Angus who was father to Dame Margaret Douglas, Countess of Lennox, the king's mother. The said George was continually about the king, as his mother's brother, and put in his head such suspicion against Riccio that the king was won to give his consent over easily to the slaughter of Signor David. This the Lords of Morton, Lindsay, Ruthven and others had devised, to become that way masters of the court, and so to stop the parliament.

The king was yet very young, and not well acquainted with the nature of this nation. It was supposed also that the Earl of Lennox knew of the said design. For he had his chamber within the palace, and so had the Earls of Atholl, Bothwell and Huntly, who escaped by leaping down out of a window towards the little garden where the lions were lodged. This vile act was done upon a Saturday [9 March 1566] about six hours, when the queen was at supper in her cabinet. A number of armed men entered within the close, before the closing of the gates, and took the keys from the porter. One part of them went up through the king's chamber, conducted by the Lord Ruthven and George Douglas; the rest remained in the close with drawn swords in their hands, crying, 'A Douglas, A Douglas' for their slogan, for it was in the gloaming of the evening. The king was before gone up to the queen and was leaning upon her chair, when the Lord Ruthven entered with his helmet upon his head, and George Douglas entered in with him, and divers others, so rudely and irreverently that the table, candles, meat and dishes were overthrown. Riccio took the queen about the waist, crying for mercy; but George Douglas plucked forth the king's dagger that was behind his back and struck Riccio first with it, leaving it sticking in him. He, making great shrieks and cries, was rudely snatched from the queen, who could not get him safe neither for threats nor fairness. He was forcibly drawn forth of the cabinet and slain in the outer hall, and Her Majesty kept as a captive.

That same night the Earl of Atholl, the laird of Tullibardine, secretary Lethington and Sir James Balfour were permitted to retire themselves out of the palace of Holyroodhouse and were in some fear of their lives. The next morning, being Sunday, I was let forth at the gate, for I lay therein, and passing through the outer close, the queen, looking forth from a window, cried unto me to help her. I drew near, and asked what lay in my power. She said, 'Go to the provost of Edinburgh, and bid him in my name convene the town with speed and come and relieve me out of these traitors' hands. But run fast', says she, 'for they will stay you.' As this word was spoken, one Mr Nisbet, master of the household to the Earl of Lennox, was sent with a company to stay me. To whom I gave good words, saying that I was only going to sermon at St Giles's church, for it was Sunday. But I went in haste to the provost, and told him my commission from the queen. He answered that he had another commandment from the king; but that he should draw the people to the tolbooth,* and see what they would do, though he expected no help from their hands, because the most part of them were so discontent with the present government that they desired a change. Yet he convened them, though in vain, and showed me their answer. Which I made Her Majesty to understand by one of her ladies, whom she sent again unto me, and said that she supposed that my Lord of Moray and his associates, who were yet banished, remaining at Newcastle, would be sent for by those who were about her; willing me at his coming to admonish and persuade him not to defile himself as to join with them but to hold himself free, and be her friend in this strait; which doing should be his great advantage, and win her love and favour as ever he had it. Which commission I executed at his coming upon the Monday; but he was more moved at his meeting with Her Majesty, who embraced and kissed him, alleging that if he had been at home he would not have suffered her to have been so uncourteously handled. Which so moved him, that the tears fell from his eyes. He knew also that it was not for his cause, but for their own particular ends, that the greatest part who had made that enterprise had therein engaged. Yet he and his company kept the day to the which they were summoned to the parliament.

In the mean time, the king repented his folly, whereupon Her Majesty took occasion to persuade him to abandon those lords who had committed so odious a crime as to put her in hazard of her life,

* The town-house, where the burgh council met.

together with his child which was in her womb. Nevertheless she was resolved to forgive them, and give them what security they would devise. The lords, seeing the king drawn from them and my Lord of Moray not so bold for them as they expected, were fain to do the next best, and consented that a pacification should be penned, which was divers times written over again to put in and out certain heads and clauses, to drive time until the writing might appear plausible and at a point. Her Majesty caused the king to advise them to discharge the guard that kept her, that their security might be passed, she being at liberty, or else it would not avail them. So that night, which was Tuesday, they went all to their rest; but the queen, king, Traquair and Arthur Erskine, master stabler for the time, went out of Holy-roodhouse at midnight toward the castle of Dunbar, and left word with one of her ladies to me, that I should be earnest to keep the Earl of Moray from joining with the other lords. They the next morning found themselves greatly disappointed, without any appearance of a settlement or pacification. In the mean time Her Majesty used diligence to send out of Dunbar Mr John Hay, Abbot of Balmerino, to my Lord of Moray, willing him to take my help to draw my Lord of Moray utterly from the late offenders, and in so doing to be pardoned, he and all his part-takers. They on this manner being destitute of all assistance, were compelled to flee to England, to Newcastle, where in a manner they might find the other lords' nests yet warm.

A few days before, my Lord Duke, my Lords of Argyll, Glencairn and Rothes had obtained their pardons; for they were divided during their banishment, and Her Majesty thought not meet to have so many lords against her; as now again, when the Earl of Moray was drawn from the Earl of Morton and his accomplices, because he had for the time a great friendship and many dependers, she might be the more easily revenged upon that most detestable deed of murdering her servant in her presence. As she was big with child, it appeared to be done to destroy both her and her child; for they might have killed the said Riccio in any other part, at any time they pleased. My Lord Moray and his dependants desired me to carry their humble thanks and consent unto Her Majesty's desire and to signify unto her how he had discharged himself unto them that had committed that vile act; and would promise Her Majesty never to have to do with them, nor intercede for them.

I rencountered Her Majesty coming from Dunbar to Haddington, and was very favourably received with great thanks for my continual care of her honour and welfare. That night in Haddington she sub-scribed divers remissions for my Lord Moray and his dependers, lamenting unto me the king's folly, ingratitude and misbehaviour and also my Lord of Lennox's part, which I supposed had been pardoned; and I excused the same the best I could, imputing it to his youth, and laid the blame upon George Douglas and others; praying Her Majesty, for many necessary considerations, to remove out of her mind all causes of ill-feeling against him, seeing that she had chosen him herself against the opinion of many, and promised him favour again of new. But I could perceive nothing but a great grudge that she had in her heart. That night in Haddington, the king enquired of me if the Lord of Moray had written to him. I answered that his letter to the queen was written in haste, and that he esteemed the queen and him but one. He said, 'He might have also written to me.' Then he enquired what was become of Morton, Ruthven and the rest of that company. I told him I believed they were fled, but I knew not whither. 'As they have brewed,' says he, 'so let them drink.' It appeared that he was sorry that he had deserted them, finding the queen's favour but cold. The next day they came to Edinburgh and lodged within the castle, where some were apprehended and executed who had been in the close of the palace and had kept the gates that night wherein Riccio was slain.

Her Majesty was now far gone with child, and went to Stirling, intending to lie in there. Thither the king followed her, and from that to Alloa. At length she came back to the castle of Edinburgh. It was thought that she fled from the king's company. I travailed earnestly to help matters betwixt them, and was so importunate that I was thought so troublesome that Her Majesty desired my Lord of Moray to reprove me, and charge me not to be familiar with the king; who went up and down all alone, and few durst bear him company. He was misliked by the queen and by all such as secretly favoured the late banished lords; so that it was a great pity to see that good young prince cast off, who failed rather for want of good counsel and experience than of evil will. It appeared to be his destiny to like better of flatterers and ill company than plain speakers and good men: which hath been the wreck of many princes, who with good company would have produced worthy effects.

About this time the Queen of England was so far visited with a hot fever, that none believed any other but death to be the end of it: all that kingdom was thereby in great perplexity. But a thing is to be marked, that two contrary factions there for the time had both determined, unknown to each other, to send for our queen, and set the crown of England upon her head. My brother Sir Robert Melville was then ambassador there resident, and I served in place of secretary here at home, because secretary Lethington was absent under some suspicion. He sent home continual advertisements how to proceed, and I again returned the answers at Her Majesty's direction.

JAMES HEPBURN, FOURTH EARL OF BOTHWELL, 1566

III

Mary and Bothwell

Now the Earl of Bothwell's favour increased, to the great dissatisfaction of many. He and the Earl of Huntly and the Bishop of Ross envied the favour that the queen showed unto the Earl of Moray; for they were upon contrary courses. The queen on the other hand knew what favour was borne unto him both in England and Scotland, and that she would be better liked in both kingdoms then for his sake; following and taking up again the former advice and information sent her by Sir Nicholas Throckmorton; and she forgot not the late help he had made her at his home-coming. These two earls, with the foresaid bishop, took occasion, when the time of Her Majesty's delivery drew near, to persuade her to imprison my Lord of Moray, to remain no longer than she should be delivered; alleging that they were assuredly advertised that he and his dependers were minded to bring in the banished lords, even at the very time of her child-bearing; for they thought, if once he were warded, they should find devices enough to cause him be kept and disgraced, ever the longer the more when he should be absent, and not have opportunity of answering and resisting their calumnies. . . .

The Queen Majesty's reckoning being near run out, she caused make my dispatch for England, to be in readiness to announce the good news of her delivery to that queen; leaving a blank in her letter, to be filled up with either a son or a daughter, as it should please God to grant unto her; and to require the Queen of England to send hither, in her name, such of hers as she knew to be best addicted to entertain good love and friendship betwixt them, to be gossips* (for so they are called in England), as also to satisfy her concerning the most part of Killigrew's demands in her name.†

All the while I lay within the castle of Edinburgh, praying night and day for Her Majesty's good and happy delivery of a fair son. This prayer being granted, I was the first who was thereof advertised, by

* Godparents.

† Henry Killigrew had recently been sent by Elizabeth as her ambassador to Scotland.

the Lady Boyne, in Her Majesty's name, to part with diligence the 19
of June 1566, betwixt ten and eleven in the morning. It struck twelve
hours when I took horse, and was that night at Berwick. The fourth
day after I was at London; and did first meet with my brother Sir
Robert, who that same night sent and advertised secretary Cecil of my
arrival and of the birth of the prince; desiring him to keep it quiet
until my being at court, to show it myself unto Her Majesty, who was
for the time at Greenwich, where Her Majesty was in great merriness
and dancing after supper. But so soon as the secretary Cecil whispered
in her ear the news of the prince's birth, all merriness was laid aside for
the night; all present marvelling what might move so sudden a change;
for the queen did sit down, with her hand upon her cheek, bursting out
to some of her ladies that the Queen of Scots was lighter of a fair son,
while she was but a barren stock.

The next morning was appointed for me to get audience. At that
time my brother and I went by water to Greenwich, and were met by
some friends who told us how sorrowful Her Majesty was at my news
and what counsel she had got to show a glad countenance: which she
did, in her best apparel, saying that the joyful news of the queen her
sister's delivery of a fair son, which I had sent her by secretary Cecil,
had recovered her out of a heavy sickness which had holden her for
fifteen days. Therefore she welcomed me with a merry countenance
and thanked me for the diligence I had used. All this she said, before I
had delivered unto her my letter of credence. After that she had read
it, I declared how the queen had hasted me towards Her Majesty,
whom she knew of all her friends would be most joyful of the good
news of her delivery, albeit dear bought with the peril of her life, for I
said that she was so sore handled that she wished she had never been
married. This I said by the way, to give her a little scare from marriage:
for so my brother had informed me, because sometimes she threatened
to marry the Archduke Charles of Austria, when any man pressed her
to declare a second person. Then I requested Her Majesty to be a gossip
to the queen, for our cummers are called gossips in England; to which
she gladly condescended. Then I said that Her Majesty would have a
fair occasion to see the queen, which she had so oft desired. Whereat
she smiled, saying she wished that her estate and affairs might permit
her, and promised to send both honourable lords and ladies to supply
her room. Then I gave Her Majesty, in my queen's name, most hearty
thanks for her friendly visiting and comforting of the queen by Mr
Henry Killigrew. She enquired if I had left him in Scotland, and what
was the cause of his long stay. I answered that the queen took to child-
bed shortly after his arrival, which was the chief cause of his delay. But
I had in commission to tell Her Majesty something thereabout, to

satisfy her mind in the mean time, and to thank Her Majesty for the putting away of the Scots rebels out of her country, albeit there were some reports that they were yet secretly entertained by some of her subjects, though I believed not that any of her subjects durst be so bold or so disobedient. She affirmed they were out of her country, and if it might be otherwise tried, it should not pass without rigorous punishment....

Before I took my leave to return, I entered with Her Majesty concerning the title; for my Lord of Leicester was become my queen's avowed friend, and had been twice in hand with the Queen of England a little before my coming, desiring her to declare the Queen of Scots second person; alleging it would be her greatest weal and security, and said in anger that Cecil would undo all. Likewise the Duke of Norfolk, the Earl of Pembroke and several others showed themselves more openly her friends, after they understood the birth of the prince; so that Her Majesty's matters in England were for the time far forward. Therefore I was advised to say unto Her Majesty that I was assured she had delayed declaring the queen second person only till she might see such succession of her body as now God had graciously granted; praying Her Majesty to take the same fair opportunity of satisfying the minds of many, as well in England as in Scotland, who desired to see that matter out of doubt, and the rather because that the queen my mistress would never seek any place or right in England, but by Her Majesty's favour and furtherance. She answered that the birth of the prince was to her a great spur to cause the most skilful lawyers in England to use greater diligence in trying out that matter, which she esteemed to belong most justly to her good sister, and that she wished from her heart that it should be that way decided. I replied that at my last being there, Her Majesty was upon the same terms; but that as I had brought her good news from the queen, I was very desirous to be so happy as to carry home with me unto Her Majesty the good tidings of that so long delayed declaration. She answered that she hoped to satisfy the queen further in that matter by such noblemen as she should send into Scotland for the baptism of the prince. All this I perceived to be but shifts, and so took my leave, because my brother was to remain there. The next day Her Majesty sent unto me two grooms of her chamber, with her writing and present of a fair chain....

About this time Her Majesty was advertised by my brother's letters that the Earl of Bedford was upon his journey toward Scotland with an honourable company, as also the ambassadors of France and Savoy, for the baptism of the prince; which moved Her Majesty to pass to Stirling with the prince, for the solemnizing thereof. But she was still sad and pensive for the late foul act committed in her presence so irreverently, she being their born queen, and then in such hazard of losing the fruit of her womb. So many great sighs she would give, that it was pity to hear her; and over few were careful to comfort her.

Sometime she would declare part of her grief to me; which I essayed to put out of her mind by all possible persuasions, in telling her how I believed that the greater multitude of friends that she had got in England should have caused her to forget in Scotland the lesser number of enemies and unruly offenders, unworthy of her wrath; and that her excellent qualities, in clemency, temperance and fortitude, should not suffer her mind to be suppressed with the remembrance of their vile offences; but that rather she should bend up her spirit by a princely and womanly behaviour, whereby she might best gain the hearts of the whole people and subjects, both here at home and afield; humbly requesting Her Majesty, first to consult with her God, next with her honour, and thirdly with her interest, in the establishing of her estate and in joining the kingdoms of Great Britain in a happy monarchy, which she knew to be so near a point to be brought to pass in her person; seeing also the banished estate of the offenders so miserable, they not having a hole to hide their head in, nor a penny to buy their dinner, that the most noble natures would almost think them sufficiently punished.

How seemly it is to a queen to be pitiful and a woman to want vengeance, I would report to her own judgment: 'and whether presently it be meeter for your honour and greatness to cease from any desire or pursuit of any further revenge, whereupon may ensue more desperate enterprises; or to give place unto necessity and reason, to rule over the beastly passions of the mind. Wherefore are princes called divine persons? No prince can pretend to this title, but he who draws near the nature of God by godliness and good government, being slow to punish and ready to forgive. It is manifestly known that all wise princes have no feud at their enemies longer than they see it may be needful for the weal of their affairs and estate; and they can change their favour and hatred according to time and occasions. Your Majesty may remember that many things might have been better managed: I speak this with love and reverence. Your Majesty might well have been as well obeyed as ever was any king in Scotland, if you had taken such princely care as was requisite. You know how that by Your Majesty's own express commandment I did show you long before what inconveniences were like to fall out upon the grudges and appearances I perceived before the slaughter of Riccio; and God is my witness I did what lay in my power to have them eschewed and prevented. And since that time Your Majesty hath repented that my opinion for the time was not followed; I pray God that the like repentance fall not out again too late. At my being in England, your adversaries were beginning to make their vantage upon vain reports that our westerly winds had blown east among them; so that my brother and I had enough to do to beat it out of the heads of divers who were devotedly addicted to the advancement of your title.'

This communing began at the entry of her supper in her ear, in French, when she was casting great sighs and would not eat for any persuasion that my Lords of Moray and Mar could make to her. The supper being ended, Her Majesty took me by the hand, and went down through the park of Stirling, and came up through the town, ever reasoning with me upon these purposes. And albeit she took hardly with them at first, she began to alter her mind, thinking fit that my Lord of Bedford should intercede for her rebels; they to be banished out of England and Scotland during her pleasure, and to be better unto them with time, according to their future deportments: and for her part, she purposed to proceed with such a gracious government as might win the victory over herself and all her competitors and enemies in time coming, as she had done at her first home-coming and could do as well as any prince in Europe. But, alas! she had over evil company about her for the time. The Earl of Bothwell, who had a mark of his own that he shot at, as soon as he understood of her wise and merciful deliberations, took occasion to bring in the Earl of Morton and his associates, to make them his friends, and by them to fortify his faction. For apparently he had already in his mind to perform the foul murder of the king, which he afterwards put in execution, that he might marry the queen. Both which he brought to pass to his own utter wreck and confusion, and brought on also great trouble and mischief to the country; and was at last the queen's wreck, and the hindrance of all our hopes in the hasty obtaining of all her desires concerning the crown of England, for a time.

The Queen's Majesty being advertised that the Earl of Bedford was come as far as Berwick on his journey to the baptism, sent me well accompanied with diligence to meet him at Coldingham, to be his first convoy, and to inform him rightly of all her proceedings, and to overthrow all evil bruits invented by the malice of her enemies. All this of my own head, by way of the long familiarity between him and me, for, as I have said, it was a perverse time; and the more that the number of her friends increased in England, the more practices her enemies made, and the more lies were invented against her. So the good earl gave me more credit than he did to any wrong report that was made, and was at this time become one of the surest and most affectionate friends she had in England.

There came with him Mr Carey, eldest son to my Lord of Hunsdon; Mr Hatton, greatest in favour with the Queen of England for the time; and one called Mr Lignish, greatest in favour with the Duke of Norfolk; and a good number of knights and gentlemen of Yorkshire, with the most part of the captains of Berwick. Her Majesty was sufficiently informed by my brother's writing to her and me, what kind of language and entertainment was most proper for the earl and each of them.

When all the rest of the ambassadors were come, they envied to see the Englishmen more friendly and familiarly used than themselves. For then she had more to do with England than with France. And the French earl who was sent was no courtier, but a simple man. And Monsieur de Morat, the Duke of Savoy's ambassador, being far off, came after the baptism. During their abode at Stirling, there was daily banqueting, dancing and triumph. And at the principal banquet there fell out a great grudge and cause of ill-feeling among the Englishmen: for a Frenchman called Bastian devised a number of men formed like satyrs, with long tails, and whips in their hands, running before the meat, which was brought through the great hall upon a trim engine, marching as appeared alone, with musicians clothed like maids, singing and playing upon all sorts of instruments. But the satyrs were not content only to make a way, but put their hands behind them to their tails, which they wagged with their hands in such sort as the Englishmen supposed it had been devised and done in derision of them; stupidly apprehending that which they should not have appeared to understand.* For Mr Hatton, Mr Lignish and the most part of the gentlemen desired to sup before the queen and great banquet, that they might see the better the whole order and ceremonies of the triumph; but, so soon as they perceived the satyrs wagging their tails or romples, they all sat down upon the bare floor behind the back of the table, that they might not see themselves derided, as they thought. Mr Hatton said unto me, if it were not in the queen's presence and hall, he would put a dagger to the heart of that French knave Bastian, who he alleged had done it out of despite that the queen made more of them than of the Frenchmen. I excused the matter the best I could; but the noise was so great behind the queen's back, where Her Majesty and my Lord of Bedford did sit, that they heard and turned about their faces to learn what the matter meant. I informed them that it was occasioned by the satyrs, so that the queen and my Lord of Bedford had both enough to do to get them appeased. It fell out unhappily at such a time, and the English gentlemen committed a great error to seem to understand it was done against them. But my Lord of Bedford was discreet and interpreted all things to the best.

* The Scots professed to believe that Englishmen had tails.

My Lord of Bedford was rewarded with a rich chain of diamonds, worth 2000 crowns; Mr Carey with a chain of pearl and a ring with a fair diamond; Mr Hatton had a chain with Her Majesty's picture, and a ring; Mr Lignish and five others of quality had all chains. I was commanded with many others to attend them to the boundary road. They parted all very well content and satisfied with the Queen's Majesty, but lamented that they saw so little account made of the king. My Lord of Bedford desired me to request Her Majesty to entertain him as she had done at the beginning, for her own honour and the advancement of her affairs; which I forgot not to do at all occasions.

[Her Majesty being at Jedburgh, to visit the Earl of Bothwell, who was overthrown by the thieves and hurt unto the death, as was supposed – yet he recovered again to work greater mischief – Her Majesty fell there deadly sick, and made a very wise and discreet testament, and many godly prayers, and gave many good documents to my Lord of Moray; which all I set out in writing and sent into England at divers times; which my brother showed to divers noblemen and other favourers of Her Majesty, who all desired copies of the said letters; whereof my brother advertised Her Majesty, to cause me continue, alleging that it laid down divers evil rumours that her enemies spread abroad; for the days were evil, and it was a busy time.]*

After the baptism and parting of the ambassadors, Her Majesty, desirous to put good order upon the Borders, sent the Earl of Bothwell before, who in the pursuit of thieves was hurt. Her Majesty passed afterward to Jedburgh herself, where the Earls of Bothwell and Huntly enterprised the slaughter of the Earl of Moray, but the Lord Hume came there with forces and prevented that enterprise. Her Majesty returned by the Merse, and desired to see Berwick afar off, where she was honoured with many shots of artillery; and Sir John Foster, warden upon the English border, came then and conferred with Her Majesty for keeping of good order. And the mean time while he was speaking with Her Majesty on horseback, his courser did rise up with his fore legs, to take the queen's horse by the neck with his teeth, but his fore feet hurt Her Majesty's thigh very ill. Incontinent the warden lighted off his horse, and sat down upon his knees craving Her Majesty's pardon; for then all England did much reverence her. Her Majesty made him rise, and said that she was not hurt, yet it compelled Her Majesty to tarry two days at the castle of Hume until she was well again. The king followed her about where she rode, but got no good countenance; and therefore he passed to Glasgow, where he fell sick –

* This passage, written earlier in the MS and marked to be inserted at this point, overlaps with the succeeding paragraph. In fact the visit to the Borders took place before and not after the prince's baptism.

for displeasure, as was alleged, not without some rumour of an ill drink by some of his servants.

In the mean time the Earl of Bothwell ruled all at court, and brought home some of the banished lords, and packed up a quiet friendship with the Earl of Morton. After Her Majesty's return to Edinburgh, she renewed a friendship again between the Earls of Moray, Bothwell, Huntly, Argyll and others. From that Her Majesty went to Stirling to see the prince, and returned again to Edinburgh, whither the king was afterward brought and lodged in the Kirk o' Field, as a place of good air, where he might best recover his health. But many suspected that the Earl of Bothwell had some enterprise against him, few durst advertise him, because he told all again to some of his own servants, who were not all honest. Yet Lord Robert, Earl of Orkney,* told him that if he retired not hastily out of that place, it would cost him his life; which he told again to the queen; and my Lord Robert denied that ever he spoke it: this advertisement moved the Earl of Bothwell to haste forward his enterprise. He made a train of powder, or had made one of before, which came under the house where the king lay, and in the night did blow up the said house with the powder; but it was spoken by a page that the king was first taken forth and brought down to a low stable, where a napkin was stopped in his mouth and smothered by holding in of his breath, and afterwards laid under a tree, and [then they] blew up the house.

Everybody suspected the Earl of Bothwell, and those who durst speak freely to others said plainly that it was he. Whereupon he drew together a number of lords to be a led assize,† which acquitted him; some for fear, some for favour, and the greatest part for commodity. This way being acquitted, he remained still the greatest favourite at court. My Lord of Moray was retired from the court certain days before. Her Majesty kept her chamber for a while. I came to the chamber door the next morning after the murder, and the Earl of Bothwell said that Her Majesty was sorrowful and quiet. He came forth and told he saw the strangest accident that ever chanced, to wit that thunder had come out of the sky and had burnt the king's house, and himself found lying dead a little distance from the house under a tree. He desired me to go up and see him, how that there was not a hurt nor a mark on all his body. But when I went up to see him, he was laid within a chamber, and kept by one Alexander Durham; but I could not get a sight of him.

The rumour began to rise that the Queen would marry the Earl of

* Lord Robert Stewart, although he held the lands of Orkney at this time, was not created Earl until 1581.

† An assize managed, or manipulated.

Bothwell, who had six months before married the Earl of Huntly's sister, and would part with his own lady. Whereat every good subject who loved the queen's honour and the prince's safety had sore hearts, thinking Her Majesty would be dishonoured, and the prince in danger to be cut off by him who had slain his father. But few or none durst speak in the contrary. Yet my Lord Herries, a worthy nobleman, came to Edinburgh well accompanied, and told Her Majesty what rumours were going through the country of the Earl of Bothwell's murdering the king and how that she was to marry him, requesting Her Majesty most humbly upon his knees to remember her honour and dignity and the safety of the prince, which all would be in danger of loss in case she married the said earl, with many other great persuasions, to eschew such utter wreck and inconveniencies as would be thereby occasioned. Her Majesty marvelled of such rumours without purpose, and said that there was no such thing in her mind. He asked pardon, and prayed her to take his honest meaning in a good part. And immediately took his farewell, fearing the Earl of Bothwell should get word thereof. He had fifty horse with him at the time, and caused his men to buy as many new spears in Edinburgh, and rode home.

I was about to have said as much to Her Majesty; but in the mean time there came a letter to me from one Thomas Bishop, a Scottishman who had been long in England and was a great persuader of many in England to favour Her Majesty's title. He used oft to write unto my brother and me informations and advertisements. At this time he used even the like language that my Lord Herries had spoken, but more freely, because he was absent in another country. He adjured me to show the said letter unto Her Majesty, declaring how it was bruited in England that Her Majesty was to marry the Earl of Bothwell, who was the murderer of her husband, another wife's husband, a man full of reproach and grangoir,* with many other reproaches that he alleged; rumours he could not believe, by reason of her noble wit and qualities and the honourable mark that she shot at; and in case she married him, she would lose the favour of God, her own reputation, the kingdoms of England, Ireland and Scotland; with many other dissuasions and examples of history, which would be tedious to rehearse. I had been absent, but I went to court to show this letter to Her Majesty, protesting that she would take it in good part.

After that Her Majesty had read the said letter, she gave it me again without any more speech, but called upon the secretary Lethington, and told him that I had shown her a strange letter, desiring him also to see it. He asked what it could be. She answered, a device of his own, tending only to the wreck of the Earl of Bothwell. He took me by

---

* Venereal disease.

the hand, and drew me aside to see the said letter; which when he had read, he asked what was in my mind, and said, 'So soon as the Earl Bothwell gets word, as I fear he will, he will not fail to slay you.' I said it was a sore matter to see that good princess run to utter wreck, and nobody to forewarn her. He said I had done more honestly than wisely. 'I pray you,' says he, 'retire diligently before the Earl of Bothwell comes up from his dinner.' Her Majesty told him at her first meeting, having first engaged him to promise to do me no harm. But I was flown and was sought but could not be found till his fury was quenched, for I was advertised there was nothing but slaughter in case I had been gotten. Whereat Her Majesty was dissatisfied, telling him that he would cause her to be left of all her servants; whereupon he promised that I should receive no harm; whereof I being advertised, I went again unto Her Majesty, showing her that she had never so much injured me as by thinking that I had invented the said letter, assuring her that it came from the said Thomas Bishop; and albeit it had not come from him, I was minded of duty to have told Her Majesty my opinion about it in all reverence and humility. She said that matters were not that far forward, but she had no will to enter in the terms.

Shortly after Her Majesty went to Stirling, and in her back-coming betwixt Linlithgow and Edinburgh the Earl of Bothwell rencountered her with a great company and took Her Majesty's horse by the bridle; his men took the Earl of Huntly, the secretary Lethington and me, and carried us captives to Dunbar; all the rest were permitted to go free. Then the Earl of Bothwell boasted he would marry the queen, who would or who would not; yea whether she would herself or not. Captain Blackater, who had taken me, alleged that it was with the queen's own consent. The next day in Dunbar I obtained permission to go home. Afterwards the court came to Edinburgh; and there a number of noblemen were drawn together in a chamber within the palace, where they all subscribed that the marriage between the queen and the Earl Bothwell was very meet, he having many friends in Lothian and upon the Borders, to cause good order to be kept.* And then the queen could not but marry him, seeing he had ravished her and lain with her against her will. I cannot tell how nor by what law he parted with his own wife, sister to the Earl of Huntly.†

A little before this the Earl of Moray had desired licence to go to France. The secretary Lethington had been long in suspicion absent

* This is apparently a reference to the bond usually said to have been signed in 'Ainslie's tavern'.

† In two concurrent cases, before different courts, the Countess of Bothwell obtained a decree of divorce on the ground of her husband's adultery and he obtained a decree of nullity on the ground of consanguinity.

KIRK O'FIELD, 1567

from court, and was brought in again by my brother Sir Robert's persuasion, for the great credit and handling he had with many noble-men in England, favourers of Her Majesty's title; albeit that he had as great credit and influence himself, he would not follow the custom of ambitious courtiers who would have all the thanks to themselves, unwilling to suffer a companion. He knew also that he was suspected, because the Earl Bothwell was not his friend. Always Lethington was again brought in; but not long after the Earl of Bothwell thought to have slain him in the queen's chamber, had not Her Majesty come betwixt and saved him; but he fled the next day and tarried with the Earl of Atholl. As for me I tarried not at court but now and then, yet I chanced to be there at the marriage. When I came that time to the court, I found my lord Duke of Orkney* sitting at his supper, who said I had been a great stranger, desiring me to sit down and sup with him, the Earl of Huntly, the justice clerk and divers others being sitting at table with him. I said I had already supped. Then he called for a cup of wine and drank to me, that I might pledge him, like a Dutchman. He bade me drink it out to grow fatter, 'for', said he, 'the zeal of the commonwealth hath eaten you up, and made you so lean.' I answered that every little member should serve for some use, but the care of the commonwealth appertained most to him and the rest of the nobility, who should be as fathers to the same. 'I knew well,' says he, 'he would find a pin for every bore.' Then he fell in discoursing of gentlewomen, speaking such filthy language that I left him, and went up to the queen, who was very glad of my coming.

The marriage was made in the palace of Holyroodhouse, at a preach-ing, by Adam Bothwell, Bishop of Orkney, in the great hall where the council uses to sit, according to the order of the reformed religion, and not in the chapel at the mass, as was the king's marriage.

After the marriage, he who was Earl of Bothwell, now Duke of Orkney, was very earnest to get the prince in his hands, but my Lord of Mar, who was a true nobleman, would not deliver him out of his custody, alleging that he could not without consent of the three estates; yet he was so oft pressed by them that had the authority in their hands, that he was put to great strait, after that he had made divers refusals; among others he made his moan to me, praying me to help to save the prince out of their hands who had slain his father and had already made his vaunt among his familiars that if he could get him once in his hands he would warrant him from revenging his father's death. I said that I would wish that it lay in my power to make any help in that; he asked if I could find any outgate.† I answered that I was intimately acquainted with Sir James Balfour, and that I knew

* Bothwell's new title.   † Way out, solution.

how matters stood betwixt Bothwell and him; for I understood by the
laird of Whitelaw that there were some jealousies and suspicions
arisen betwixt them. I assured him, as the said laird told me, that the
Earl Bothwell would have the castle out of his hands;* the earl and he
had been great companions, and he was also great with the queen, so
that the custody of the castle of Edinburgh was committed to him; but
afterwards he would not consent to be present, nor take plain part
with the murderers of the king, whereby he came in suspicion with
the Earl of Bothwell, who dared no more credit him, so that he would
have had the castle out of his hands, to have committed the charge
thereof to the laird of Beinston.†

This my Lord of Mar made one of his excuses, that he saw not a
sure house to keep the prince in case he would deliver him. Whereupon
I took occasion, when I returned to Edinburgh, to deal with Sir James
Balfour not to part with the castle, whereby he might be an instrument
to save the prince and the queen, who was so disdainfully handled,
and with such reproachful language, that in presence of Arthur Erskine
I heard her ask for a knife to stab herself, 'or else,' said she, 'I shall
drown myself.' Now, said I to Sir James Balfour, there was no security
for him to be out of suspicion but to keep the castle in his own hands
and to be the good instrument both of saving queen and prince and in
assisting the nobility, who were about to crown the prince and to
pursue the Earl of Bothwell for the king's murder. I told him that unless he took part with them therein he would be holden as art and part
of the said murder, by reason of his long familiarity with the Earl of
Bothwell; that it was a happy thing for him that the said earl was become in suspicion of him; assuring him that I had intelligence, by one
who was of the Earl of Bothwell's council, to wit, the laird of Whitelaw,
captain of the castle of Dunbar, that the Earl of Bothwell was determined to take the castle of Edinburgh from him, and make the laird
of Beinston captain thereof, and then to put the prince there in his
keeping. Sir James Balfour gave ear incontinent to my proposition, and
consented to help to pursue the murderer with the rest, upon condition
that the laird of Grange would promise to be his protector, in case the
nobility should alter upon him; for he and many of them had formerly
run contrary courses, so that he durst not credit them.

The Earl of Mar was hereof advertised by his brother Alexander
Erskine, who was true and careful of the prince's safety and came
secretly to me at midnight; for the days were dangerous for all honest
men. Now my Lord of Mar being continually required and threatened
to deliver the prince out of his hands, at length granted (only to drive

* Balfour was at the time keeper of Edinburgh Castle.
† Beinston was a Hepburn and a dependant of Bothwell.

time) upon condition that an honest responsible nobleman should be made captain of the castle of Edinburgh; because he saw no other sure house to keep the prince in, he should deliver him unto the queen, his mother, which he was not minded to do as long as he might resist. Albeit, he was not a good dissimuler, but thought it a meet answer to drive a little time and assuage the present fury, until the nobility might convene to pursue the murderers and to crown the prince, as they had already concluded at a secret meeting among themselves; which was not so secret but that one of the said lords gave advertisement thereof to the Earl of Bothwell, how that they were minded to environ the palace of Holyroodhouse and therein to apprehend him. Whereupon he forgot enquiring after the prince, being only now concerned how to save himself; therefore he fled out of Edinburgh to the castle of Borthwick and from that to the castle of Dunbar, taking always the queen with him wherever he went.

All Scotland cried out upon the foul murder of the king; but few of them were careful how to get it revenged, till they were driven thereto by the crying out of all other nations generally against all Scottishmen wherever they travelled either by sea or land. Among other princes, the King of France sent hitherto his ambassador Monsieur du Croc, a grave, aged, discreet gentleman, advanced by the house of Guise, a letter, marvelling that such a foul murder being committed upon the person of a king, so few honest subjects were found apparently to find fault with the same, far less to seek after any sure trial or see the same punished. Whereupon the lords who had the enterprise in their heads were hasted forward to take arms; and in the mean time they obliged themselves, by a writing under their hands, which they delivered to the said Monsieur du Croc to send to the king his master, that they should do their utmost diligence to try out the authors of that foul murder of their king; and in the mean time convened to the number of 3000 men, and came first to Edinburgh, and there set out a proclamation of their just quarrel. Also sundry libels were set out both in rhyme and prose, pitiful and persuasive, to move the hearts of the whole subjects to assist and take part in so good a cause.

The Earl of Bothwell, having the queen in his company, convened a greater number out of the Merse and Lothian, and out of all parts where he had interest or friendship, over Her Majesty's proclamation, which was not well obeyed for the time; and so many as came had no hearts to fight in that quarrel. Yet the Earl of Bothwell marched forward out of Dunbar toward Edinburgh, taking the queen with him. The lords again with their companies went out of Edinburgh on foot, with great earnestness and fierceness to fight. Both armies lay not far from Carberry: the Earl Bothwell's men camped upon the hill head, in

a strength very advantageous; the lords camped at the foot of the hill.
And albeit Her Majesty was there, I cannot call it her army, for many
of those who were with her were of opinion that she had intelligence
with the lords, especially such as understood of the Earl of Bothwell's
mishandling of her and many indignities that he had both said and
done unto her since their marriage. He was so beastly and suspicious
that he suffered her not to pass one day in patience, without making
her shed abundance of salt tears. Thus part of his own company detested him; other part believed that Her Majesty would fain have been
quit of him, but thought shame to be the doer thereof directly herself.

   In the mean time the laird of Grange did ride about the hill with
200 horsemen, who came there with Drumlanrig, Cessford and Cowd-
ingknows, thinking to be betwixt the Earl of Bothwell and Dunbar,
and was minded to make an onset that way, which was plain and even,
in the mean time that the lords should come up the hill to the part
where their adversaries were camped.

   When the queen understood that the laird of Grange was chief of
that company of horsemen, she sent the laird of Ormiston to desire him
to come and speak with her under surety; which he did, after he had
sent and obtained leave of the lords. As he was speaking with Her
Majesty, the Earl of Bothwell had appointed a soldier to shoot him,
until the queen gave a cry, and said that he should not do her that
shame, seeing she had promised that he should come and return safely.
He was declaring unto the queen that all of them would honour and
serve her upon condition that she would abandon the Earl of Bothwell,
who had murdered her husband and could not be a husband unto her,
as he had but lately married the Earl of Huntly's sister. The Earl of
Bothwell hearkened, and heard part of this language, and offered the
singular combat to any who would maintain that he had murdered the
king. The laird of Grange promised to send him an answer shortly
thereunto. So he took his leave of the queen, and went down the hill
to the lords; who were content that the laird of Grange should fight
with him in that quarrel; for he first offered himself, and sent up word
that he would challenge him and fight with him upon that quarrel.
The Earl of Bothwell answered that he was neither earl nor lord, but a
baron; and so was not his equal. The like answer made he to Tullibardine. Then my Lord Lindsay offered to fight him, which he could
not plainly refuse; but his heart grew ever colder as time passed. Then
the queen sent again for the laird of Grange, and said to him that if the
lords would do as he had spoken to her, she should put away the Earl
of Bothwell and come unto them. Whereupon he asked the lords if he
might in their name make Her Majesty that promise; which they
willed him to do. Then he rode up again, and saw the Earl of Bothwell

part; and came down again, and assured the lords thereof. They desired him to go up the hill again, and receive the queen: who met him, and said, 'Laird of Grange, I render myself unto you, upon the conditions you rehearsed unto me in the name of the lords.' Whereupon she gave him her hand, which he kissed, leading Her Majesty's horse by the bridle down the hill unto the lords, who came forward and met her.

The noblemen used all dutiful reverence; but some of the rascals cried out against her despitefully, till the laird of Grange and others, who knew their duty better, drew their swords, and struck at such as did speak irreverent language; which the nobility well allowed of. Her Majesty was that night convoyed to Edinburgh, and lodged in the midst of the town, in the provost's lodging. As she came through the town, the common people cried out against Her Majesty at the windows and stairs; which was a pity to hear. Her Majesty again cried out to all gentlemen and others who passed up and down the street, declaring how that she was their native princess, and that she doubted not but all honest subjects would respect her as they ought to do, and not suffer her to be mishandled. Others again showed their malice in setting up a banner or ensign whereupon the king was painted lying dead under a tree, and the young prince upon his knees, praying, 'Judge and revenge my cause, O Lord.' That same night it was alleged that Her Majesty did write a letter unto the Earl of Bothwell, and promised a reward to one of her keepers to see it surely convoyed to Dunbar unto the said earl, calling him her dear heart, whom she should never forget nor abandon for absence; saying that she had sent him away only for his safety, willing him to be comforted, and be upon his guard: which letter the knave delivered to the lords, though he had promised the contrary.* Upon which letter the lords took occasion to send her to Lochleven to be kept; which she alleged was contrary to promise. They on the other hand affirmed that by her own handwriting she had declared that she had not, nor would not, abandon the Earl of Bothwell. Grange again excused her, alleging that she had in effect abandoned the said earl but that it was no wonder that she gave him yet a few fair words; not doubting but if she were discreetly handled, and humbly admonished what inconveniencies that man had brought upon her, she would leave him by degrees and ere long detest him. But they said that it stood them upon the security of their lives and lands, and when that time came that she should be known to abandon and detest the Earl of Bothwell, it would be then time to reason upon the matter.

Grange was yet so angry, that had it not been for the letter, he had

 * *Marginal Note:* Some suspected this letter to have been invented.

instantly left them; and, for the next best, he used all possible diligence to make her and them both quit of the said earl, causing to make ready two ships to follow after him, who had fled first to the castle of Dunbar, and from thence to Shetland. In the mean time Her Majesty sent a letter to the laird of Grange out of Lochleven, lamenting that promises had been broken to her. Whereunto he answered that he had already reproached the lords for the same; who showed unto him a letter sent by her unto the Earl of Bothwell, promising, among many other fair and comfortable words, never to abandon or forget him; which, if it was written by Her Majesty, as he could scarcely believe, it had stopped his mouth, marvelling that Her Majesty considered not that the said earl could not be her lawful husband, being so lately before married with another, whom he had deserted without any cause of separation, although he had not been so hated for the murder of the king her husband; and he requested Her Majesty to put him clean out of mind, or else she would never get the love and obedience of her subjects; with many other loving and humble admonitions, which made her bitterly to weep; for she could not do it so hastily, which process of time brought to pass.

Now the laird of Grange's two ships being in readiness, he made sail toward Orkney; and no man was so ready to accompany him as the laird of Tullibardine and Adam Bothwell, Bishop of Orkney. But the earl was fled from Orkney to Shetland. There also they followed him, and came in sight of Bothwell's ship, which moved the laird of Grange to desire the skippers to hoist up all the sails, which they were loath to do, because they knew the shallow water thereabout. But Grange, willing to come a time, compelled the mariners; so that, for too great haste, the ship wherein Grange was did break upon a bed of sand, without loss of a man. But Bothwell had leisure in the mean time to save himself in a little boat, leaving his ship behind him; which Grange took, and therewith the laird of Tallo, John Hepburn of Bolton, Dalgleish, and divers others of the earl's servants.* He himself fled to Denmark, where he was taken, and kept in strait prison; wherein he became mad, and died miserably. But Grange came back again with Bothwell's ship and servants, who were the first who gave most knowledge of the manner of the murder; which the lords thought fit to let the King of France understand, and of their diligence, according to the promise made by them. . . .

* This is inaccurate. Dalgleish had been arrested in Edinburgh in June and the laird of Tallo escaped in a fishing boat to Pittenweem, where he was apprehended.

IV

Regency of Moray

M Y Lord of Moray had obtained liberty to pass into France shortly
after the murder of the king; for he did foresee the great trouble
like to ensue and he had promised never to come in the queen's contrary. The rest of the lords enterprisers, after they had put the queen
in Lochleven, began to consult how to get Her Majesty counselled to
demit the government to the prince her son; and for that effect they
dealt first with my brother Sir Robert, because he was sometimes
allowed access to Her Majesty: and after that he had refused flatly to
meddle in that matter, they were minded to send the Lord Lindsay,
first to use fair persuasions, and, in case he came no speed, to enter in
harder terms. The Earls of Atholl, Mar and secretary Lethington, and
the laird of Grange, who loved Her Majesty, advised my brother to
tell her the verity, and how that any thing she did in prison could not
prejudge her, being once again at liberty. He answered, he would not
persuade her, nor speak anything but as her true and faithful servant;
always, he said, he should tell her the opinion of so many as were her
friends. But she refused utterly to follow that advice, till she heard
that the Lord Lindsay was at the new house* and was upon a threatening humour; then she yielded to the necessity of the time, and told my
brother that she would not strive with them, seeing it could do her no
harm when she was at liberty. So at my Lord Lindsay's coming she
subscribed the signature of renunciation and demission of the government to the prince, and certain lords were named in the said signature
to be regents to the prince and country, every one after another; Her
Majesty desiring my Lord Moray, who was absent in France, to be the
first regent.

This being past, the lords concluded to crown the prince; and sent
letters to France for the Earl of Moray to come home. In the mean time
there were a number of lords convened at Hamilton, as my Lord
Hamilton,† my Lord Paisley,‡ John Hamilton, Bishop of St Andrews,

* Apparently a house near the castle of Lochleven where Mary was imprisoned.
† Lord John, second son of the Duke of Châtelherault.
‡ Lord Claud, third son of Châtelherault.

my Lord Fleming, Boyd, and divers others, to whom the lords who were to crown the prince would have sent me. Which commission at the first I refused, till the secretary Lethington, the laird of Grange and other secret favourers of the queen advised me to take in hand, alleging that it was meet to join all the country together in quietness; fearing that in case civil wars entered among us it might endanger Her Majesty's life; for those who were at Hamilton appeared to lean to the queen.

At my coming to Hamilton, I told them my commission in the name of the other lords, how that, the king being murdered, all neighbour nations cried out upon the whole nation, but especially the King of France and the Queen of England admonished them to enquire after, and punish, the murderers; how that they had found that it was the Earl of Bothwell, who was fled, and some of them who had assisted him, who were punished; and what was passed since thereupon was known to the whole country: that the Queen's Majesty had demitted over the government to the prince her son, whom they were minded to crown shortly; whereof they thought fit to warn all the nobility, as being minded to hurt no man nor to prejudge no nobleman of his rights, titles or prerogatives; requesting them who were there convened to come to Stirling and be present at the said coronation, for retaining their own privileges, the weal and quiet of the whole country. Some of the youngest lords answered and said that they would not believe that the Queen's Majesty had demitted the government; and if she had done it, it would be found for fear of her life. But the bishop, who had more experience than they, reproved them, and said that those noblemen had dealt very reasonably and discreetly with them. So he drew the rest aside to advise, and then returned and delivered their answer and said:

'We are beholden to the noblemen who have sent you with that friendly and discreet commission; and, following their desire, we are ready to concur with them, if they give us sufficient security of that which you have said in their name; and in so doing they give us occasion to suppose the best of all their proceedings past and to come: so that if they had made us foreseen of their first enterprise of punishing the murder, we should have taken plain part with them. And whereas now we are here convened, it is not to pursue or offend any of them, but to be upon our own guards, understanding of so great a concourse of noblemen, barons, burghs, and other subjects: for, not being made privy to their enterprise, we thought fit to draw ourselves together till we should see whereto things would turn.'

When I returned back to Stirling and declared this answer, it was thought very good by all wise and peaceably-minded men; but others said that however they minded to do, I had painted out a fair story for them, and in their favours: so that I perceived them already divided in factions and opinions. For so many of our lords as leaned to England desired not the stability of our state; others had particular designs against the Hamiltons, and expected to get them ruined, thereby to gain advantage by fishing in troubled waters; so that the Hamiltons were ill used; for they would fain have agreed with the rest, but their friendship and society was plainly refused at this time, and they not admitted to come to the coronation, nor yet to take instruments that they should not be prejudged in any sort;* which occasioned great trouble afterward in the country. For they perceiving themselves cast off, and their friendship and assistance refused, made the endeavours and plans that they might for their own security and defence; and such other noblemen as favoured them and had not yet joined with the new enterprises were the more easily drawn upon that side (who were afterward called the queen's lords), when they understood of such disdainful proceeding with the Hamiltons.

I have before related that my Lord Moray was written for to come home; and so soon as he came to London the lords were advertised, who desired me to ride and meet him at Berwick, and show him how that the office of regent was appointed for him. Which journey I accepted with the better will, in that some friends who were best inclined thought meet to give him good counsel in due time. My commission from the lords was to inform him of all their proceedings, and of the present estate, and to desire him to do nothing without them, especially with the queen; for they feared that he would do as any other wise man would have done, in respect that he had not offended the queen of late, that he might perchance keep her in hand in good hope some day of relief and not run so hard a course against her as most of them were minded to do. Another sort of the said lords (that did still bear a great love unto the queen and had compassion upon her estate, and who entered upon that enterprise only for safety of the prince and punishment of the king's murder, as the Earl of Mar, the Earl of Atholl, the secretary Lethington, the lairds of Tullibardine and Grange) sent their instructions with me to my Lord of Moray, praying him in their name to bear himself gently and humbly unto the queen, and to procure so much favour of her as he could. Not that they would wish him to forget any part of honest duty to the lords, so long as they kept touch with him; but that in case they, or any part of them, would be

* The Hamiltons were heirs to Mary, but it was arguable that James's heir was his uncle Charles, Darnley's brother, and it was in the Hamiltons' interest that James's coronation should not prejudice their rights. A formal protest was, however, made on their behalf, and Melville's statement is wrong.

offended at him afterwards, for the refusal of some casualty,★ benefice, or for some other particularity, they would come to themselves again, seeing the queen and him in so good terms, lest he should set her at liberty upon account of their misbehaviour. And further, that Her Majesty, being now free of evil company and of a clear wit and princely inclination, was beginning already to repent her of many things past, and time might bring about such an occasion that they should all wish her at liberty to rule over them; and what had he lost for his discreet and friendly behaviour to her? He appeared to like very well of this advice, and promised that he should follow it forth, but to accept upon him the regiment he would not grant at the first but refused it plainly, albeit I was informed by some of his company that he was right glad when he understood first that he was to be regent. There came home with him a French ambassador of my acquaintance, called M. de Lingueroles, who was sent to see how matters passed, to comfort the captive queen and to intercede for her; but he did it very slenderly: for he said to the lords, he came not to offend any of them, alleging that the old league betwixt France and Scotland was not made with any one prince, but betwixt the estates of the two kingdoms, and with those who were commanders over the country for the time.

After that my Lord of Moray had met with all his friends, he granted to accept the government. But when he went to see the queen in Loch-leven, instead of comforting her and following the good counsel he had gotten, he entered instantly with Her Majesty in reproaches and such injurious language as was like to break her heart. So many of us as found fault with that manner of procedure, lost his favour. The injuries were such, that they cut the thread of love and credit betwixt the queen and him for ever.

You have heard how that the lords who were in Hamilton were cast off, and refused to be accepted into society with the rest, against the opinion of the fewest in number, though the wisest men and least factious. But the worst-inclined and manyest votes obtained their intent. Whereupon the lords who were refused in friendship drew themselves together at Dumbarton, under the pretext to procure by force of arms the queen their sovereign's liberty, and banded themselves together against the king's lords; which they would not have done, if they could have been accepted in society with the rest. . . .

The signatories of the bond made at Dumbarton, undertaking to restore the queen to liberty, were John Hamilton, Archbishop of St Andrews; the Earls of Argyll and Huntly; Lord John Hamilton, Commendator of Arbroath;

★ Some property or right which had fallen to the crown under feudal law or in consequence of escheat following on judicial process.

Alexander Gordon, Bishop of Galloway; John Leslie, Bishop of Ross; Lord Fleming; Lord Herries; James Cockburn of Skirling; Gavin Hamilton, Commendator of Kilwinning; and Sir William Hamilton of Sanquhar.

This small number were the first who banded themselves together, and afterwards all those who were malcontent, or had any particular question, claim, or feud with any of the king's lords, drew to these new confederates, hoping by time to win their intent against their adversaries, in case their faction might prevail. And some drew to both the factions who desired never to see either king or queen in an established estate.

The court of England, again, left nothing undone to kindle the fire, and to furnish both the factions with hope of assistance in case of need. For oft times, besides their ambassador ordinary who was resident here, they upon some new occasion would send in another openly to deal with the king's faction, because it was strongest and greatest, and under-hand to deal with the queen's faction and allege that their quarrel was most just and right and that Her Majesty's authority was only lawful. No man can tell this better than I, who was so long acquainted, during their banishment in France in Queen Mary's time, with all the ambassadors who were sent to Scotland for the time; as with Mr Randolph, Sir Nicholas Throckmorton, Mr Davison, [Mr Killigrew] and the marshal of Berwick. Among the which number Sir Nicholas Throckmorton dealt most honestly and plainly, for he shot at the union of the whole isle in one monarchy. . . .

Now my Lord of Moray having accepted the government upon him, pressed to have the strengths in his hands, as the castles of Edinburgh, Dunbar and Dumbarton. The castle of Edinburgh was still in the hands of Sir James Balfour, who had assisted the noblemen who pursued the murder, and now took plain part with them, and likewise assisted the new made regent. Yet the regent desired to have the castle out of his hands; which he was content to deliver up upon condition that the laird of Grange should be made captain thereof, upon whose constant friendship he reposed most; which was easily granted by the regent and all the rest. After this, Dunbar was also rendered to him by the lairds of Whitelaw and Wauchton. Then he took great pains to steal secret raids upon the thieves and held justice ayres in the in-country:* but he took no care to settle the differences among the nobility, and to draw them, by a discreet and equitable behaviour, to the obedience of the king's authority, which might have been easily done, if they had seen security for their persons and prospects for their

* That is, to lead expeditions to the unruly Border country and hold criminal courts in areas far from the capital.

affairs and actions. But such as happened to be about him, having their own ambitious and covetous ends, counselled him otherwise, thinking by the wreck of others to make up themselves. They were so blinded by their affections and greedy appetites that they thought all would succeed prosperously to their claims, without any resistance. Thus rushing forward, the regent's rough proceedings uncircumspectly and improvidently gave occasion to many to draw to the contrary faction and to make practices how to draw the Queen's Majesty out of Lochleven before the time was ripe to set forward their particularities against the regent and his partisans; whereof the regent was oft and frequently warned, even by divers who were upon the counsel of her out-taking, who desired that way to win thanks at his hands. But he would credit none but such things as came out of the mouths of those who had grown into his conceit and favour by flattery.

In the mean time the queen was convoyed out of Lochleven by George Douglas, the laird's brother and the regent's half brother, who was for the time in some evil terms with them. The old lady his mother was also thought to be upon the counsel. My Lord Seton and some of the house of Hamilton, and divers others of their dependers, received Her Majesty at her landing out of the loch, and convoyed her to Hamilton.

The regent being for the time at Glasgow holding justice ayres, proclamations and missives were incontinent made and sent abroad by both sides to convene so many as would act for them in the country. A French ambassador was come to Edinburgh ten days before, called Monsieur de Beaumont, knight of the order of the cockle, whom I had convoyed to Glasgow, and procured that he might see the queen captive, in vain. He said to me that he never did see so many men so suddenly convened; for he rode to Hamilton to the queen, and dealt between the parties for peace, but was not heard. Her Majesty was not minded to fight, nor hazard battle, but to go unto the castle of Dumbarton, and by little and little to draw home again unto her obedience the whole subjects. But the Bishop of St Andrews and the house of Hamilton, and the rest of the lords there convened, finding themselves in number far beyond the other party, would needs hazard a battle, thinking thereby to overcome the regent, their great enemy, and be also masters of the queen, to command and rule all at their pleasure. Some alleged that the bishop was minded to cause the queen to marry my Lord [John] Hamilton,* in case they had obtained the victory. And I was since informed by some who were present that the queen herself feared the same; therefore she pressed them still to convoy her to

* Second son of the Duke of Châtelherault and, with the insanity of his elder brother, heir of the house of Hamilton.

Dumbarton, and had sent me word with the French ambassador and also caused my brother, Sir Robert, to write a letter unto me, the same morning before the battle, to draw on a conference for concord, by the means of the secretary Lethington and the laird of Grange; and for her part she would send the lord Herries and some others. But the queen's army came on so fiercely that there was no stay.

The regent went out on foot, and all his company except the laird of Grange, Alexander Hume of Manderston and some Borderers to the number of 200. The laird of Grange had already viewed the ground, and with all possible diligence caused every horseman to take on behind him a footman of the regent's guard, and rode with speed to the head of the Langside hill, and set down the said footmen with their culverins at the head of a strait lane, where there were some cottage houses and yards of great advantage. Which soldiers with their continual shot dropped down divers of the vanguard led by the Hamiltons, who, courageously and fiercely ascending up the steep hill, were already out of breath when the regent's vanguard joined with them. There the worthy Lord Hume fought on foot with his pike in his hand very manfully, well assisted by the laird of Cessford, his brother-in-law, who helped him up again, when he was strucken to the ground off his feet with many strokes upon his face, by the throwing of pistols at him after they had been discharged. He was also wounded with staves and flacons* and had many strokes of spears through his legs; for he and Grange, at the joining, cried to let their adversaries first lay down their spears, to bear up theirs; which spears were so thick fixed in others' jacks† that some of the flacons, pistols and great staves that were thrown by them which were behind, might be seen lying upon the spears.

Upon the queen's side the Earl of Argyll commanded the battle, and the Lord of Arbroath the vanguard. On the other part the regent led the battle, and the Earl of Morton the vanguard. But the regent committed to the laird of Grange the special care, as an experimented captain, to oversee every danger, and to ride to every wing, to encourage and make help where greatest need was. He perceived at the first joining the right wing of the regent's vanguard put back and give ground, like to fly, whereof the greatest part were commons of the barony of Renfrew; whereupon he came to them, and told them that their enemies were already turning their backs, that were behind the rest, and requested them to stay and debate, till he should bring them fresh men forth of the battle. Whither he did ride in diligence alone, and told the regent, or alleged, that the enemy were dispersing and flying away behind the little village, and desired a few number of fresh

* ? Powder flasks.   † Defensive coats, of leather.

men to come with him. Where he found enough willing, as the Lord Lindsay, the laird of Lochleven, Sir James Balfour and all the regent's servants, who followed him with diligence and reinforced that wing which was beginning to fly; which fresh men with their loose weapons struck their enemies in their flanks and faces, which forced them incontinent to give place and turn back, after long fighting and pushing others to and fro with their spears. There were not many horsemen to pursue them; and the regent cried to save and not to slay; and Grange was never cruel, so that there were but few slain and taken. And the only slaughter was at the first rencounter, by the shot of the soldiers that Grange had planted at the lane-head behind some dykes.

After the loss of the battle, Her Majesty lost all courage, which she had never done before, and took so great fear that she never rested till she was in England, thinking herself assured of refuge there, in respect of the many fair promises formerly made to her by the Queen of England by words to her ambassadors and by her own hand-writ both before and after she was captive in Lochleven. But God and the world knows how she was kept and used: for not only she [Elizabeth] would not see her, of whom she appeared so oft to desire a sight and a meeting, but also caused keep her prisoner and at length suffered her life to be taken, or else it was subtly taken against her intention. . . .

After the battle of Langside, the regent went through the country, and took up the escheats and houses of those who had assisted at the said battle, and caused cast down divers of their houses, distributing all their lands to his servants and dependers.

The council of England being crafty, and in special the secretary Cecil, they knew what kind of commodious men had most credit about him for the time, and thereupon took occasion to deal with the least honest, most ambitious and covetous of that number and society, who had joined and banded themselves together to assist each other, whereby to advance themselves and to disgrace all such true and honest men as had ever assisted and helped him in all his troubles. This sort of men were soon persuaded and corrupted to move the regent to pass into England and accuse their native queen before the queen and council of England, to the great dishonour of their country and prince. For the Queen of England, who had no just cause to retain the queen, who had fled to England in hope of getting refuge and the assistance which had been so oft promised her both before and after her captivity in Lochleven, was very desirous to have some colour whereby she might make answer to the ambassadors of sundry princes, who reproached her for her unkindly and unprincely proceeding therein.

Because the most part of those who had the regent's ear were gained to this opinion, and the number few who were of a contrary mind, he went forward to England, accompanied with the Earl of Morton, the Lord Lindsay, the laird of Lochleven, the Bishop of Orkney, the Abbot of Dunfermline, Mr James Macgill, Mr Henry Balnaves, Mr George Buchanan, the laird of Pittarrow, George Douglas, Bishop of Moray,* Mr John Wood, the regent's secretary, a great ringleader, Mr Nichol Elphinston, secretary Lethington, the provost of Lincluden, Alexander Hay, Alexander Hume of North Berwick, the laird of Cleish, with divers other barons and gentlemen, who went there to see the manner and some to wait upon the regent and lords; and some, who could not get the regent dissuaded from this extreme folly at home, went with him to England to see if by any assistance of such as were friends there to the union of the isle, and to the title of Scotland, might perchance make them some help to get the accusation stayed. For those who were the queen's lords, who came there to defend the queen's part, had no credit nor familiarity with the chief faction in England concerning the title, nor durst open their minds but to such as by long acquaintance they were well assured of their honesty and secrecy. The names of the queen's lords were the Lord Herries, the Lord Boyd, the Lord Fleming, the Lord Livingston, the Bishop of Ross, and some others, with my brother Sir Robert, who attended to do all the good he could.

The Duke of Norfolk, the Earl of Sussex, Sir Walter Mildmay and several other counsellors were sent down to York to hear the regent's accusation, and to be as judges between the king and queen's lords.

The first day of meeting, the Duke of Norfolk required that the regent should make homage in the king's name to the crown of England, thinking he had some ground to demand the same, seeing the said regent there to plead his cause before the council of England. Whereat the regent grew red, and knew not what to answer; but secretary Lethington took the speech, and said that in restoring again to Scotland the lands of Huntingdon, Cumberland and Northumberland,† with such other lands as Scotland did of old possess in England, that homage should gladly be made for the said lands: but as to the crown and kingdom of Scotland, it was freer than England had been lately, when it paid St Peter's penny to the Pope.

It appeared still that the duke drove time with us, as having no inclination to enter upon the terrors of accusation. . . .

Norfolk's reluctance to accept a formal accusation of Mary arose from his

---

* He did not become Bishop of Moray until 1574.

† These three earldoms were held by King David I (1124–53). Before Henry II of England became king, he undertook to secure the Scots in Northumberland, Westmorland and Cumberland, but in 1157 he insisted on incorporating them in his own kingdom.

fears that her claims, and those of her son, to the English succession, might be prejudiced if she were to be condemned as an adulteress and murderess. Lethington was likewise anxious to withhold a formal accusation, possibly because an enquiry might disclose his own part in conspiracies against Darnley. It was therefore with Lethington's approval that Norfolk told Moray that he was critical of Elizabeth for her reluctance to settle the English succession and advised him not to make any accusation without an undertaking by Elizabeth that she would convict Mary should the charges against her be proved.

When the duke demanded the accusation to be given in, the regent asked for his security the Queen of England's seal and hand-writing, as was advised; of which the rest of his faction gave Lethington the full blame, because it drew on a delay until the post was sent to the court, and come back again. The queen's answer being come, it was told that she was a true princess, her word and promise would be sufficient enough. The secretary Cecil and Mr John Wood, secretary to the regent, thought strange of this manner of the regent's proceeding, and therefore caused him and the lords on both sides to go from York toward the court, a far way, that the matter might there be treated, where the queen was more able to give ready answers and replies. . . .

The regent being arrived at the court of England, which was for the time at Hampton Court, he was daily pressed to give in his accusation. . . .

Moray had agreed with Norfolk that Mary would not be accused and that Norfolk would obtain Elizabeth's approval of Moray's position as regent of Scotland. But Norfolk disclosed this agreement to Mary, one of whose retinue passed on the news to Morton, who was indignant at Moray's bargain and instructed John Wood to inform Cecil of all that had passed.

Mr John Wood said that it was fit to carry in all the writs to the council house, and he would keep the accusation in his bosom, and would not deliver it unless all conditions were also kept to him. The rest of the regent's lords and counsellors had concluded among them that so soon as the Duke of Norfolk, as chief of the council, would enquire for the accusation, they should all with one voice cry and persuade the regent to go forward with it.

Secretary Lethington and a few others reminded the regent how far he had obliged himself to the Duke of Norfolk. He said he would do well enough, and that it would not come to that length. So soon as he with his council were within the council-house, the Duke of Norfolk asked for the accusation; the regent desired again the assurance of the conviction by writ and seal, as is said. It was answered again that the

THE BATTLE OF CARBERRY, 1567

Queen's Majesty's word, being a true princess, was sufficient. Then all the council cried out, 'Would he mistrust the queen, who had given such proof of her friendship to Scotland?' The regent's council cried out also in that same manner. Then secretary Cecil asked if they had the accusation there? 'Yes,' says Mr John Wood; and with that he plucks it out of his bosom, 'But I will not deliver it till Her Majesty's hand-writ and seal be delivered to my lord regent for what he demands.' Then the Bishop of Orkney snatcheth the writ out of Mr John Wood's hand. 'Let me have it,' says he, 'I shall present it.' Mr John ran after him, as if he would have taken it again, or torn his clothes. Forward goes the bishop to the council-table, and gives in the accusation. Then said to him my Lord William Howard, chamberlain of England, 'Well done, bishop Turpy, thou art the smartest fellow among them all, none of them will make thy leap good'; scorning him for his leaping out of the laird of Grange's ship.* Mr Henry Balnaves only had made resistance, and called for secretary Lethington, who waited without the council-house. But so soon as Mr Henry Balnaves had called for him, he came in and whispered in the regent's ear that he had shamed himself, and put his life in danger, by the loss of so good a friend [as the Duke of Norfolk] and that he had lost his reputation for ever.

The regent, who, by his facility, had been brought to break with the Duke of Norfolk, repented himself thereof so soon as Lethington had shown him the danger, and desired the accusation to be rendered up to him again, alleging that he had some more to add thereto. They answered that they would hold what they had, and were ready to receive any other addition when he should please to give it in. The Duke of Norfolk had enough ado to keep his countenance. Mr John Wood winked upon secretary Cecil; who smiled again upon him. The rest of the regent's company were laughing one upon another; the secretary Lethington had a sore heart. The regent came forth of the council house with tears in his eyes, and went to his lodging at Kingston, a mile from court, where his factious friends had enough ado to comfort him.

The Queen of England having obtained her intent, received thereby great contentment. First, she thought she had matter for her to show wherefore she detained the queen. Then she was glad of the queen's dishonour; but in her mind she detested the regent and all his company, and would not know him nor hear any more of him. She sent also incontinent to the queen to comfort her, praying her to look on herself in a better case there, albeit for a while restrained, than to be in

* An allusion to the wreck of Grange's ship in Shetland in 1567 (p. 70 above). Bishop Bothwell made a spectacular leap to safety from the sinking vessel.

Scotland, among so unworthy subjects, who had accused her falsely and wrongfully, as she was assured; and that neither should they be the better nor the worse for any thing they had done, for she would neither be judge nor give out any sentence thereupon; nor should any part of the said false accusation be made known by her, or her council, to any; praying her to take patience in her gentle ward, where she was nearer at hand to get the crown of England set upon her head, in case of her decease, who was but the eldest sister.

Thus the regent won no other thing for his labour but to be despised by the queen and council of England, detested by the Duke of Norfolk, and reproached by his best and truest friends, suffered to lie a long time at Kingston, in great displeasure and fear, without money to spend, and without hope to get any from the queen. . . .

Word of the negotiations between Moray and Norfolk reached Elizabeth, and the duke, 'finding himself disappointed by the regent and his purposes discovered to the queen', began to avow his belief in Mary's right to the English succession and to boast that he would marry Mary.

But, according to Melville, Norfolk was also able to prevail on Elizabeth to give Moray £2000. Then, after he had left the English court, Moray was persuaded to send to Elizabeth any letters he received from Norfolk.

After the regent's safe return to Scotland, Mr John Wood, his secretary, procured, upon the first occasion, to be sent to England, with all the letters that could be got that might serve to undo the Duke of Norfolk. . . .

*This led to the imprisonment of Norfolk, 'who after long captivity was executed, ending his life devoutly in the reformed religion'.**

Shortly after Mr John Wood's returning out of England, there was a great convention held at Perth, where the regent was minded to accuse secretary Lethington as being of counsel with the Duke of Norfolk. But he had so many friends for the time, that they durst not lay hands on him; albeit from that hour forth, he retired from the court and remained with the Earl of Atholl, where the regent entertained him with friendly letters. And upon a time being at Stirling, he wrote for him to come and help to make a despatch for England; whither being come, Captain Crawford was directed to accuse him before the privy council, of the late king's murder; and being accused of so odious a crime, he was committed to ward. Sir James Balfour was also taken out of his own house, when he expected no less.

* On 2 June 1572.

Then my Lord of Doune wrote to the laird of Grange to be upon his guard, for the regent would take the castle of Edinburgh from him, and make the laird of Drumwhasel captain, whereof he had advertised the laird of Grange of before, as also of the design to take the secretary and Sir James Balfour. . . .

So the regent came to Edinburgh, and brought the secretary with him, intending, as Grange was informed, to make the secretary a steall guse* to draw Grange down out of the castle to the town the next morning to receive the secretary to be convoyed up to the castle, and then to retain Grange also till the castle should be delivered unto the laird of Drumwhasel to be keeper thereof, and to send Grange home to his house, and reward him with the priory of Pittenweem. But the Earl of Morton had appointed four men to slay Grange at the entry of the regent's lodging, without the regent's knowledge. But Grange was loath yet to believe the worst of the regent; and being of opinion that the regent's gentle nature was forced by the lords, as he had sent him word, and understanding that they were minded to carry the secretary to Tantallon,† he came down out of the castle with a company, and seized the secretary out of the hands of his keepers and convoyed him up to the castle. . . .

The regent and his counsellors, when they understood how that Grange had taken the secretary to the castle, were in great perplexity, supposing all their counsels to be disclosed. They knew not how to help the matter; but they advised the regent to cover his anger until a better opportunity, causing him to go up to the castle the next morning, for he durst trust Grange. But Grange durst no more trust him, albeit at [their] meeting the regent gave him more fair words than he was wont to do, which Grange took in evil part.

After this there were many devices how to entrap Grange some time in his down-coming to the regent, but he was ever advertised, and upon his guard; so as the regent lost daily of his best friends, and the number of his enemies increased. For the Duke of Châtelherault (who was agreed with him by the influence of the Lord Herries), when the said duke and the Lord Herries came to Edinburgh, as was appointed at the agreement, to concur with the regent in council, and otherwise, for the quieting of the country, they were both warded in the castle, against promise. . . . The captivity of the duke and my Lord Herries made many enemies to the regent, who took the greater boldness to conspire against him when they perceived him to lose and cast off his oldest and best friends.

It was a grievous thing to see that good regent, once so well inclined

* A decoy goose.

† Tantallon Castle in East Lothian, about 20 miles from Edinburgh.

to do good offices in religion and commonwealth, so deflected and drawn after other men's vain pretences and affections; employing therein the whole time of his government, to his own utter wreck, to the wreck of many worthy persons, and to their wreck at length who led him in these ways. The regent's misbehaviour through evil counsellors, as giving ear only to flatterers, and would not suffer his true friends to tell him the verity, made many conjecture that his ruin was at hand. . . .

Melville put before Moray a scheme for conciliation, and Moray denied that he had any hostility to Kirkcaldy and Maitland, whom he visited in the castle. But in his professions of friendship he was dissembling, and he did not deceive Kirkcaldy and Maitland.
Melville proceeds to describe Moray's character.

Himself was at the first of a gentle nature, well inclined, good with good company, wise with wise company, stout with stout company, and contrariwise with others of the contrary qualities, so that as company chanced to fall about him, his business went right or wrong. In his first uprising, his hap was to light upon the best sort of company: for in his beginning, full of adversity, true honest men stuck by him, because he was religiously brought up. Again, when he was regent, flatterers for their profit drew to him, and puffed him up into too good an opinion of himself. His old true friends, who would reprove him, thereby lost his favour. I would sometimes say to him that he was like an unskilful player in a tennis-court, running ever after the ball; whereas an expert player would discern where the ball will light, where it will rebound, and with small travail will let it fall on his hand or racket. This I said, because he took very great pains in his own person to small effect. After he had gotten divers advertisements of his enemies' conspiracies, yet in vain, for he would credit nothing but what came from his own familiars, who told him nothing but of fair weather, and of the best government that could be, and so rendered him careless and secure: which encouraged the good-man of Bothwell-haugh, called [James] Hamilton, to lie in his way as he was passing through Linlithgow, who shot him, whereof he died that same night.★ All his counsellors and familiars were as well advertised as he was, both of the man, the place and the time; and yet were so careless of him that they would not be at the pains to search the house where the man lay to shoot him, but suffered him to escape upon a speedy horse.

I have written thus far of him, because every one knows not the verity how he was led out of the right way; and because St Augustine says that all kind of ignorance is neither worthy of pardon nor excuse,

★ 23 January 1569/70.

but only such as have not the means to be instructed, nor to get knowledge. I was sometimes compelled to recite divers sentences of Solomon to this good regent (for so he was, and is yet called): how that an heavy yoke was ordained for the sons of Adam, from the day they go out of their mother's womb till the day that they return to the mother of all things; from him who is clothed in blue silk and weareth a crown, even to him who weareth simple linen; wrath, envy, trouble and unquietness, rigour, strife and fear of death in the time of rest. . . .

'How are flatterers', said I to the regent, 'flown away with your wonted humility, and who hath puffed you up so, that you will not suffer a friendly reproof? Says not Solomon, "If thou seest a man wise in his own conceit, there is more hope to be had of a fool than of him. Exalt not thyself in the day of honour; for pride goeth before destruction, and an high mind before a fall?" Yet hear counsel and receive instruction; let reason go before every enterprise, and counsel before every action. When you followed the counsel of your old experimented friends, your affairs prospered: since you left them, to follow the flattering fetches of your wonted foes (who are now become your chiefest counsellors since you have been made regent), your credit decays, and all your business goes back. I did show you lately, coming from Dumfries, in what danger your estate and person were, of which you had taken too little notice; which danger appears to me to be ever the longer the greater, without speedy repentance and the hasty embracing of such remedies as I mentioned for the time. Therefore take this better to heart, and in good part of him, of whose fidelity you have had in all your adversities.' . . .

The most part of these sentences, drawn out of the Bible, I used to rehearse to him at all erroneous occasions;* and he took better with these off my hands than if they had proceeded from the most learned philosopher. Therefore I promised to put them in writing and give him them to keep in his pocket; but he was slain before I could meet with him.

---

* i.e. occasions when Moray fell into error.

V

Civil War in Scotland

AFTER the decease of the regent, England sent the Earl of Sussex to Berwick; whither the Earl of Lennox came also at that same time, as being sent for by the lords of the king's faction to be made regent in place of the Earl of Moray. The Earl of Sussex had with him the forces of the North, as if he had some enterprise to do and to take some advantage at this time, when the country wanted a regent.

About that same time, so many of the lords as were banded and professed the queen's authority, caused to proclaim the same at Linlithgow. As yet they of the castle of Edinburgh professed the king's authority, albeit there were secret jealousies betwixt them and so many of the rest as had been cause to draw the late regent to apprehend the secretary Lethington and Sir James Balfour, and who would also have ruined Grange because he was a friend of these two, and also because his virtues were envied and his captaincy* desired by others.

They who were within the said castle for the time were my Lord Duke of Châtelherault and my Lord Herries, warded wrongfully as I have said; therefore the laird of Grange obtained a warrant from the rest of the king's lords to set them at liberty. The Lord Hume was there to assist with those of the castle, with the laird of Grange, the secretary Lethington, his brother the Prior of Coldingham, three of my brothers, Sir Robert Melville, Captain David and Sir Andrew Melville, the lairds of Drylaw and Pittarrow, Sir James Balfour, the lairds of Fernihirst, Buccleuch, Wormiston, Parbroath, and divers other noblemen and barons, who came there at all occasions, and were ready for them when they had to do.

This company directed me to Berwick, toward the Earl of Sussex, to know what he intended to do with his forces; whether to assist any of the two factions, or to agree them? I was friendly received by him, well lodged, and my expenses by him defrayed, wanting nothing, not so much as his own night-gown furred with rich furrings, so long as I abode there. Albeit he was a great enemy to all Scotsmen, he appeared to enter in great familiarity with me, and seemed to tell me his most

* Of Edinburgh Castle.

secret thoughts, alleging his plainness to me was upon the report he had heard by sundry of his countrymen. He said that his coming with his forces was not to assist any faction, nor to decide questions and titles that were among us, but to serve the commandment of the queen his mistress, and that if he did any enterprise or harm at that time against any Scotsman, it would be against his heart. That of all Scotsmen, he liked best of those who were within the castle of Edinburgh and their dependers, especially because he knew them to have been friends to the Duke of Norfolk, his near cousin, whose part he would plainly have taken if the said duke had out of his own mouth communicated his enterprise to him, as he had foolishly done by a gentleman of his, to whose credit he durst not commit the secrecy of that weighty matter, which stood him upon his life and heritage. And that albeit he with his forces came not to set out nor to fortify any faction in Scotland, yet he durst be plain with me privately, as with a true friend, to declare that he did esteem the Queen of Scotland and the prince her son righteous heirs to the crown of England, which part of his mind he had shown to few in England.

So I returned with no direct answer, but with a firm opinion that he was sent to appear to set forward the Earl of Lennox to be regent, and to send word to the lords of the king's side that he would assist them and send in Mr Randolph here with the Earl of Lennox; and yet to deal with the lords of the queen's faction, to encourage them to hold forward their factious course, because the said Mr Randolph had a great dealing with the house of Hamilton, as he who convoyed the Earl of Arran, now visited with the hand of God,* out of France through England and home to Scotland, to assist the congregation.† He knew also what old and long hatred had been betwixt the houses of Lennox and Hamilton; and was deliberately directed secretly to kindle a fire of discord betwixt two strong factions in Scotland, which could not be easily quenched; and to confirm the Lord Hume, who was not yet resolved to take part with the queen's faction, which England thought not yet strong enough to sustain long strife against the king's faction.

The Earl of Sussex entered the Merse with his forces, and took the castle of Hume and Fastcastle, full of riches and precious moveables, that way moving the Lord Hume to take plain part with the Hamiltons and the queen's faction. Whereby it may be seen that the conclusion to hold countries in discord, by the craft of the council of England for the time, as I have before mentioned, was now put in practice

---

* James, third Earl of Arran, son of the Duke of Châtelherault, was insane from 1562 until his death in 1609.

† In 1559.

incontinent after the decease of the Earl of Moray. For albeit the Earl of Lennox had his lady, children and lands yet in England, they would not credit him, supposing he would be a true Scotsman, as he proved indeed afterwards.

I being in Berwick when the Earl of Lennox was so far toward Scotland to be regent, as said is, I thought it my duty to visit him, for at his first coming, before the marriage of his son the Lord Darnley with the queen, he sent the present Colonel Stewart for my brother Sir Robert and me; and because my brother was absent, I went to him alone. At which time he told me that his long absence out of the country had made him as a stranger to the knowledge of the country, and that his lady at his parting from her had desired him to take my brother's counsel and mine in all his affairs, as her friends and kinsmen; so that, being familiar enough with him, I visited him at this time, and told him the state of the country. I dissuaded him from taking upon him the regiment,* fearing that in so doing it would cost him his life, as matters were like to be handled, as I should inform him more at length, being once at home. As for myself, I promised to serve and assist him, albeit I could not see the like intention by those that were in the castle of Edinburgh. He promised again to be my friend, so far as lay in his power, upon which he gave me his hand, then he enquired what was the cause that those who were in the castle would oppose him. I answered, for no particular they had against himself, but because the company of lords who had sent for him to come home and be regent by them, were not their friends, and suspected that in process of time they would move him also to be their enemy. He said that the laird of Grange had been always his good friend, and had done him sometimes great pleasure. I said I hoped he should yet be his friend, after that he had settled himself in the regiment, and might have leisure to be rightly informed of every man's part. . . .

The Commendator of Dunfermline, who had been in England to ask Elizabeth to hand Mary over to the regent's party, returned with word that Elizabeth would insist on security for Mary's life if she handed her over. But Elizabeth had added: 'I believed you had been a wise man; you would press me to speak what is no ways necessary; you may know that I cannot but for my honour require pledges for that end. I think you may judge also of yourself what might be best for me.' *Melville comments:* 'Her meaning in this might be easily judged and understood.'

The Earl of Lennox came to Edinburgh shortly after me; and, after he had accepted the government, his first enterprise was to take

* Government.

Brechin, which was kept by some companies of footmen, taken up by
the Earl of Huntly to assist the queen's faction. These soldiers, being
advertised that the new regent was coming to pursue them, fled, except
a few who kept the kirk and steeple, who were all hanged. I had made
myself ready to ride with the regent, but Mr Randolph, the English
ambassador, who came in with the Earl of Lennox, appearing to set him
forward at his power, hindered me from doing so, fearing that I would
be an instrument of persuading the laird of Grange and those in the
castle to the regent's obedience with time, to the hindrance of the
civil dissension which he intended to establish. . . . Now, I being
stayed at Mr Randolph's desire, his first proposition to me was to
desire the captain of the castle to agree with and assist the regent. I told
him that I supposed he should do it with time, but not so hastily. And
that same answer I brought to him back again, with a request from the
laird of Grange to be plain with him; for there had been also great
friendship betwixt them in France. After some ceremonies and pro-
testations of secrecy, he said, 'Tell your friend this from Mr Randolph,
but not from the English ambassador, that there is no lawful authority
in Scotland but the queen's; she will prevail at length, and therefore
her course is surest and best for him to join himself to her faction.' This
was the help he made to the regent, who expected that his only
ambassage and labours was to advance his authority and obedience
under the king. I appeared to be very satisfied with this wholesome
advice, and went up to the castle, and told the captain and his associates no more than I had assured them of at my return from Berwick.

The laird of Grange was still minded to own the king's authority,
seeing that to be factious in the queen's name, during her absence and
captivity, might do her more ill than good, and occasion great blood-
shed among the subjects, by the malice of the ringleaders of England
and partialities of a few in Scotland, and was affecting but a fit opportunity of making agreement betwixt the parties. . . .

Seeing that Grange could not yet be moved to join with the queen's
faction, according to the desire of the court of England (for the rest of
that kingdom was sorry to see this kind of dealing), the English
ambassador persuaded the regent to cast him off, by divers wrongs and
slights done to himself and his dependers. In the mean time my Lord
Duke, the Earls of Argyll and Huntly addressed themselves unto him,
making their moan, how that they, being noblemen of the country,
were refused to be admitted into the society of the rest, who sought
their ruin under pretext of the king's authority, by the regent, the Earl
of Morton, and others, not their friends, requesting him to be their
protector and to assist them during the king's minority; telling him
how that they at first would fain have assisted the king's authority,

but could not get place, nor be admitted. Thus Grange, finding himself despised by the king's lords, and sought after by the queen's, was compelled to join with that side at length, having with him the Lord Hume, malcontent, also secretary Lethington and Sir James Balfour spurring him on to take that course. Being so cast off, he was compelled, for his next refuge, to join plainly with the queen's side after that he among the rest was summoned to be forfeited, as you shall hear.

Now the two furious factions being in this manner framed, their hatred and rage grew daily greater and greater. For Mr Randolph knew the animosities which were among the nobility, and the nature of every one in particular, by his frequent coming and long residence in Scotland. Among the ladies he had a mother and a mistress, to whom he caused his queen frequently to send commendations and tokens. He also used his craft with the ministers, offering gold to divers of them. One of them that was very honest refused his gift, but he told that his companion took it, as by way of charity. I am not certain if any of the rest took presents, but undoubtedly he offered to such as were in meetest places, to cry out against factions here or there, and kindle the fiercer fire; so that the parties were not content to fight and shed one another's blood, but would revile each other with injurious and blasphemous words, and at length fell to the down-casting of each other's houses, to which England gave assistance, by a number of men of war that came in to throw down Hamilton, because of an attempt that was made by some good ministers to reconcile the two factions.

Now as Nero stood upon a high part of Rome to see the town burning, which he had caused to be set on fire, so Mr Randolph delighted to see such a fire kindled in Scotland; and by his letters to some of the court of England he gloried that he had kindled a fire in Scotland which could not be easily extinguished. . . .

Morton had for a time been absent from court because he had not been granted the revenues of the archbishopric of St Andrews (vacant by the death of John Hamilton). Randolph, with Elizabeth's support, pressed that Morton should have those revenues, and the regent gave way, whereupon Morton returned to court.

After that the Earl of Morton was returned to the court, and had by Randolph's means obtained the bishopric of St Andrews, these two suspecting the apparent agreement, which had been kept secret from them, they devised incontinent how to hinder the same, by holding a parliament wherein to forfeit all their enemies, whereby the regent should utterly ruin his ancient enemies the Hamiltons; and every one of the king's lords would get lands and gear enough. Mr Randolph promised such effective assistance from England that there could be no resistance from their adversaries. The Earl of Morton had established his leadership of the most part of the council, to persuade them to consent to a parliament, to be held at Stirling for the foresaid effect.

The queen's lords, to be equal with them, held another parliament at Edinburgh, both at one time, each one to forfeit the other. The laird of Grange in the mean time took great displeasure to see Scotsmen so furiously bent against each other, set on by the practices of England and the extreme avarice of some Scots lords who intended to augment their rents by the ruin of some of their neighbours whom they envied. Therefore he sent for the laird of Fernihirst, his son-in-law, and the laird of Buccleuch, father to this present laird, who loved the laird of Grange better than any of his own kindred; which laird of Buccleuch was a man of rare qualities, wise, true, stout and modest. These two lairds were desired to come well accompanied, and arrived at Edinburgh in an evening late. The laird of Grange had already devised an enterprise, to wit, that same night after they had supped themselves, and baited their horses, to ride all night forward with them to Stirling, to be there early in the morning before any of the lords who held the parliament were out of their beds, hoping, by the intelligence he had received, assuredly to surprise them before they could be advertised. All the lords and council found the device exceeding good, but they would in no wise grant that he should ride with them, alleging that their only comfort, under God, consisted in his preservation. He on the other hand alleged that his presence would be necessary, for he was experienced in difficult enterprises, and feared that they would not follow rightly nor carefully his direction. But they engaged to follow it most strictly, and would not suffer him to ride with them; but the Earl of Huntly, my Lord Arbroath, my Lord o Paisley and divers others went forward with the forces of the two lairds, and were at Stirling before four of the clock in the morning, and entered the town of Stirling at a little passage, led by a townsman called George Bell; which entry of theirs was immediately after the night-watches had retired to their rest.

They divided their men, and appointed such as they thought meetest to await at every lord's lodging, and a company with Captain Halkerston to wait at the market-cross to cause good order to be kept and to preserve the town-houses from being spoiled; only they appointed the stables to be cleansed by Buccleuch and Fernihirst's men and not to leave one horse in town uncarried away with them; which commission the south-land lads* forgot not to do for their part. But

* i.e. the Borderers, who had a reputation for thieving.

because Captain Halkerston came not in due time with his company to stand where he was appointed, a number of unruly servants broke up the merchants' booths and ran here and there in disorder after the spoil, leaving their masters all alone, after they had taken out all the lords from their lodgings and were leading them captives down the steep causey* of Stirling on foot, intending to mount their horses at the nether port, and ride to Edinburgh with their prisoners.

But when those within the castle perceived the great injury and shame they would endure if they did not show themselves men, and seeing the disorder of their enemies, they came down fiercely upon them and rescued all the prisoners save the regent, whom one came and shot behind his back, commanded, as was alleged, by my Lord of Paisley. The laird of Wormiston was the taker of the regent, and had been ordained by the laird of Grange to wait upon him, to save him from his particular enemies: for they all had engaged to him, as they went from Edinburgh, not to kill any man, or he would not have agreed to remain behind them. Wormiston was also killed against the regent's will, who cried continually to save him, who had done what he could for his preservation. The regent died not suddenly, but some days after and made a very godly end. They who had lost this fair enterprise for want of Grange's presence had enough to do to save themselves, and had been all taken, had not those in Stirling lacked horses to pursue after them. For those who had taken the horses did ride forward with all possible speed, leaving their masters behind them in danger.

When they were returned back to Edinburgh, they were very unwelcome guests to the laird of Grange, who greatly lamented the regent's slaughter. He said that if he knew who had done that foul deed, or had directed it to be done, his own hand should revenge it. And whereas before he used to be meek and gentle, he now burst out into harsh language against the disorder and greediness of them and called them snafflers† and beasts. For he knew the regent was inclined to peace, and was not ignorant how he was driven on by the Earl of Morton's practices and Mr Randolph to hold the said parliament, to the hindrance of concord and agreement: therefore his intention was to bring all the king's lords to the castle of Edinburgh and to set down a good agreement before they parted. But God would not permit this until our wickedness might be better punished: for the parliaments held forward, and each one of the two parties forfeited others. The king's lords came and lay at Leith, and the queen's within the town and castle of Edinburgh.

Mr Randolph would have had Morton made regent in place of Lennox; but the lords liked better of the Earl of Mar, and chose him.

* Street.   † Snaffle = seize by stealth.

For a little time there was hot skirmishing betwixt Leith and Edinburgh, and extreme hatred betwixt the two factions, and great cruelty where they could be masters of one another. And frequently the marshal of Berwick came to Leith to assist Mr Randolph privately, though publicly to find fault with his proceedings when he might get opportunity to speak or send word to them of the town of Edinburgh and castle thereof; which my Lord of Mar's friends perceived, and himself at length, whereupon he began to grow colder in the quarrel, and withdrew himself to Stirling, advising with his friends what was meetest to be done; alleging that he could see nothing but the wreck of the country, under pretext of owning the king's and queen's authority, while neither king nor queen was in any of their minds, but they were pushed only by their own partialities of ambition, greediness and vengeance, England kindling up both the parties and then laughing them all to scorn.

After this conference, Captain James Cunningham, servant to my Lord of Mar, a discreet gentleman, desired a secret meeting with my brother Sir Robert. In the mean time the most part of the king's lords went to Stirling, where the regent was, leaving my Lord of Morton in Dalkeith and my Lord Lindsay in Leith. When the wars grew colder, and notice thereof taken by the court of England, a new ambassador was hasted to Scotland, to wit, Mr Henry Killigrew, an old friend and acquaintance of mine; for Mr Randolph was returned home, because he had not such credit with the Earl of Mar and had lost the favour of both the factions, except only with the Earl of Morton, for his double-dealing was discovered.

This new ambassador being arrived at Leith upon his way toward Stirling, where the regent remained for the time, he sent up to the castle of Edinburgh to see if I was there; for they had told him in Leith that I was newly come over the water [from Fife]. He desired that I would come and speak with him, which I did, and convoyed him unto Cramond, reasoning together all the way upon such matters as he said he had in commission, chiefly how he might be a good instrument to agree the differences that were between the two parties; albeit there was nothing less in his mind, at least in his commission. He said he had the queen his mistress's commands to deal with both parties for concord, but more carefully and with the advice of more loving friends unto them of the castle than with their contrary party; and albeit that outwardly he behoved first to go to the regent, to give him the prerogative, yet in effect my friends in the castle should be preferred, both by his first salutation by me to them and by two familiar letters, the one from my Lord of Leicester to the laird of Grange and the other from secretary Cecil to secretary Lethington, desiring me to pray them to follow and credit the advice given therein by the said lords, who loved them entirely for their virtue and old acquaintance. He willed me to tell them that after he had declared his commission to the regent he would come back again to them, and at length declare his commission from Her Majesty.

It appeared that he had intelligence how that Mr Randolph's double-dealing had been discovered, and he seemed to find fault with him, but he excused him as far as he could, until I adjured him, upon the long and great familiarity that had been betwixt us, to deal plainlier with me. I told him he might serve his mistress truly enough, without casting me and my friends upon a wrong side, which might be afterwards our ruin, who had deserved better at his hands than to put us in such danger, by the common practices of countries, as if we were untoward, dishonest, or uncounsellable, as Mr Randolph had done, forgetting the fraternity of religion so well grounded among us during his banishment in France for religion. Then he was compelled to grant to me that his commission and his mind went not one way, and that he was employed against his will, and, as a servant, he durst not disobey his princess, and said he would give me his loving counsel and warning.

He said that the queen and council of England neither built their course here upon the late regent, nor yet upon this regent, but entirely upon the Earl of Morton, as well of their own plot laid long since as by the information of Mr Randolph, who hath confirmed them in that opinion, so that they will not alter for no contrary persuasion; willing my friends and me to join our course, and band with the Earl of Morton, or else to expect no friendship from the court of England, but hurt and ruin so far as they might. For albeit he was not regent, they knew that he had a great friendship in the country, which they would increase so far as they could; so that, whoever was regent, he should get little or nothing done without his consent. In this I thought he dealt plainly; my friends of the castle were of that same judgment, yet they could not find in their heart to join with him, albeit he made suit to them, offering to hold up the queen's authority; for they thought his course unsure for the king and settling of the estate, he being too much addicted to England.

After that this ambassador had been with the regent in Stirling, and was come back again to Edinburgh, he told the rest of his commission to them of the castle, to whom he used himself but like an ambassador as he was directed. Generally he said that he found them more reasonable than the regent's party. Then he went to Dalkeith to meet with the Earl of Morton, and thereafter returned to Edinburgh, to wait all fit occasions and informations how to proceed conform to the tenor of his instructions. He had commandment to stay in Scotland for a time, to see if he could obtain as much credit as to serve their turn who sent him. And because I was of his greatest acquaintance, he came with me to my house [in Halhill], and stayed a few days to refresh his spirits; and after I had convoyed him back to Edinburgh, he showed me some articles of his instructions, one of which was,

'Item, If the captain of the castle will condescend that all the differences now in question among the Scots be referred to be decided before us and our council, as the rest of the king's lords have granted already, we shall be his good friends, maintain him in his office, and give him an honourable pension.' But he plainly refused to comply with this, saying it would prejudge his prince and country; but that and his other former refusals cost him his life afterwards.

About this time my lord regent sent a letter to me, with all diligence to come to him. At my coming he made a heavy moan for the civil troubles that were kindled in the country by the craft and malice of some in England and some in Scotland, taking the colour of this or that authority and yet were only moved by their own particularities, to the hurt both of king, queen and country; desiring me that I would go unto the castle of Edinburgh and show them, as of my own head, and not as from him, that I understood he perceived, albeit too late, how that we are led upon the ice, and that all good Scotsmen would fain agree and settle the state; and they in special, if they could get a meeting, which I could be assured they would get of him if they would ask the same. And I was to offer myself to be the instrument to bring on a good agreement between them and me, which should by God's grace take good effect upon my return with their reasonable offers and answer. Whereupon I went to Edinburgh, and found them all inclined to peace and quietness, with little need of persuasions thereto; for they were near a point before with my Lord of Lennox, and some conference had been betwixt my brother and Captain Cunningham of before.

At my return to the regent, he was very glad, saying he knew that the honest men were ever willing to cease from civil discord, seeing the queen was captive, to whom their owning her authority could do no good but evil; but that they had been by crafty practices cast against their wills upon a contrary course. Then he enquired upon what conditions the captain and his friends would agree? I said that the laird of Grange would not sell his duty to his prince and country for any advantage, but would serve the king and his regent to settle the estate, so long as the queen was detained in England; and if God pleased to grant her liberty, they doubted not but she and her son should agree betwixt themselves, to which all honest and good subjects on both sides would hold hand. They for their parts desired no man's land nor goods, but only liberty peaceably to enjoy their own livings. Only

Grange desired that the regent would cause to pay certain debts contracted for repairing of the castle and artillery; which conditions the regent promised to fulfil, and to be an assured friend to Grange and those in the castle in particular. And without any further ceremonies the regent called the laird of Tullibardine, his brother-in-law, and, after he had declared unto him how far we had proceeded, he put his hand in mine and did swear the peace in presence of the said Tullibardine, who had also been a good instrument to the said agreement, together with his man of law, Mr Clement Little, a very honest man, brother to William Little, afterwards provost of Edinburgh. No more were made privy thereto but my Lady Mar and Captain James Cunningham.

After this the regent went to Edinburgh to convene the lords of council, to show them the calamities that the civil wars produced, and to let them see how necessary agreement and a settled state would be to the whole country. In the mean time, until the appointed council-day, he went to Dalkeith, where he was nobly treated and banqueted by the Lord of Morton; shortly after which he took a vehement sickness, which caused him to ride suddenly to Stirling, where he died, regretted by many. Some of his friends and the vulgar people spoke and suspected he had gotten wrong, and others that it was for displeasure.*

The Earl of Morton, after the decease of the Earl of Mar, was made regent, England helping it with all their might. So soon as he was chosen he sent for me, declaring how that against his mind and will the lords had burdened him with that troublesome office, which seeing he behoved to accept, he would wish that he might stand the country and commonwealth in some stead. First he would desire the help of all good and honest men, to draw on peace and concord to the quieting of the state, praying me, as one for whom he had ever good liking, to travail with my friends of the castle for that effect, and to persuade them to go forward with him, as they were minded to do with the Earl of Mar; assuring me that none of the former regents had at any time been more willing than he was presently to put an end to the civil troubles, nor that I should remember less the partialities past; and that the regent should not revenge the Earl of Morton's quarrels. But whoever would serve the king and be his friend, he would embrace them, upon what faction soever they had formerly been. And he was willing to give whatever conditions the Earl of Mar had offered, or better; that I should have the priory of Pittenweem for my pains; the laird of Grange the bishopric of St Andrews and castle of Blackness;

* The suspicion was that he had been poisoned at Morton's banquet. The alternative explanation was that he died broken-hearted because of his failure to restore peace.

and every one within the castle should be restored to their lands and possessions as of before.

It was very hard to bring on this agreement with the Earl of Morton, for the evil opinion which was conceived of him, and for the foul and hurtful marks they supposed by proofs and appearances that he would shoot at, being by nature too covetous and too great with England, and over fearful that the king would be his ruin, concerning which a lady, who was his leman, had shown him the answers of the oracles. Yet the laird of Grange, who was ever willing to see concord in the country, was easily persuaded; the Lord Hume and Lethington made some resistance at the first, but were also at length content. So that after I had past twice or thrice between them, they appeared to be agreed in their hearts; and for superabundance the laird of Grange said he would cause all the rest of the queen's faction to agree with the regent; but he refused to take the bishopric of St Andrews and the castle of Blackness, desiring nothing but his own lands.

When I returned to the regent with this answer conform to his desire, he was marvellously glad; but when I declared that the laird of Grange would be a good instrument to cause all the rest of the queen's faction to agree also with him, he answered that was not meet. And when I reasoned against him, and showed him how that I had spoken in his name that he was resolved to agree all Scotland, and that Grange had no quarrel of his own, but to help a number of noblemen who required his protection during the king's minority, and had requested the regent once to agree with them altogether, for Grange's honour; and afterwards he and all these of the castle should band with him and lay aside all other bands. The regent answered, and said, 'James, I will be plain with you, it is not my will to agree with them all, for then their faction will be as strong as ever it was, whereby they may some day circumvent me, if they please, therefore it is my will to divide them. And moreover there have been great troubles in this country this while bygone, and during them great wrongs and extortions committed, for the which some fashion of punishment must be made, and I would rather that the crimes should be laid and light upon the Hamiltons, the Earl of Huntly, and their adherents, than upon your friends; and by their wreck I will get more profit than by that of those in the castle, that have neither so great lands nor escheats for us to win and to be the reward of our labours. Therefore show Grange and your friends that either they must agree without the Hamiltons and the Earls of Huntly and Argyll, or the said lords will agree without him, and these of the castle.' To this I answered that I understood him, his speeches being very plain. With this I went again to the castle, and rehearsed our whole reasoning. Grange said it was neither godly or just dealing, to lay the blame upon those that were richest, for their lands and goods, and not upon them who were guiltiest, seeing these noblemen had been ever willing to agree, after that the queen was kept in England, but could not be admitted. And yet if now they would abandon him, and agree without him and those in his company, he had deserved better at their hands; yet he had rather that they should leave and deceive him, than that he should do it unto them.

When the Earl of Morton perceived that Grange stood stiff upon his honesty and reputation, he appeared to like him the better, and seemed that he would go forward with those of the castle. He sent up Car-michael, at my desire, to hear out of their own mouths so far as I had spoken in their name; they of the castle likewise sent Pittarrow to the regent, to hear out of his own mouth so far about the agreement as I had said to them in his name. This I did for my discharge, whatsoever might chance afterwards.

The regent asked at what time the castle of Edinburgh should be delivered to him? I said, 'Within half a year.' 'What security', said he, 'shall I have for that?' I said I should be a pledge if he would accept me. Then he enquired wherefore I sought so long delay. I answered in the first place, till all articles and promises might be performed, and like-wise because he said that he ever esteemed the laird of Grange an honest man, yet by wrong reports and practices the ministers were stirred up to cry out and preach against him; therefore to make him more able and give him the greater courage to serve for the future, it would be some satisfaction to his mind to let the world see that, as well after the agreement as before, he should be esteemed alike honest and worthy to keep the house, and then at the time appointed the regent should be requested to receive the castle out of his hands. He appeared to be very well content with this manner of dealing, and gave me great thanks for the travail I had made, desiring me to go home, and he in the mean time would convene the rest of the noblemen of his side, and acquaint them with his proceedings, and take their advice and consent to this good purpose, which he doubted not to procure; and thereafter he would send for me again, and put the form of the agreement in writing.

But he took immediately another course, and sent a fit man to the Hamiltons, the Earls of Huntly and Argyll, and their dependers and assisters, and offered them the pacification, not including Grange and those in the castle; which condition they gladly accepted of, without many ceremonies, and sent their letters instantly from Perth to the laird of Grange, lamenting that the straits they were reduced to had compelled them to accept that agreement which the regent had offered them, praying him not to take it in evil part, seeing they had no house nor strength to retire themselves to. They gave him many thanks for the help and assistance he had made them, which they would never forget so long as God would lend them their lives.

This was the recompence this good gentleman obtained for the great help, hazard and charges done and made for these lords, not imagining that the regent would be so malicious as to cast him off, and not accept of his friendship, which he incontinent offered, after the rest were agreed. But from that time forth the regent would hear none of his offers, persuading the rest of his faction that these of the castle were so proud and wilful that they would not grant to serve the king, or acknowledge him as regent. And this was published and preached; and yet the contrary was true, for they would have taken any reasonable appointment. What rage was in the regent's mind for greediness of their lands and goods, or what should have induced him to bring an army from England to besiege the castle of Edinburgh, I know not, it being to the dishonour of his prince and country; which castle was offered a little of before to the Earl of Rothes, to be instantly delivered unto his hands, to be kept to the regent's behoof; which was refused. So that apparently he had some other fetch in his head than a man esteemed so wise should have had, seeing he might have obtained his intent without the help of England, having all Scotland at his devotion saving that few number within the castle, who would have agreed upon any reasonable condition.

Thus the castle of Edinburgh was straitly besieged with an English army under the conduct of the marshal of Berwick, assisted by all Scotland. These within, seeing they could not be received upon any composition, debated so long as they had victuals and water: for their draw-well dried by the droughty summer, and they had no other water but what they fetched, letting men with cords down over the walls and rock of the castle to a well on the west-side, which was afterward poisoned, whereby so many as escaped the shot died, and the rest fell deadly sick. Yet the laird of Grange undertook with eight persons to keep the castle untaken by force, of the which number were the Lord Hume, my two brothers Sir Robert and Andrew, the laird of Pittarrow and his brother Patrick Echlin. This resolution being taken, the laird of Cleish and Matthew Colville, his brother, were sent to the castle, under the pretext of making offers of agreement; but their intent was to get intelligence of the state of the house and to seduce the soldiers who were yet alive; which they did, so that some fled out over the walls, and others were shot forth. For the captain thought the house in a surer state, both for victuals and otherwise, when they were forth.

The marshal of Berwick, seeing no appearance to succeed, entered into contention with the ambassador, alleging that the queen his mistress would be dishonoured, and said he would wait no longer;

whereupon they without* entered on a new communing, and sent up again the laird of Cleish to offer them conditions to come forth with their armour and bag and baggage, which was agreed to, and that they should be restored to their lands; and because for the time their lands were in other men's possession, it was referred to themselves whether they would go to England with the marshal of Berwick or remain in Scotland among their friends, until such promises as were made them might be fulfilled. The Englishmen desired that the castle should be put in their hands; but Grange sent secretly to Captain Hume and Captain Crawford, desiring them to come and lie within the bulwark betwixt the house and the Englishmen; and so he put the castle in hands of Scotsmen, and his person to go to England with the marshal, who was his friend, until all promises might be kept to him and the rest by the Queen of England's means. In this manner they came forth, after that George Douglas, natural brother to the regent, had received the house; they had all their swords and weapons about them, and were three days at liberty. My brother Sir Robert lay with me at his own lodging; the laird of Grange and the secretary Lethington remained yet with the marshal of Berwick at his lodging for their greater security, because that the people of the town of Edinburgh were their great enemies. For except a few that tarried within the town during the civil troubles between the parties that lay in Edinburgh and Leith, the most part of the richest men and merchants left the town and went to Leith, to take part with the regent; therefore their houses were spoiled, upon which account they did bear great hatred to those in the castle.

But at the end of three days they were all laid hands upon, and kept as prisoners. For some of their most malicious enemies put it easily in the regent's head, and the ambassador's, that it was well done to request the Queen of England to cause deliver the whole company to the regent, to be disposed upon at his pleasure, alleging they had no security but a naked promise, which they needed not to keep; and because those of the castle confided most on the marshal's promise, the marshal's writing was so forestalled by the ambassador that the Queen of England's sharp letter came to the marshal to deliver up them of the castle to the regent. And he durst not disobey, but delivered them up with great regret, by reason of his promise, and returned malcontent to Berwick. And they of the castle were committed to strait ward; and thereafter new letters were purchased by the regent from the queen, that he might execute them, which she willingly permitted, for she would have been quit of my Lord Hume and Grange, as being two true Scotsmen, unwonable to England to do any thing against their king or country, and of the secretary Lethington, but he died at Leith

* i.e. outside the castle.

before that the rest were delivered to the shambles, some supposing he took a drink and died as the old Romans were wont to do. . . .*

On this manner both England and the regent were revenged upon that worthy champion [Grange], whom they had sometimes in great estimation, who had done such notable service in France, being captain of an hundred light horsemen, that he was extolled by the Duke of Vendôme, Prince of Condé, and Duke of Aumale, governors and colonels then in Picardy: that I heard Henry II point unto him and say, 'Yonder is one of the most valiant men of our age.' Also the king used him so familiarly, that he chose him commonly upon his side in all pastimes he went to; and because he shot fair with a great shaft at the butts, the king would have him to shoot two arrows, one for his pleasure. The great constable of France would never speak to him uncovered, and that king gave him an honourable pension, whereof he never sought payment. England had proof of his qualities both against them upon the Borders, where he gave them divers ruffles, and by single combat he vanquished Lord Yvers' brother† between the two armies of Scotland and England. He afterwards debated so manfully the liberty of his country against the Frenchmen, when they pretended to erect the land into a province. He had lately refused the demands of Mr Randolph and Mr Killigrew, as is before mentioned, and had reproached both the said ambassadors of false and deceitful dealings. Last of all, he had refused to put the castle into the hands of Englishmen, and therefore, because he was true and faithful to his prince and country, it cost him his life. For they boasted plainly to bring down that giant's pride who, as they alleged, presumed to be another Wallace. Albeit contrariwise he was humble, gentle, and meek like a lamb in the house, but like a lion in the fields.

He was a lusty, strong and well proportioned personage, hardy and of a magnanimous courage, secret and prudent in all his enterprises, so that never one that he made or devised mischanced where he was present himself. When he was victorious he was very merciful, and naturally liberal, an enemy to greediness and ambition and a friend to all men in adversity. He fell frequently in trouble to defend innocent men from such as would oppress them, so that these his worthy qualities

* Sir James does not mention the fate of his brothers, Robert and Andrew, who were in the castle when it fell. Robert was handed over to Morton, but his life was spared at Queen Elizabeth's intercession, he was set at liberty in 1574 and his estates were restored in 1579. Andrew had to leave Scotland, but entered Mary's service in England.

† The brother of Lord Evers or Eure. The first lord, who died in 1548, had a son, Ralph, who was killed at the battle of Ancrum in 1545, and he was succeeded by his grandson.

were also partly causes and means of his wreck; for they promoted him so in the opinion of many, that some loved him for his religion, uprightness, and manliness, others again depended upon him for his good fortune and apparent promotion, whereby divers of them hoped to be advanced and rewarded, supposing that offices and honours could not fail to fall to him. All which he lacked through his own default, for he fled from avarice and abhorred ambition and refused sundry great offices, even to be regent, and benefices and great pensions. Thus, wanting place and substance to reward, he was soon abandoned by his greedy and ambitious dependers: as soon as they saw him at a strait, they drew to others, whom they perceived to aim at more profitable marks. On the other hand, he was as much envied by those who were of a vile and unworthy nature as he was beloved of all honest men. Then, as many have made tragical ends for their too great avarice and ambition, as shortly after did the Earl of Morton, this good gentleman perished for being too little ambitious and greedy. But so soon as the king's majesty came to perfect age, and understood how the estate of the government and country had been handled during his minority, he caused to restore the heirs of the said laird of Grange, who he said was wrecked contrary to the appointment made with the regent and the marshal of Berwick; and also ordered his bones to be taken up, and buried honourably in the ancient burial-place of his predecessors in Kinghorn.

After his death the marshal of Berwick took so heavy displeasure, because of the breach of his promise, and that the appointment which he had made with the castle of Edinburgh was not kept, that he would tarry no longer in his office at Berwick, seeing he had lost his credit and reputation; for he was a plain man of war, and so loved Grange with his heart, that at his request he spared to cast down the houses of Seton and Niddrie, when he came in to cast down the house of Hamilton. Likewise all the officers of Berwick lamented the loss of so worthy a captain.

The regent triumphed for a while, because of the great assistance that England made to him, which they had never done to any of the former regents, but rather stirred up factions and parties against them to keep the country in discord. . . .

This regent held the country in an established estate, under great obedience, better than for many years before or since. For there was not another Earl of Morton to stir up the subjects in factions, as he used to do against the rest of the regents, which made him so proud and disdainful that he despised the rest of the nobility. And, using no man's counsel but his own, he became ungrateful* to all his old friends and servants. . . .

★ i.e. not *persona grata*.

VI

Intrigues around the Young King James

Now the young king was brought up in Stirling, by Alexander Erskine and my Lady Mar. He had for principal preceptors Mr George Buchanan, Mr Peter Young, the Abbots of Cambuskenneth and Dryburgh,* descended from the house of Erskine, and the laird of Drumwhasel, master of the household. Alexander Erskine was a nobleman of a true, gentle nature, well loved and liked by all men for his good qualities and great discretion, no ways factious nor envious, a lover of all honest men, and desired ever to see men of good conversation about the prince, rather than his own nearer friends, if he thought them not so meet. The laird of Drumwhasel again was ambitious and greedy, his greatest care was to advance himself and his friends. The two abbots were wise and modest.

My Lady Mar was wise and sharp, and held the king in great awe; and so did Mr George Buchanan. Mr Peter Young was more gentle, and was loath to offend the king at any time, and used himself warily, as a man who had mind of his own weal, by keeping of His Majesty's favour. But Mr George was a stoic philosopher, who looked not far before the hand: a man of notable qualities for his learning and knowledge in Latin poesy, much honoured in other countries, pleasant in company, rehearsing at all occasions moralities short and effective, whereof he had abundance, inventing where he wanted. He was also of good religion for a poet, but was easily abused, and so facile that he was led by every company that he haunted for the time, which made him factious in his old days; for he spoke and wrote as those who were about him for the time informed him, he was become slippery and careless, following in many things the vulgar opinion; for he was naturally popular, and extremely revengeful against any man who had offended him, which was his greatest fault. He did write despiteful invectives against the Earl of Menteith, for some particulars that were between him and the laird of Buchanan. He became the Earl of Morton's great enemy, for that a hackney of his chanced to be taken from his servant during the civil troubles, and was bought by the regent,

* These 'Abbots' were laymen who held the abbey property.

who had no will to part with the said horse, he was so sure footed and so easy, that albeit Mr George had oft-times required him again he could not get him. And though he had been the regent's great friend before, he became his mortal enemy, and from that time forth spoke evil of him in all places, and at all occasions. Drumwhasel also, because the regent kept all casualties* to himself, and would let nothing fall to others who were about the king, became also his great enemy; and so did they all who were about His Majesty.

The regent again, ruling all at his pleasure, made no account of any of them that were about the king, until a discreet gentleman called Mr Nichol Elphinston advertised him that he was envied of many, and hated of every man, especially by those who were in Stirling with the king, advising him, albeit too late, to bestow part of his gold unto so many of them as he believed were wonable. He gave to one that was in mean rank twenty pieces of gold, at twenty pound the piece. What he gave to others I cannot tell: but such as had spoken ill of him before durst not alter their language, because of the king's wit and good memory, who could check any that he perceived had first spoken evil and then began to speak good again; as His Majesty had done to one of the company, alleging that he had changed his coat, as I was informed for the time: so that the regent was too long in dealing part of his gold to those about His Majesty, who increasing in years and knowledge, sundry gentlemen began to suit service, and were on-waiters. Among others, James Stewart, son to the Lord Ochiltree, a young man of a busy brain, a quick tanter,† with merry conceits and an aspiring spirit, through time won great favour and credit with His Majesty, though not so well liked by those of the castle of Stirling. Yet he was the more overseen, because he gave continually evil information to His Majesty of the Earl of Morton; and so did also my Lord Robert, Earl of Orkney, who had been warded and hardly handled by the regent for some underhand dealing with Denmark, as was alleged.

The regent being in this manner brought in disfavour with His Majesty even when he was upon the height of the wheel, the Earls of Argyll and Atholl were secretly practised,‡ and drawn to Stirling by Drumwhasel, with the consent of Alexander Erskine, Master of Mar, and Mr George Buchanan; by whose advice and counsel His Majesty was easily moved to depose the regent from his office; who yielded and granted easilier thereto than any man would have believed, against the opinion of divers of his friends, retiring himself to the house of Loch-

* Property and revenue casually accruing to the crown either through the operation of the feudal system of land tenure or through proceedings in courts of law.   † Banterer.   ‡ Brought to engage in a plot.

leven within the loch, for the surety of his person, until he might understand what was like to follow thereupon, and what might be the next best for him to do.

The King's Majesty, having attained unto the age of [twelve] years, ordained a council to sit at Edinburgh for the affairs of the realm; the Earl of Atholl to be chancellor, because the Lord Glamis was a little before slain in Stirling by the Earl of Crawford, as was suspected, though he denied the deed and purged himself thereof as far as he could. The Earl of Argyll and the Master of Mar stayed in Stirling with the King's Majesty.

During the time that this new council sat in Edinburgh, the Earl of Morton, who was quiet in Lochleven, making the alleys of the garden even, his mind was in the mean time occupied in crooked paths, with a complot how to be brought again to be master of the court; which was accomplished upon a night at midnight. When he came to the gates of the castle of Stirling, they were opened unto him by the two abbots and a faction that they had drawn in there with them. Albeit the Master of Mar and Earl of Argyll made what resistance they could, where the master's eldest son died in the throng, yet the enterprisers prevailed, and brought in again the Earl of Morton, and put out the Earl of Argyll, the Master of Mar, Drumwhasel and such others as they misliked, and so made a new change at court; where the Earl of Morton handled the matter so discreetly and moderately as he could, that the alteration should not appear to be over sharp or violent. The new chosen council scattered incontinent, some of them retiring home, and some joined with the Earl of Morton, hoping never to see a turn again.

About this time came here out of France my Lord of Aubigny, who was afterward made Duke of Lennox, who was brother's son to the Earl of Lennox and obtained afterward great credit and favour. James Stewart of Ochiltree, of whom I formerly made mention, assisted him through process of time to persuade the King's Majesty to desire to ride out of Stirling, and make a progress among the rest of his subjects; which the Earl of Morton would not resist, supposing that it lay in his power to frame the court at his pleasure, by his great wealth to gain so many as he judged necessary, and by the multitude of his friends to bear out his business, however the court was ruled after he had obtained a discharge and allowance of his handling [of finance] during the time that he was regent, remaining always strongest about the king. But my Lord Aubigny and James Stewart were most in favour, who by their continual rounding in the king's ear against the Earl of Morton engendered at last a greater dislike in the king of him than he had before. And as James Stewart was the stirrer up of the other, so afterwards, when he thought the time convenient, he took occasion to accuse the said earl, before the council, of the late king's murder. Whereupon the Earl of Morton was made prisoner, and sent first to the castle of Edinburgh, and afterwards to the castle of Dumbarton; which was thought strange, in respect of his many friends that were in court for the time, who were then found to be but friends to his fortune. For he was loved by none, and envied and hated by many; so that they all looked through their fingers to see his fall.

England was also angry at him for the time, because of his slowness to complete such turns as they hoped for at his hands, having put the king and country in his power. Yet they made some countenance to assist him; which was rather the cause to hasten his ruin. For they sent down some companies to the Borders, to the number of 1800, boasting to send a greater number and to declare open war, in case the Earl of Morton was not set at liberty and the Lord Aubigny put out of Scotland. Mr Randolph was sent in with this ambassage. His Majesty again having these two young men about him, who knew of no perils, raised a taxation to pay hired soldiers, and caused make a proclamation for every man to be in readiness; which moved the English to retire, and leave off any further procuring or making of assistance; encouraging thereby so many as were deadly enemies to the Earl of Morton to ride to Dumbarton, with the forces of 1000 waged hagbutters, besides their own friends, and brought the Earl of Morton back again to Edinburgh, to undergo an assize and to be justified.* Some of the earl's friends convened, but were not strong enough to seize him out of their hands. They might have done it, had it not been the forces of hagbutters which had been newly levied, occasioned by countenance and threatenings which England had made. Being brought to Edinburgh, he found few friends to act for him. His gold and silver was transported long before, by his natural son James Douglas and one of his servants called John Macmorran. It was first carried in barrels, and afterwards hid in some secret parts; part whereof was given to be kept by some who were looked upon as his friends, who made ill account of it again: so that the most part thereof lighted in bad hands, and himself was so destitute of money that when he went through the street to the Tolbooth,† to undergo his assize, he was compelled to borrow twenty shillings to distribute to the poor who asked [alms of him] for God's sake. The assize condemned him to death, as being art and part in the king's murder and as being of counsel with the Earl of Bothwell, who brought him out of banishment when he was absent for the slaughter of David Riccio. He granted that he was made privy thereto;‡ but was

* i.e., to have justice done on him.
† The town-house of Edinburgh, where courts were held.
‡ i.e., to the murder of Darnley.

not a deviser thereof. And as concerning the young king, he purposed to send him to England for his weal, that he might the rather obtain his right to the crown of England, being within the country, and brought up among them. He died resolutely, and had ended more perfectly if he had declared and confessed his worldly practices and fetches to nourish the civil troubles, partly at the devotion of England, and partly for his own particular profit, during the government of the first three regents, which occasioned great blood-shedding, that commonly cries to heaven for vengeance. . . .

After that the Earl of Morton, the last of the four regents, was deposed, the King's Majesty, being yet young, of [fourteen] years, took the government into his own hands. My Lord of Aubigny, being made Lord of Dalkeith and afterwards Duke of Lennox, was chiefest about His Majesty, and James Stewart, formerly mentioned; who afterwards took unto himself the style, and then the earldom, of Arran, thinking that he had deserved well for accusing and wrecking the Earl of Morton. He also took unto him the Earl of March's wife, both* without any great right or reason.

The duke was of nature upright, just and gentle, but lacked experience in the state of the country. At first he was most guided by the said James Stewart and his wife; who both began secretly to envy him and see how they might cast him off, that they might attain to the sole management of affairs; and for this end they gave him wrong advice, and sinister informations against sundry of his best friends, moving him to sudden wrath, without true trial, to start at them; which being perceived by some that loved him for the king's cause was often remedied and other times forestalled; but it was so often renewed again that at length it took the desired effect, not without the practices also of England, who by their ambassador stirred up sundry against him, alleging him to be a papist, altogether at the Duke of Guise's devotion, and therefore a dangerous man to be about His Majesty. But his chiefest fault was that, being true to the king, he was thought unwonable to their behoof, as he was indeed. . . .

Then the rest of the nobility were dissatisfied to see these two young lords chiefly in favour with the king, supposing them both to aim at noblemen's lives, for their lands. And albeit some of them misliked the Earl of Morton's proceedings, yet they judged the taking of his life an hard preparative. Therefore a number of them consulted together, before they had sufficient proof of the Duke of Lennox's good qualities, to displace both the duke and the Earl of Arran, to send them both home, the one to France and the other further off, if he escaped with his life. In the mean time they would throng themselves in about

* i.e. both the earldom and the wife.

the king and keep him, under pretext of a necessary reformation; and His Majesty being environed with their forces, to present unto him a humble supplication, so soon as he came to Dunfermline, whither he had appointed to come at his return out of Atholl, where he was for the time at the hunting. . . .

At this highland-hunting His Majesty was very quiet, only accompanied by his domestics. The Duke of Lennox tarried for the time at Dalkeith; the new Earl of Arran at Kinneil. Many of the council were appointed to hold justice ayres* in divers shires of the country. I was appointed to hold the justice ayre of West-Lothian at Edinburgh with my Lord Newbattle, Mr David Macgill and Mr John Sharp. There came to my bed-side timely in the morning a gentleman, alleging that I had formerly done him pleasure which till now he was never able to recompense, that he would make me the instrument of saving the King's Majesty my master out of the hands of those who were upon an enterprise to take and keep him. I said I could not believe that; but I feared that the Duke of Lennox might be in hazard, who was to go to Glasgow to hold justice ayres, because of the hatred against him, especially for the maintaining the two [arch]bishops of St Andrews and Glasgow.† He answered, 'They will lay hands on the King's Majesty, and then the duke and the Earl of Arran dare no more be seen, their insolency and misbehaviour being the cause of the present disorder; and there is an enterprise to present a supplication against them to His Majesty.' After he had told me the names of the noblemen, he willed me not to declare his name, though to tell the matter to His Majesty. He said that the turn would be done in ten days; and as I started up to put on my clothes, he slipped out with a short farewell.

Because the duke was at Dalkeith, I did ride thither, and showed him the whole matter, advising him to ride himself to His Majesty with this advertisement, for his own security; but he chose rather to direct a gentleman with all possible diligence to His Majesty, willing me also to write unto the Earl of Gowrie; for the gentleman had not named him to me with the rest [of the enterprisers], either out of forgetfulness, or else because he was but lately won to that purpose by the laird of Drumwhasel, who assured him that the Duke of Lennox was determined to slay him at the first meeting; persuading the earl, upon this ground, to join with the rest of the noblemen who were determined to reform the estate. Unto the which invented advertisement he too easily gave credit, and so joined with the rest of the nobility who were minded to present the forenamed supplication to the king at his coming to Dunfermline. . . .

* Itinerant courts for criminal justice.
† He supported the archbishops against the presbyterians.

It is certain the Duke of Lennox was led by evil counsellors and wrong informations, whereby he was moved to meddle in such hurtful and dangerous courses that the rest of the nobility took suspicion, and feared for their estates by a hard alteration. As for the Earl of Arran, they detested his proceedings, and esteemed him the worst and most insolent instrument that could be found out, to wreck king, kirk and country. The duke had been tolerable, had he happened upon as honest counsellors as he was well inclined of himself; he loved both the king and commonwealth, but he wanted experience, and was not versed in the affairs of state, nor brought up in our religion, which apparently he was like to embrace by time. But the Earl of Arran was a scorner of religion, presumptuous, ambitious, needy, careless of the commonwealth, a despiser of the nobility and of all honest men; so that every man was expecting a sudden change; which should have been made in Dunfermline, in presenting the above specified supplication. What moved the lords to surprise His Majesty within the house of Huntingtower, [I know not]; some alleged it was to embark the Earl of Gowrie [whose house it was], more deeply in their bond; others say that the lords, fearing their enterprise to be discovered, made the greater haste, and stayed His Majesty in that place; [the enterprise] was afterward called the Raid of Ruthven.*

After that the Duke of Lennox was advertised of this enterprise, he sent for the Earl of Arran, who was peaceably passing his time in Kinneil. He took in hand to ride out and save the king, boasting that he would chase all the lords into mouseholes; but he was chased, and saved himself in the house of Ruthven, where they had shortly made an end of him, but for the Earl of Gowrie, whose destiny it was to keep him alive to be his own wreck afterwards. The Duke of Lennox being advertised that His Majesty was in [their] hands, retired himself to Dumbarton; and His Majesty was conveyed to Stirling, and there retained. . . .

The lords in the mean time thought meet to hold a council, and reasoned upon their best, and resolved that their enterprise was good service to His Majesty, the kirk and commonwealth; which His Majesty granted also to be true; whereupon an act of council was formed. At that same time the general assembly of the kirk was held at Edinburgh, to the which His Majesty was moved to send two commissioners, to testify that he had allowed for good service the said lords' enterprise, willing likewise the kirk to find it good for their parts, and to ordain the ministers, and commissioners of every shire,†

* Ruthven was the Earl of Gowrie's family name.
† Overseers appointed by the general assembly to perform some of the functions normally carried out by bishops.

to publish the same to their parishioners and to get the principal gentlemen's subscriptions to maintain the same. Nevertheless, His Majesty took the matter further to heart than any man would have believed. He lamented his mishandling to sundry noblemen and others; and at length made some of them privy that he intended to relieve himself through time out of their hands who held him as captive. He desired divers of them that he trusted in to assist him with their counsel and help.

The lords again who were joined together for the reformation of the state, being rid of the Duke of Lennox, who had passed through England to France, where he shortly after died of a sickness contracted through displeasure, and being also rid of the Earl of Arran, whom they kept captive in the custody of the Earl of Gowrie, they retired themselves from the court to their houses, that His Majesty should not think himself any way detained by them; for they had got some intelligence of his inward grief for his taking and retaining. Whereupon His Majesty took occasion to appoint a convention to be holden in St Andrews. . . . To the which convention His Majesty, by missives, invited some of the nobility, but none of the lords who had lately left him, supposing that they would not come unwritten for; and that way he thought he might slip himself out of their hands, and hold about him such lords as he had written for, to wit, the Earls of Argyll, Huntly, Montrose, Crawford, Rothes and March (who was an indweller in St Andrews for the time) and the Earl of Gowrie, of whom he judged himself assured, though for some respects he would not employ him till afterwards, lest the rest of his associates should allege that he had left them unhonestly. For the said earl had repented him sore that he had suffered himself to be drawn by Drumwhasel to join with the rest, after he had sure information that the Duke of Lennox was not laid for his slaughter, as was alleged. Therefore he repented his folly, and offered at all occasions to His Majesty to help to set him at liberty.

So His Majesty thinking himself assured of all these noblemen, the day appointed for the convention drawing near, it pleased him to send Colonel Stewart to my house, showing that His Majesty, having one of the greatest turns to do that ever he had, directed him unto me as to one of his most faithful servants, of whom he had good proof, by the true warning I had made him before the alteration. As a sworn gentleman of his chamber, [he desired] that I would now help him to his liberty, which he was determined to attain at his being at St Andrews, whither he was to go shortly to a convention; he desired my assistance and advice, His Majesty being minded to follow my counsel so long as he lived, willing me be resolved not to refuse any service that His Majesty would propose to me at meeting, after I had resolved to be at

His Majesty in Falkland with all possible diligence. This commission was to me very unpleasant, for I had taken my leave of the court, as being tired and wearied with the many alterations I had seen, both at home and in foreign countries, and had got great trouble and damage by them for other men's causes. Therefore I was determined and inclined to lead a quiet, contemplative life the rest of my days, which this purpose of my prince and master was like to put me from. In this perplexity I had recourse by humble prayer to God, so to direct my doings as they might tend to his glory and to the weal of my prince and country. And thereafter, according to my dutiful obedience, I went unto His Majesty. When I came to him at Falkland, he told me of his intention and deliberation, lamenting his hard state and mishandling by his own subjects, and what displeasure he had taken, and that he was thought but a beast by other neighbour princes, for suffering so many indignities. . . .

Melville advised James not to commit himself wholly to the faction opposed to the Ruthven Raiders, and to pardon the latter. James was determined 'to liberate himself fully or die in the attempt', but he agreed to make an act of oblivion for offences committed during his minority.

His Majesty engaged also to be secret, constant, and counsellable; for the first, it was thought expedient, that he should be in St Andrews some few days before the convention, that being free there, proclamation might be made to forbid any nobleman or other to come to the convention without being expressly called by letter. For this end it was devised that the Earl of March should invite His Majesty to be at St Andrews two or three days before the convention, by reason of his preparation of wild meat and other fresh fleshes, that would spoil in case His Majesty came not to make good cheer with him some days before. Whereupon His Majesty went forward, contrary to the opinion of some that were about him, who durst not be so bold as to stay him; but part of them spoke, and said that it was not meet that His Majesty should ride before the lords who were absent might be advertised. Nevertheless he went on, and had appointed the Earl of March, the provost of St Andrews and other barons to attend him at Dairsie. Where meeting them, His Majesty thought himself at liberty, with great joy and exclamation, like a bird flown out of a cage, passing his time in hawking by the way after his meeting them, thinking himself sure enough, albeit I thought his estate far surer when he was in Falkland. For when he came to St Andrews he lodged in the old inns, a very open part, the yard dykes being his greatest strength;* few of the lords he

* i.e. there was little defence except the walls at the ends of the yards or gardens.

had written for the second time to be at St Andrews as soon as he were yet come, except only the Earl of Crawford, who was near.

In the mean time I perceived the folly, and went to the provost of the town, to know what forces he had within the town at his devotion. He answered, very few, and that the commonty were not to be trusted to. I asked who was in the castle? He told me, the bishop; who was dealt with incontinent to have the castle in readiness to receive His Majesty; which he promised to do. But when I returned to His Majesty, believing that the proclamation had been made that no man should come to the convention but such as had been written for, I found that the Abbot of Dunfermline was arrived out of Lochleven and the Earl Marischal out of Dundee. The Earl of Mar was still with His Majesty; but all the lords were advertised with diligence from Falkland that His Majesty was ridden so suddenly to St Andrews, desiring them to make haste to go thither, else they would be too late. The said abbot for his part was soon enough there, and behaved himself so, extolling His Majesty's enterprise, that he retained so much credit as to cast down all their devices who were upon the king's course; for he was a special doer for the contrary party, and said it was not fit by proclamation to stay the nobility, but rather to write missives to them not to come accompanied with any more than ten persons with every nobleman.

When His Majesty told me this, I was very angry, and showed that this was the ready way to put him again, by craft and without thanks, in their hands from whom he had lately fled; and that without purpose, proceeding so carelessly as to follow their own counsel against themselves, assuring His Majesty that they were coming forward very strong and in arms, and were like to be sooner there than those lords he had written for, and they might come in quietly themselves, and cause their companies to come in by twos and threes to the town, whereas it had been better to let them come in all together, that their whole forces might be seen. Yet His Majesty was loath to enter within the castle that night for his greater security, until it was very late after supper, giving those that were there already time to advise, and to enterprise that same night to take him again, in case he had gone to the abbey yards to walk, as they had persuaded him, till the castle was prepared. And some were already entered the said yard for that effect in armour, whereof some suspicion was taken, and therefore His Majesty, being advertised, changed his purpose, and passed by the yard-gate to the castle.

The next day the whole lords, as well sent for as unsent for, arrived at St Andrews; the king's lords quiet, without armour, the other lords strongly armed. The Earls Marischal and Mar and the Abbot of Dunfermline lodged within the castle with His Majesty, where the

crafty abbot counselled the king to let none of the lords come within
the castle accompanied with more than twelve persons. He ever
appeared to favour the king's opinion, and therefore his crafty counsel
was followed. The next morning the castle was full of men; for those of
the contrary party, being well armed, had already taken the stair-heads
and galleries, intending again to be masters of the king and all the rest;
which being too late foreseen, diligence was used to bring within the
castle incontinent all the Earl of March's gentlemen, with the young
laird of Dairsie, the lairds of Balcomy, Segie, Forret, Barns, the good-
man of Fengis and so many of the town as were at the provost's
devotion; which for the night prevented the enterprise.

The Earl of Gowrie was also a great stay in that matter; for albeit
he came thither as strong and as angry as any of the lords, yet he was
advertised of the king's good will towards him, and so was won and
drawn from the rest. That dangerous day being past without any harm
done, the next day such order was taken that His Majesty was master
of the castle, following no more the said abbot's counsel, but declared
his moderate intentions to all the lords, to the Fife barons, and towns
upon the coast side, who had been sent for, and likewise to the ministers
and masters of the college: that, albeit he had been detained against
his will for some time, yet he intended not to impute it as a crime, nor
to remember any thing done in his minority, but would put in oblivion
all that was past, satisfy the church, agree parties and carry himself
to all his subjects equally, knowing none of them to bear him any
evil will, and that they had been driven to enterprise any thing they
had done by the force of their factious partialities; using many other
words of clemency and discretion, to all their contentments. Thereafter he ordained four lords, two of every faction, to retire them for a
while, to wit, the Earls of Angus, Mar, Bothwell, Huntly and Crawford; retaining all the rest about him, as indifferent, for his ordinary
council, by whose advice he was resolved to settle his estate, and thereafter to bring again to court the whole lords above named. Then His
Majesty called for me before a number of the said lords, and gave me
greater commendation and thanks than I had merited, as the only
instrument, under God, of his liberty. His Majesty caused also to make
a proclamation, conform to his former speeches and moderate intention: but I took no pleasure to be praised in presence of so many,
answering to His Majesty that I had the ill will already of so many as
were upon the purpose of his detention.

Now matters being settled in appearance, and like to take good
success, some of the king's lords who had been slow in coming (and
when they were come, finding the lords of the contrary faction at St
Andrews strong and in armour) denied that they knew any thing of

His Majesty's enterprise, laying the whole burden upon Colonel Stewart and me. But when they saw appearance of a prosperous success, they took the matter stoutly upon them, and began in plain council to tell how long they had been upon the counsel of that enterprise with His Majesty, and long waiting for his advertisement.

Of a truth His Majesty was of a merciful mind, and gently inclined toward all the nobility, intending to win all their hearts by his own discreet behaviour, and to that effect he went first to the house of Ruthven, to let the country see that he was entirely reconciled to the Earl of Gowrie; who, after he had made His Majesty a great banquet, fell down upon his knees, lamenting that His Majesty should have been retained in that unhappy house at his last being there, which, he said, fell out rather by accident than deliberation, only for the safety of the Earl of Arran's life; alleging that he knew no other thing than that at His Majesty's being at Dunfermline they were all minded to present him an humble supplication, asking pardon for that accidental fault: which His Majesty graciously promised never to impute to him, knowing how blindly he was brought upon it, by the practices of others.

VII

The Ascendancy of Arran

IN the mean time James Stewart, Earl of Arran, had obtained the favour to be warded in Kinneil, his own house for the time, and sent and congratulated His Majesty's liberty, desiring that he might have access to come and kiss his hand; which was plainly refused . . . And at length I was requested by his agent James Stewart, now Sir James of [   ], to be an instrument to deal with His Majesty to permit the said earl to come again to the court . . . Whereupon I went unto His Majesty, and showed him what language the Earl of Arran's servant had to me concerning his master's coming to court, and that His Majesty laid too great a burden upon me, as to say that he would do nothing without my consent. Thereupon His Majesty took me to the gallery of Falkland, lamenting, as he had been informed, the loss of many of his best friends, as the Earls of Lennox, Atholl, and Duke of Lennox: 'And now', says he, 'they will not permit the Earl of Arran, who hazarded his life to come and relieve me, to come and see me.' He desired me to acquaint him what might be the occasion they hated him so much. My answer was, that to tell the verity perilled myself, to conceal the truth endangered His Majesty. He would needs know my meaning therein. I said, 'Because the Earl of Arran is one of the worst instruments that could come about you, whereof Your Majesty hath had too hard a proof, his misbehaviour being the only occasion of the late enterprise; and if he ever get place again, the like or worse will follow. And my peril for telling Your Majesty the verity is that you will be my deadly enemy, in case it be shown unto him again.' Then His Majesty desired to let him come and kiss his hand, promising he should tarry no longer; willing me to deal with my Lord of Gowrie, that he would also grant that he might but once come to court, and he should incontinent return to his house without any tarry. I said I should cause him to yield to His Majesty's pleasure.

In the mean time I took occasion to declare unto His Majesty how that many princes are wrecked by their ambitious counsellors, who will rule all alone, taking upon them a greater burden than they can bear. For remedy whereof, His Majesty should spend every day but one hour to hear a chosen number of honest counsellors reason upon his affairs; then himself to give his opinion that he can well enough judge and understand to be the best and meetest to be followed forth, as the King of France used to do. Which His Majesty granted very willingly, and so long as he kept that order by the ordinary council-days, his turns went rightly forward. The whole lords who had assisted His Majesty were of his council, Sir Robert my brother, Colonel Stewart, the laird of Segie and myself.

But as soon as the Earl of Arran got access to His Majesty, he not only stayed at court against promise, but also within a short time altered all this kind of privy conference, to do all affairs himself. At his first entry he carried himself very humbly; for after he had kissed His Majesty's hand, he embraced me and kissed my cheek, giving me many thanks in His Majesty's presence, alleging that the whole name of Stewarts was obliged to me for the notable service, he alleged, I had done His Majesty: as for him, he said, he should never take any thing in hand but be directed by my brother and me and the laird of Segy. But Colonel Stewart and he spoke not together until His Majesty willed me to agree them, which I did at length. At first the colonel swore a great oath that if His Majesty suffered that villain to remain at court, he would yet again undo all. For a while he kept himself quiet; but there was no appearance of his home-going. Sometimes he would reprove my gentle kind of procedure in His Majesty's affairs, and could not endure to see them handled by a number. He put into His Majesty's hand that he would find it a troublesome business to be encumbered with many contrary opinions. He desired him to recreate himself at hunting, and he would tarry in and hear us and report again, at His Majesty's return, all our opinions and conclusions.

This he observed two or three times, and so in a very short space changed the former order and took no man's advice but his own; yet he said to His Majesty that he had all our counsel and consent to cause His Majesty to follow a violent course, directly against His Majesty's first deliberation, intention, and proclamation of clemency and forget-fulness of all things that fell out in His Majesty's minority; and he caused to make contrary proclamations against those of the Raid of Ruthven, ordaining them all to take remissions for that which before was allowed for good service, moving divers noblemen and others to withdraw far from the court, for fear, to some place of security. When he caused to be read before the council his new invented proclamation, I opposed myself to it, saying that it was directly against His Majesty's mind and promise. Whereupon he leapt out of the council house in a rage, and said I would wreck the king by my manner of doings. I answered, 'Either you or I'; with other sharp pricking language, so that for that time it was stayed. Afterward he waited a meet occasion to get it passed, by a flattering faction that assisted him, turning all upside down, a great number of noblemen and others being put thereby in fear of their estates. And when any of us who were devoted to His Majesty's quiet and prosperous estate would show the dangerous and impertinent proceedings of the earl, His Majesty would be very sorry, saying that the earl made him believe that he did nothing but by common consent of the council. And when His Majesty understood the contrary, he was very earnest and willing to amend the disorder, but was still circumvented by the said earl and such as for fear, flattery or profit, advanced all his pretences. . . .

The Earl of Arran obtained the keeping of the castle of Stirling and obtruded himself so far forward that he took upon him the whole management of affairs, and caused sundry noblemen to be banished, as the Earls of Mar and Angus, the Master of Glamis, and divers others; and by his insolency he drove the Earl of Gowrie from court, against His Majesty's intention for the time; who sent me for him to his house, to bring him again to court, which was for the time at Cupar in Fife, where His Majesty agreed him and the Earl of Arran. But no promises were kept to Gowrie, so that he was so vexed and put at, that he took purpose to leave the country. . . .

His Majesty, being at Stirling, asked frequently for me, regretting that I was not continually with him. Whereupon the Earl of Arran devised that I should be sent ambassador to the Queen of England, as well to absent me from His Majesty as to take occasion upon my return to bring me in disgrace, because he was assured that I could do no good at that time. And commonly, when men's commissions take no good effect, they are calumniated by their enemies and enviers as unfit instruments, unskilful and indiscreet. Which calumnies get oft-times too much credit, when matters succeed not conform to the desire of the master. Before His Majesty's letter came to my hands for the said voyage, I had indited a long letter to have sent unto His Majesty, as a remembrance of his former promises and proclamations; showing what inconveniencies were like to ensue the setting forward of a contrary course, together with such salutary and sudden remedies as I could judge meetest for the time.

The tenor of His Majesty's letter to me was that he had some matters to communicate to me, wherein he intended to employ both my advice and pains; and therefore he desired me to come to Stirling with all convenient expedition after the sight of the said letter, where I should understand more amply the occasion of my being sent for, as I would do him acceptable pleasure and good service. Written from the castle of Stirling, the 22d of October 1583.

After the receipt of this letter, I did ride unto His Majesty, and took with me the letter which I had penned before, as I have said; whereof the copy followeth.

'SIR,

As it hath pleased Your Majesty heretofore to accept of my good will for agreeable service, even so I hope that Your Highness's constant favour shall continue towards me now and in time coming, notwithstanding my present absence and disease. For albeit that, during Your Majesty's young age, I was suffered to live happily at home, from the troublesome handling of public affairs; yet I knew myself obliged to bear my proportionable burden in your service so soon as it should please Your Majesty to command and charge me therewith, being then most assured to walk in a just and lawful vocation; wherein, to give continual testimony of my dutiful obedience, not presuming to give Your Majesty counsel, I have only taken the boldness to present to you in these few lines my simple opinion of things that are apparently to fall out upon Your Majesty's late proceedings.

'For when it pleased Your Majesty, at your first going to St Andrews, to take upon yourself the free government of your affairs, Your Majesty's gracious intention and proposition then was not only most agreeable to all the lords, barons and ministers there present for the time, but also to the rest of your good subjects, when as they understood of your reasonable inclinations. Which being now otherwise fallen out and interpreted than was either first intended or determined, is able to breed cumber* and disorder, unless Your Majesty by wisdom and dexterity prevent the apparent inconveniencies. For it pleased Your Majesty then openly to declare how that you only sought, with your own reputation and security, the weal and safety of your whole subjects, as most willing to give satisfaction to the church, to agree parties, to blot out of memory the name of factions and put in perpetual oblivion all crimes committed in Your Majesty's minority, acknowledging all such as chanced to be done during the same but to have fallen out betwixt subject and subject, for such particular respects as Your Majesty never purposed to impute; but to reign over them all in times coming as a gracious father, and that by the advice of the least factious and best affected of the nobility, barons and other sufficient subjects; no man to be placed or preferred about Your Majesty by favour or surname, kin, friend or ally, but for sufficiency, virtue and loyalty; as also, if any were absented, or sent home for a time, it should not be done at the instance of any envious suiter of his office, or particular party, but for Your Majesty's honour and security, during your

* Trouble.

pleasure; leaving them still in hope, through good behaviour, to obtain again familiar access about Your Majesty, as formerly.

'If this calm course had been followed, there was appearance of a quiet state. But altering and changing this gentle kind of doing into a sharp and violent pursuit of sundry, by seeking out over many faults in the persons of so many great and active men, hath bred such discontent and so furious a faction, that, if sudden remedy be not provided, civil dissension and desperate enterprises ought to be looked for by all such as have sufficient experience of the nature of Scotsmen, and seemly intelligence of the deportment of divers, which the necessity of their unsure estate might well drive them hastily to take in hand.

'It is true that the standing of commonwealths consists much in the rewarding of the good and punishing of the wicked. No doubt but faults enough have been done during your nonage; but to seek them out narrowly, and to punish them straitly, in such cases and at such times, in matters wherein many have dipped, is not best. Yet, if Your Majesty were willing, as I know you are not, I cannot see any way how you can get it done against so great a number, having so small substance and forces, and so mighty and advantageous neighbours lying still at wait upon all such controversies and occasions, whereby to serve their own turn. This consideration also ought presently to be respected, that the wonted reverence borne by the subjects unto the princely authority of their sovereigns is much decayed in this kingdom, by reason of the queen's [Mary's] youth and long absence; and even so in Your Majesty's time for some of the like causes, chiefly because that Your Majesty, being yet young, has been accompanied this time past with the youngest and meanest sort of your nobility; who, albeit they be faithful and affectionate to set forward your service, yet the rest of your subjects, alleging them to be factious, ignorant and needy, doubt of their discreet behaviour, seeing their intentions are to rule by force. Hardly may a prince assure himself at all occasions to choose a sure course, wherein there shall be no peril; for commonly men, thinking to escape out of one inconveniency, fall oft-times into another: therefore prudence consists in understanding the quality of dangers, and in choosing the least evil for the best.

'Some kingdoms and countries are governed by force, some by fairness; on the other part, subjects obey either for awe, or love. That prince is reputed either ineffective or fearful who cannot win the hearts of his subjects by one of these two: for either must the means be taken at once from such as are suspected deservedly, whereby they may do harm; or else they must be satisfied in such sort as in reason they ought to be content that they neither need to desire nor think it convenient for them to seek any change or alteration. No man will deny but that country is most happy and stable wherein the subjects rejoice and are content and serve for love and not for awe. So that it is easy to judge which of these two kinds of governments may be meetest for Your Majesty.

'The Emperor Trajan, being demanded wherefore his subjects loved and honoured him above his predecessors, answered, "Because I forgive them who offended me, and never forget any who may have done me good service." Julius Pollux, preceptor to Caesar, points out a true prince to be of divine countenance, godly, merciful, just, equitable, careful of his affairs, constant in his deeds, true in his promises, subject unto reason, master over his affections, forceful and fatherly towards his subjects, of easy access, gentle to be spoken to, ready to forgive, slow to punish, princely, liberal, subtle, secret, and sharp of ability.

'Now, because it appeareth Your Majesty in youth hath been sufficiently versed in many of these virtuous precepts, I wish from my heart that such impressions might be as well taken of them that are presently about you, seeing that princes are commonly deemed to be like those whom they make their most familiars.

'Therefore, Sir, for eschewing all those evils, and to put the nearest remedy unto all the appearing inconveniencies, it is fit, so soon as it may please Your Majesty, to pass to Edinburgh, to convene the most ancient of your nobility and barons of best reputation, by whose advice, together with those that are already in court, your country may be quieted and your subjects satisfied. For now, as matters are handled, to speak of clemency, by causing them to take remissions, it will want credit, and be ill interpreted, as not conform to Your Majesty's first declaration.

'The Emperor Hadrian sought after all men of great age and experience, and helped himself by their many perils.

'Alexander Severus would perform no matter of importance, but with advice of the most ancient and best experimented. He never went out of Rome unaccompanied with four or five of the most honourable, ancient and grave personages, that none should need to fear that he would commit any error or reckless turn. He never suffered the senate to conclude any weighty purpose unless fifty of them had been present. He caused all his counsellors to put their opinions in writing, to see if any were possessed with passions or particularities. He changed oft his chief familiarity with sundry of the senate, lest he who had always and only the prince's ear might be overcome with importunate presents, bribes and partiality.

'The urgent necessity of the time, most noble and excellent prince, causeth me to be so lengthy and tedious. Humbly craving pardon, and heartily kissing Your Majesty's hands, I pray the Eternal, Sir, to grant you a long and happy life.

'From Halhill, this
15 of October 1583.

Your Majesty's most humble
and obedient servitor,
JAMES MELVILLE.'

When I came to Stirling, and showed His Majesty this letter, he not only liked well of it, but engaged to follow the advice therein contained. He lamented the partial dealing of many that were about him; only he said that my brother Sir Robert was upon a sound course for quieting of the estate; and that some noblemen, against whose partialities he had opposed himself, had discorded with him in His Majesty's presence. It pleased His Majesty also to tell me the cause why I was written for was to be sent to England, to travail with the queen there for entertainment of mutual amity and increase of her favour and good-will concerning the title and succession to the crown of England, and assistance to help to establish his estate, perturbed by the insolence and partialities of his subjects, bred and engendered among them during his minority.

I answered that the time was unmeet and that England would make no account presently of him, nor of any that might be sent from him, until first he would let it be seen and heard that he could settle his own estate, and, by wisdom, render his own subjects ready to obey him; this being done, they would dread and esteem him. And that the best and readiest way to obtain also one day the crown of England was to guide Scotland so well that they might yearn and wish to be under the government of such a prince. By this language, His Majesty was satisfied that my voyage should be stayed till a more convenient time. So I returned from court to my own house. . . .

The Ruthven Raiders had been strongly pro-English, and Elizabeth had written to James reproaching him for his attitude to them after his escape. James, in his reply, indicated that he was not going to submit to dictation from England. But Elizabeth had said in her letter that she would send an envoy to James, 'willing him to stay from any strict proceeding against the lords who were pricked at for the Raid of Ruthven', and in an effort to reassert English influence in Scotland she sent north her secretary of state, Francis Walsingham. 'But he was of a sickly complexion, and was not able to endure riding post, therefore he was long by the way, being carried in a chariot.'

So soon as His Majesty was advertised of the arrival of Sir Francis Walsingham, I was sent for to come to court, and directed to ride and welcome him in His Majesty's name, to bear him company and convoy him about by Stirling to St Johnston,* where His Majesty thought

* Perth.

most meet to give him audience; desiring me also to say unto him that His Majesty was very glad of the coming of such a notable personage, who was known to be endued with religion and wisdom, whom he esteemed his good friend, being assured that his tedious travail in his long voyage (being diseased as he was) tended to some more substantial points for the confirmation of the amity between the queen his sister and him than had been performed at any time before.

The secretary Walsingham answered me again that the great desire he had to establish an assured amity betwixt the two princes and countries moved him to undertake the ambassage himself, His Majesty being the prince in the world that he loved next unto the queen his mistress, and wished most to see and be acquainted with. And he hoped that his commission should succeed the better, because he met first with me, his old friend and only acquaintance in Scotland. For we had been companions in other countries, and divers times when I was sent to or passed through England he would have me to lodge and lie with himself at London, which occasioned that we had more familiar conference. Whereupon I did write two several letters, that His Majesty might be the better provided to make answer to such heads as he would propose. Then we took our journey through Linlithgow to Stirling, and from that to Perth. He had heard that my Lords Seton and Livingston were written unto to convoy him; but he requested me to stay them, that he might have the more conference by the way with me, otherwise he would be compelled to entertain the noblemen. It may be that it was also to let his own great company be seen, for he had eight score horse in train. Being near the court, His Majesty sent out two of the council to meet him, to wit my Lord of Doune and my brother Sir Robert.

The next day His Majesty gave him audience, accompanied with Mr Bowes, ambassador resident in Scotland. Their first reasoning was upon His Majesty's liberty, and wherefore he had left the company who were about him, being the best and most religious sort of the nobility and of Her Majesty's best acquaintance, and by whom she would deal in his affairs more friendly than she could do with others, whom she could not so well credit; with hard and sharp speeches conform to his former writing. Whereunto His Majesty made answer off-hand so gravely and directly that Walsingham wondered. The next day His Majesty appointed four of the council, and myself to be with them, to reason with him and to see what he would be at. But he refused to deal with any but His Majesty, who heard him again alone, without Mr Bowes. Where he discoursed long with His Majesty; and when he came forth from His Majesty, he took me by the hand and said that he was the best content man that could be, for he had spoken with a notable young prince, ignorant of nothing, and of so great expectation that he thought his travail well bestowed. The Earl of Arran desired to enter into familiar conference with him, but he refused to speak with him; and made no longer stay, but took leave of His Majesty, who commanded me to accompany him to the ferry.* At our parting, he promised at all occasions to write to me, and lamented that the Earl of Arran was again in court, and in such credit with His Majesty. Which if he had understood before he took his journey, he would have stayed, and suffered some other to have been sent, for he could see no sure course could be taken between their Majesties so long as such instruments had greatest credit about him. For he esteemed the said earl a scorner of religion, a sower of discord, and a despiser of true and honest men; and therefore he would not speak with him, nor enter into acquaintance; for he was of a contrary nature, religious, true, and a lover of all honest men.

Therefore Arran, to be revenged upon him, spared not to do a great dishonour to His Majesty. First, for despite that he refused to speak with him, he caused refuse to permit the captains of Berwick and divers honest gentlemen, who came to convoy the secretary Walsingham, the entry of His Majesty's chamber door. And then he caused to prepare a scornful present for him at his leave-taking, to wit, a ring with a stone of crystal, instead of a rich diamond which his Majesty had appointed for him, valued at 700 crowns, which he was oft-times minded to send back unto His Majesty, rather to let him see how he was abused, than how he was used. Some promise was also made unto him about the repairing some wrongs done by Scotsmen upon the Borders, which he alleged was not kept. For Arran did what he could to displease him and to render his commission in all points unprofitable and his travail in vain. Nevertheless he made so good report of His Majesty's virtues and qualities that it put him in some suspicion at his return to the court of England, where shortly after he took sickness and died.†

My opinion is that if God had granted him longer life he would have been found a great friend to His Majesty, who marvelled that the chief secretary of England, burdened with so many great affairs, sickly and aged, should have enterprised so painful a voyage without any purpose. For he could not yet perceive what was his errand, save only that he gave His Majesty good counsel. But he, being religious and of a good conscience, was so desirous to see and understand assuredly such qualities to be in His Majesty as he heard oftimes by report that he returned with great contentment in his mind for that part; but very sorrowful for the company that he found in greatest favour and credit about His Majesty; which was unexpected, by reason of a letter that His Majesty had sent unto the queen his mistress, promising not to

* Queensferry.   † Walsingham did not die until 1590.

bring in again to court the Earl of Arran without her advice and consent. For my part I never saw such appearance of a prosperous estate for His Majesty's honour, surety, love and obedience of his own subjects, increase of the number of his friends in England to the advancement of his title, neither before that time nor since, if the said Arran had not been brought again to court; which I left not undeclared to His Majesty divers times, not without some danger.

Indeed His Majesty's intention was not that he should stay at court, but . . . he remained at court, and minded to make himself and his assisters rich by the wreck and spoil of others, who had taken His Majesty at the Raid of Ruthven; and then he and they were to guide all at their pleasure. . . .

Melville thoroughly disapproved of Arran's influence over the king, and believed that Arran frustrated James's own intention of settling his government on the principle of conciliation all round. After a bitter quarrel with Arran, during which Melville said 'I would get more honest men to take my part than he would get throat-cutters to assist him', Melville resolved to retire from the court. 'At my leave-taking His Majesty said he doubted not but I would return when called for. By which I understood that I should not come back till sent for.'

Now the Earl of Arran triumphed, being chancellor, and captain of the castles of Edinburgh and Stirling. He made the whole subjects to tremble under him, and every man depended upon him, daily inventing and seeking out new faults against divers, to get the gift of their escheats, lands, benefices, and to procure bribes. He vexed the whole writers and lawyers to make sure his gifts and acquisitions. Those of the nobility who were now in fear of their estates, fled; others were banished. He shot directly at the life and lands of the Earl of Gowrie: for the Highland oracles had shown unto his wife that Gowrie would be ruined, as she told to some of her familiars. But she helped that prophecy forward as well as she could: for Gowrie had been his first master, and despited his insolent pride, oppression and misbehaviour plainly in council, which few others durst do; therefore he hated his person, and loved his lands, which at length he obtained.

For Gowrie had taken purpose, being compelled, to pass out of the country with His Majesty's favour and licence. But as he was making his preparations too longsomely and slowly in Dundee (as he was of nature over slow), where his ship was to receive him, he was advertised by some factioners that the Earls of Angus and Mar and the Master of Glamis had an enterprise to come home out of Ireland and take the town and castle of Stirling; having correspondence with divers nobles and others their friends, who were in the country, malcontents, so that they were in hope to make a party sufficient against the Earl of Arran. Which moved the Earl of Gowrie to stay, with intention to take part with them for the great disdain and despite that he had against the Earl of Arran. There was at this time an universal miscontent in the country, and a great rumour of an alteration. . . .

These rumours and advertisements made His Majesty be upon his guard, and to use means to get intelligence. The lingering of the Earl of Gowrie in Dundee gave ground of suspicion. His Majesty had also been advertised that he was not minded to take ship, but to wait upon the incoming of the banished lords. His Majesty also dreamed a dream that he saw the Earl of Gowrie taken, and brought in prisoner before him by Colonel Stewart; and he thought his estate was thereby settled: which indeed for that time came true, because the lords who had taken Stirling, so soon as they understood of the taking of the Earl of Gowrie, fled incontinent out of Stirling, and again out of the country, believing that the said earl had been taken willingly and supposing his affection to have been so great to His Majesty, as a near kinsman, come of the house of Angus, his mother being a natural daughter of the said house; as also that he was never upon the first design of any enterprise, but drawn in afterwards by the craftiness of others. Therefore His Majesty had compassion upon him, and had no intention of taking his life. But the Earl of Arran was resolved to have his lands, which he divided afterwards with others, to get their votes and consents that he might be ruined. At his death upon the scaffold, he showed himself a devout Christian and a resolute Roman, much regretted by many that were present and heard his grave harangue, and did see his constant end.

After his death there was quietness for a while, though without appearance of long continuance. During this little while of fair weather, there was a parliament held to forfeit the banished lords, at the instant desire of such as hoped to be the better by other men's ruin.

Among others, I was written for and graciously received by His Majesty, who, remembering some of my speeches, took me alone into his cabinet, and enquired how I now relished his proceedings. I answered that he had great cause to thank God, and no good guiding, and that there would be yet more enterprises; that they who took Stirling, and had retired again, would never cease to make enterprise upon enterprise, till they might see themselves in a better security. His Majesty replied that they had gained so little by their last incoming that they would never commit such a folly again. I answered that had not the taking of the Earl of Gowrie fallen out, who they believed was taken by his own desire, to bewray their enterprise, they had gained their intent, for even some who were then upon His Majesty's own side would have concurred with them to put the Earl of

Arran out, whom they assisted for awe and not for love, and were beginning to envy and hate his insolency, and could not see a sure outgate* how to stand by him; and had made secret promises to them, by such as went betwixt them: but seeing the Earl of Gowrie in hands, and the said lords thereby so discouraged as to fly away, such as had made the said promises took up a new deliberation, showing themselves boldest in their contrary.

The Lord Burghley, chief ruler in England at this time, caused send here one Mr Davison to be an agent, to see what new business he could brew, who was afterwards made secretary. For after the decease of Walsingham, secretary Cecil being advanced to be Lord Burghley and great treasurer of England,† two secretaries were chosen, one called Mr Smith, and this Davison,‡ whose predecessor was a Scotsman, whereby he was thought more able to acquire credit here. He had been in Scotland before, and was at my house, in company with Sir Henry Killigrew, my old friend, when he was resident in Scotland. At which time he made a secret confession to me that he was come of Scotsmen and was a Scotsman in his heart, and a favourer of the king's right and title to the crown of England. He desired me to keep all secret from Mr Killigrew, promising, if he could find the means to be employed here, that he would do good offices.

His Majesty was for the time at Falkland, and wrote for me, to be directed to ride and meet the said Davison; whom I was commanded to convoy to Cupar, there to remain till His Majesty had time to give him audience. Afterwards I convoyed him to my own house, and from that to Falkland, where His Majesty found but little effect in his commission. But because Walsingham had refused, at his being here, to speak with the Earl of Arran, albeit the said earl had offered by me to give satisfaction to him in all his desires, so that he would deal and confer with him (which Walsingham still refused), Mr Davison was directed at this time to deal with the Earl of Arran, to see what advantage might be had at his hand; for my Lord Burghley was not content that Walsingham was so precise. Therefore Davison entered into familiarity with him and was made his gossip, and heard his frank offers, and liked well of them; for after that the lords were fled to England, and forfeited, the council of England thought they had some ground to build a new strong faction upon, to trouble the king and his estate. And whereas the said Davison had promised before to show himself a kindly Scotsman, I perceived him clean altered, and a very practiser against the quiet of this state; which I showed unto His Majesty.

* Way out, solution.
† Cecil had become Lord Burghley in 1571 and treasurer in 1572.
‡ Davison became a secretary in 1586, in Walsingham's lifetime.

After his return, England appeared not to take such a scare as it had formerly had at the Earl of Arran. For there was a meeting drawn on at the Borders, betwixt the Earl of Hunsdon* and the Earl of Arran, who had long and privy conference together, to keep a great friendship betwixt the two princes and countries; with a secret plot that the Earl of Arran should keep the king unmarried for three years, under this pretext that there was a young maid of the blood in England, who about that time would be ready for marriage; with the which the queen would declare His Majesty second person.

This was a deceitful traffic, and kept secret from everybody, the design thereof being to hinder the king to deal for any other honourable and profitable match. The Earl of Arran thinking himself settled, being in friendship with the Queen of England, as he supposed, moved His Majesty to send thither the Master of Gray, who was entered in great favour and familiarity with His Majesty by some secret dealing and intelligence he had with the queen his mother in England, by means of some of her friends in France, he being there. Being lately returned, he brought some letters directed from Her Majesty to the king her son, and conveyed the answers back again, by an interest he had in England with some who favoured Her Majesty. He was a great dealer also between Her Majesty and some catholics in England. He was a proper gentlemen, of a trim spirit and fair speech, and so well liked by His Majesty that Arran thought fit to absent him from court by this ambassage. Nevertheless he employed him also in the course begun betwixt him and the Earl of Hunsdon, as said is. And yet when he was at the court of England, so well esteemed and treated, as was reported by such as were sent back, it was alleged by some of the Master of Gray's friends that the Earl of Arran began to envy him, and misreport him unto His Majesty, as if he had discovered unto the Queen of England a great part of the Queen of Scotland's purposes and proceedings. However the said master returned again well rewarded, and commended for his behaviour, qualities and discretion, unto the king's Majesty, to the great increase of his credit with the king. Not long after his return, he was informed what misreport had been made of him in his absence; which he recompensed the best he could with court charity at such convenient times that by little and little he began to put Arran out of favour.

The Master of Gray also forewarned His Majesty of a notable personage who was upon the way, sent unto His Majesty by the Queen of England to do him honour and to bear him company, to entertain a stricter friendship between that queen and him than had been made at any time before; and that the said ambassador, called Mr Wotton, would not trouble His Majesty with business or country affairs, but

* Henry Carey, first Baron Hunsdon; he was not an earl.

with honest pastimes of hunting, hawking and horse-riding, and with friendly and merry discourses, as one come lately from Italy and Spain, expert in languages and customs of countries; and a great lover of His Majesty's title and right to the crown of England. So that His Majesty was ravished to love him before he did see him, and caused to write to me to come with diligence and entertain the said ambassador.

At my return to court, I was the better taken with, that Arran was a little disgraced. The Master of Gray was then my great friend: for His Majesty had told him that I had ever resisted the Earl of Arran's furious proceedings. His Majesty desired me, as I would do him acceptable service, to bear good company to the said ambassador, declaring unto me all his properties and good qualities above specified; willing me also to banquet him at my house. . . .

But Melville had encountered Wotton before, and knew him as the nephew of Dr Wotton, ambassador in France for Mary Tudor. The constable of France, Melville's master, had reproached Dr Wotton because Mary was helping her husband, Philip of Spain, with men and money, against the French, and the ambassador had replied that the English troops in Flanders were volunteers. Dr Wotton on his side alleged that France was helping English rebels and fugitives and inciting them against their queen, and the constable in turn denied this charge. Dr Wotton therefore brought to France his brother's son, aged twenty-one, who, without revealing his identity, had an interview with the constable in which he said that a third of the people of England were willing to accept the French king as their sovereign and expounded a plot to put Calais into French hands. The constable refused to have anything to do with such a violation of the 'sworn peace' between France and England.

This is he now who was sent hither to bear His Majesty company, as one who will not meddle with practices, but with pastimes. But when I forewarned His Majesty to beware of him, and told how that he, being little above twenty years old, was employed to beguile the wise old constable; now he was fifty years, and His Majesty but twenty, it was to be feared he would go about to beguile him. Yet His Majesty would not believe me, but believed the said Mr Wotton to have great love and friendship for him, and so he became one of his most familiar minions, waiting upon him at all field pastimes; and he despised all busy counsellors and meddlers in matters of state, as he was instructed by such as said he would please His Majesty best to seem to be so. But he had more hurtful fetches in his head against His Majesty than any Englishman that came in hither had at any time before, always for the service of his princess and country, according as the course of their affairs and pretences pressed them for the time.

VIII

The Marriage of James VI

YOU have heard before of a meeting that was drawn on at the Borders, betwixt the Earl of Hunsdon and Arran; where, at their secret conference, Arran was required, by the craft of the Lord Burghley and his faction [in the English council], to stop the king from any marriage for three years, upon many fair feigned promises; and also to be declared second person, at which time again Arran granted all that was desired, he was so glad to get the Queen of England's friendship. About that time the Queen of England, by her intelligence from Denmark, was advertised of a great and magnific ambassage sent by the King of Denmark to Scotland, viz. three ambassadors, with six score persons, in two brave ships. Whether she suspected, or had heard, that it was to draw on a marriage, I cannot tell; but this far I learned, that her council feared it was at least to confirm a greater familiarity and friendship betwixt the two kings and their countries, which was one of the causes that moved them to send this Mr Wotton to Scotland, to use all his wiles to disturb and hinder any greater amity that might proceed from the said commission and negotiation between the two kings and their countries. For England trusted nothing to the Earl of Arran's promise; for they esteemed him of an inconstant capacity, as is already declared.

So soon as the Danish ambassadors arrived by ship in this country, His Majesty ordered me to entertain them and bear them company. And because they were three joined in commission, he willed me to choose any other two whom I thought meetest, to bear them company with me. I named unto His Majesty the laird of Segie, one of the Session,* and William Shaw, Master of Work. The names of the Danes were Manderupius [Parsberg], Henrych Bello and Doctor [Nicholas] Theophilus; the first two were councillors.

First, at Dunfermline they congratulated His Majesty in the king their master's name, with a long discourse of the old amity, bond and mutual friendship between the two kings and their kingdoms. And last of all, they required the isles of Orkney to be restored again to the

* A judge of the Court of Session, the central court for civil justice.

crown of Denmark, alleging they were mortgaged, to be redeemed again for the sum of 50,000 florins.*

Their coming and demand was diversely regarded; some supposing wars would ensue unless the said isles were rendered; others thought that their intention was to bring on a marriage with the King of Denmark's daughter.

Now, albeit His Majesty was determined to treat them well and honourably, they were nevertheless mishandled, ruffled, trifled, drifted and delayed here the space of [   ] months, to their great charges and discontent: for they lived upon their own expenses, and were not defrayed by His Majesty, as all other ambassadors of that nation have been since....

The principal of the three ambassadors was a wise, grave and ancient counsellor. Henrych Bello was furious in his speeches. The third cried out, 'The king our master is injured, and will be revenged.'

I took Manderupius apart, requesting him to hear me patiently; for he spoke good Dutch,† but mine was not so good. Therefore I desired that he would give more attention to my meaning than to any wrong words, and be more careful to cause his friendly commission to take effect, that he might return home with happy success, than start and steal away, to be called unhappy instruments of discord, at the pleasure of a few scornful factioners, who had laid their heads together to cause them part‡ dissatisfied, and to be as instrumental in doing evil as they were minded at their coming to do good offices.

I told him how that the Queen's Majesty of England was a wise, well inclined and politic princess, and that there were as many honest and good men in England as in so much bounds in the whole world; albeit there was in it divers opinions and factions, shooting at sundry marks, as they do in all other parts. And because that their queen would never marry, to bear succession of her own body, they all took great care to know who after her should reign over them. [I continued:]

'The most part of the country expects that it shall be our king, and wisheth his welfare and prosperity, as being righteous heir to the crown of England, both by the father and mother's side. But those who have the chief management of the court shoot at other particular marks of their own, minding to set forward some of themselves or of their friends, to enjoy the kingdom. And for that cause, they make all the hindrance they can to our king; also because of their unmerciful dealing to his mother they fear some day to be punished, when he comes to be King of England. For all these respects, they practice to keep him from marriage, and from all foreign friendship and alliance. This ambassador

* This was true, by a treaty of 1468.   † Deutsch or German.   ‡ Go away.

of England is a very ill instrument, both himself and his gentlemen; and, hunting daily with His Majesty, make the worst reports they can. . . .'

After this, I showed unto His Majesty what inconveniences might ensue upon the long delaying and strange handling of the Danish ambassadors; and yet that I marvelled not that he made so little account of them, in respect of the great care and fine practices that were used to cast them and him asunder by the English ambassador and his assistants, who had His Majesty's ear for the time. At the first His Majesty was impatient to hear this language spoken of persons he had so good liking of, and said that he was informed that the King of Denmark was descended but of merchants, and that few made account of him or his country but such as spoke the Dutch* tongue. For this was cleverly put in his head to prevent lest any of my persuasions in their favour should get place or credit. I answered that neither could the King of France or Queen of England speak Dutch, and yet they made great account of the King and country of Denmark, France having their ambassador ordinary lying there, and paying yearly to the King of Denmark a great sum of gold, to the value of 16,000 or 20,000 crowns. His Majesty said the more shame was his. I said, 'Rather to the King of France, who must buy his kindness. Neither could the Queen of England,' said I, 'speak Dutch; yet she made much account of the King and country of Denmark, and durst not offend him, nor none of his ships, both by reason of the strait passage at Elsinore† and also because he had great ships to take amends, in case she did him or his any wrong!' Then His Majesty said that he spoke but by way of reasoning. I said again, by way of wrong information; and said, moreover, 'Whereas it hath been reported to Your Majesty the race of their kings not to be of noble and royal blood, I shall show Your Majesty that it is but manifest invention to cause you to despise them. . . . And whereas he requires again the isles of Orkney, it is for the discharge of his oath, because every King of Denmark, at his election, that is one of the articles that is presented unto him by the estates to swear to claim again the said isles, which he hath done for the fashion, and for no other effect but to draw on a greater familiarity and friendship. Or else he had not sent so honourable a company, but rather an herald of arms, if he had been earnestly bent either to get the said isles, or to discord and fight for them.'

After that His Majesty had heard this discourse, far different to his former informations, he was exceeding glad, and said he would not for his head but that I had shown and declared this verity unto him. And

* German.   † A reference to the narrows of Öresund, where Denmark controlled the entrance to the Baltic.

that same afternoon he sent for the said ambassadors, and showed them how near of kin he was to the King of Denmark; he excused their long delay, and promised to see them instantly despatched himself, and that within three or four days: he sent for his afternoon [drink], and did drink to them, and sent them to their lodgings well content and satisfied. He commanded a banquet to be prepared for them; which His Majesty's comptroller and officers were quietly forbidden to do, and allege the scantness of provisions: but the laird of Segie and I dealt with the Earl of March, who prepared a great banquet for them in His Majesty's name, to the great dissatisfaction of Mr Wotton and his partisans, who durst not appear, but would not suffer His Majesty to be present at the banquet, but to dine in his own chamber; yet His Majesty, being informed by me how matters went, rose from his own chamber and went to the banquet-house, and drank to the King, Queen and ambassadors of Denmark, and so contented them more and more. And he caused their despatch to be in readiness, conform to his promise. But when I advertised His Majesty that there was no present prepared for to reward them withal he was marvellous sorry and said they would shame him who had the management of his affairs.

Now at this time was the Earl of Arran at court, not so much in favour as formerly. During the which time there chanced a reckless misrule to fall out at a day of meeting between the two wardens upon the Borders; where Sir Francis Russell upon the English side was killed. Whereupon the English ambassador took occasion to lay the blame upon the Earl of Arran, alleging that the laird of Fernihirst, who was warden upon the Scots side, had married the Earl of Arran's brother's daughter; and that the said earl had caused the slaughter to be made, that the Borders might break [loose]. In this complaint the said ambassador was well assisted by the Master of Gray and his companions; so that the Earl of Arran was commanded to ward within the castle of St Andrews, and was kept straitly there three or four days: so that, being in fear of his life, he sent for Colonel Stewart, the laird of Segie and me, and lamented to us his hard handling, purging himself, as he might justly do, of that accident that fell out upon the Borders, requesting us to procure his liberty.

He declared unto us a secret to be shown unto His Majesty, in case his life was taken from him; which was, a promise made unto the Queen of England that the King should not marry with any party for the space of three years, whereof I have formerly made some mention. Nevertheless he forgot not to travail for himself, for he sent his brother Sir William to the Master of Gray at midnight, promising to get unto him the abbacy of Dunfermline, so that he would obtain his liberty at His Majesty's hand. Which was incontinent granted, and also the said benefice disposed unto the said master. Whereat the English ambassador was in a great rage at the master, but their discord was afterward agreed by Mr John Maitland, secretary, and the justice-clerk; and the Earl of Arran was ordered to retire home to his house. But before Arran's journey, His Majesty was informed to desire him, with all possible diligence, to lend him a great chain which he had got of before from Sir James Balfour, which weighed 750 crowns, to be given unto the Danish ambassadors. Which if he had refused to do he would have lost His Majesty, and in delivering it he should lose the chain.

In the mean time, the ambassadors understanding that their despatch was in readiness, took their leave of His Majesty, who was also ready to part from St Andrews. I informed His Majesty not to deliver them the despatch, because the chain was not yet come; for they were minded incontinent to make sail, in respect of their long stay and that the winter season was at hand; albeit I had shown to one of their familiar servants that certain rewards were to come there within two days, praying them to stay so long among the rest. Which they would not grant to do, but went to their ships; whither I promised to bring their writings and despatch, which I requested His Majesty to cause deliver into my hands, to be kept till the chain should come; which was divided into three parts, for it was beautiful. When I came to their ships, they were going to supper. Which being done, I delivered to them their answer in writing, with the chains, and some excuses for their long stay and small reward, always to their great contentment; assuring me that they would be good instruments of amity, albeit by the harsh usage they had met with they had once minded to do otherwise, and that their commission tended not to discord, but to bring on greater friendship. Neither were they commanded to speak of marriage, whereof there was a vain rumour, though the king their master had fair daughters, any of which being suited as it is requisite that gentlewomen be, they supposed the claim of Orkney would go right. They thanked me for the good offices I had done, where in staying them from parting in displeasure the two countries were preserved from hot wars. This they would not fail to declare unto the king their master, with whom they would not fail to make me acquainted, not doubting but that the king my master would one day say that I had done him good service. So I did take leave, having rewarded the gunners, trumpeters and taborings.*

At my return to court I showed to His Majesty how that the Danish ambassadors had set sail for their own country well contented. I gave him an account of all other speeches that past betwixt them and me at their parting. Whereupon His Majesty took occasion shortly after to

* Drummers.

send in Denmark, offering that commission first to me; which I shifted me of, perceiving those who had His Majesty's ear, and had most credit with him, to be averse from his marriage that way, holding still on a course with England. I named Mr Peter Young, master almoner to His Majesty, as very fit for that errand; who was sent to Denmark, to thank that king and to see his daughters, that he might make report again of his liking of them, with a promise that ere long His Majesty would send an honourable ambassage.

The Earl of Arran being sent home, as said is, the English ambassador and his Scots friends (as the Master of Gray, secretary Maitland and the justice-clerk) had chief credit and handling of His Majesty's affairs. The said ambassador had acquired such favour and familiar access about His Majesty at all times, and at hunting, that he was upon an enterprise to have brought in secretly the banished lords, to have fallen down upon their knees in the park of Stirling before His Majesty, at such a time as they should have so many friends in court, as that His Majesty should have remained in their hands as masters of the court for the time. But this enterprise failed him; for they durst not yet take such hazard as to come in, till they might lay their plans more substantially.

Then the said English ambassador enterprised to transport His Majesty out of the park of Stirling unto England; and failing thereof, His Majesty was to be detained by force within the castle of Stirling, whither companies of men were sent to be there at an appointed day. Of which design the secretary, Mr John Maitland, gave some intelligence to my brother Sir Robert, who told it incontinent to the King's Majesty, giving him the names of some of the chief enterprisers. And because it came to one of their ears, who stoutly affirmed the contrary, my brother strove to maintain the same by the offer of a singular combat; which His Majesty would not permit, because the person granted it to His Majesty. Whereupon my brother persuaded His Majesty, with great difficulty, to depart out of Stirling for ten or fifteen days, and hunt at Kincardine, before the enterprise might be ripe. Which so soon as the ambassador understood, he fled in great fear and haste, without goodnight or leave-taking of His Majesty; well instructed, and furnished with the promises of such as had assisted him in our court, to persuade the noblemen who were banished in England to come home, where they should find friends enough before them at court to put His Majesty in their hands as before. The Master of Gray also absented himself, and went to Dunkeld, and there remained with the Earl of Atholl. And upon some bruits of enterprises, there was a proclamation set out in His Majesty's name, by such as had his ear, to acquire the more credit to be true and careful counsellors for His Majesty's security; which proclamation was afterwards delayed by craft, that the banished [lords] might anticipate the day, and come in and get the king in their hands, whereby they might discharge the proclamation at their pleasure.

In the mean time I received a letter to be at His Majesty with all possible diligence, and another from the Earl of Arran, to accompany him from Kinneil to the court. But I went to His Majesty; whither also the said earl came that same night, for he had procured that he might return again to court and remain about His Majesty.

At my coming to Stirling, I got intelligence from a secret friend that the said lords were already at the entry of the Borders, assisted by my Lord Hamilton, my Lord Maxwell, my Lord Bothwell, my Lord Hume and sundry others, who had not formerly joined with them. Also the Earl of Atholl, the lairds of Tullibardine, Buccleuch, Cessford, Cowdenknows, Drumlanrig and others, who were in greatest credit about His Majesty, were to join with them at their in-coming. Whereof I advertised His Majesty and Colonel Stewart, who undertook to ride unto the Borders and overthrow them before their whole forces should meet together. Which was a likely purpose, if the design had not been craftily disappointed by such as were about His Majesty, who appeared to set forward the colonel's enterprise to please His Majesty and to acquire credit; saying they would write to Cowdenknows, Buccleuch, Cessford and such others to assist him, whom they knew to be upon the contrary faction already; so that the said apparent enterprise was turned to no purpose, and His Majesty mocked. And because I had shown some of them what advertisements I had got, and how His Majesty was like to be straited with a new taking, I was answered with scornful language. And incontinent they caused His Majesty to send me a feigned errand to Dunkeld, that they might the better bring their purpose to pass without any contradiction. The pretext of my commission was to cause the Earl of Atholl to stay at home and not to join with the lords who were to come shortly to Stirling. And by the way I was to deliver a letter to the bailies of St Johnston,* to be upon their guard and not to suffer any of the king's enemies to come within their town. The bailies enquired of me, what if the Earl of Atholl and Master of Gray would desire to come within their town? I said they might let themselves enter, with ten in company, but no more. They alleged that their letter specified not that far. I showed them how that was committed to me by mouth, the conclusion of my letter willing them to credit me.

When I came to Dunkeld, I knew that the Earl of Atholl would not stay for me, who had 1000 men in readiness to take the town of St

* Perth.

Johnston and to come forward to Stirling, with the Master of Gray, who was yet with him. But I showed him that Colonel Stewart was ridden with forces to defeat the lords at their entry into the country, before they might be joined together; therefore he would do well to lie at home till he might understand the issue of the said colonel's enterprise. If that took effect, it would be folly to him to march forward; and if it did not succeed, he might do as his heart served him. He thought this counsel good, desiring me to write unto His Majesty for a licence to him and his to remain at home from the proclamation, which I did. In the mean time the Master of Gray was sent for to court, the ports* of the town of Perth being refused to his men, who were come out of Angus to assist him. At his returning to court, he was as great with His Majesty as ever he was, remaining with him within the castle of Stirling; where there were two factions, who revealed themselves so soon as they saw the malcontents and banished lords draw near unto the town of Stirling, whither they came to the number of 3000, and entered into the town without stop. His Majesty inclined most to the faction who brought in the said lords, who advised His Majesty to send some down to the town to commune and compound matters. Which was at length agreed upon that His Majesty should remain in their hands; that no rigour should be used to those who were about him. So that those who were mediators appeared to be good instruments and stayers of bloodshed. For Arran was escaped, and fled at the first entry: but Colonel Stewart, only with ten or twelve, gave them such a charge in the midst of the narrow part of the town that a little more help might have put them in great disorder, for the most part of their southland men and Borderers were busy spoiling horse and goods.

The lords, when they came into His Majesty's presence, fell down upon their knees, humbly begging pardon; for their hard handling by Arran and other partial persons about His Majesty had compelled them upon plain necessity, and for their last refuge, to take the boldness to come in arms for the safety of their lives and lands, being ever humbly minded to serve and obey His Majesty.

The king again, like a prince full [of] courage and magnanimity, spoke unto them pertly and boastingly, as though he had been victorious over them, calling them traitors, and their enterprise plain treason. Yet, said he, in respect of their necessity, and in hope of their good behaviour in time coming, he should remit their faults; and the rather, because they used no vengeance nor cruelty at their in-coming.

In the mean time, His Majesty committed and recommended the keeping of the Earls of Montrose and Crawford unto my Lord Hamilton; and the keeping of Colonel Stewart unto my Lord Maxwell. These three

* Gates.

were for a time in some danger, because they were esteemed to take too strong a part with the Earl of Arran and his particulars. The rest of His Majesty's servants were overlooked and spared. Sir Robert my brother, and his son, were both courteously used. This moderate behaviour of the lords acquired daily more and more favour from His Majesty, they pressing him in nothing but by the humble intercession of such as formerly had his ear. A parliament was proclaimed at Linlithgow for their restitution; whither His Majesty was convoyed, there to pass his time at hunting and recreate his spirits.

Many nobleman and others were written for, to come unto the said parliament. Among the rest, the Earl of Atholl, to whom I had been sent and with whom I was at the lords' coming to Stirling, where I was waiting upon an answer from His Majesty which the Earl of Atholl had desired me to ask in writing, as said is. When I came to kiss His Majesty's hand, I was gladly made welcome; His Majesty alleging that I was a corbie messenger.* I answered that my absence with the Earl of Atholl had saved all my horse, and the town of St Johnston untaken, and had kept the said earl from assisting with the rest; so that if those who remained at Stirling with him had kept the south side as well and as free as I kept the north side, their horse had been safe as well as mine was. His Majesty said that God had turned all to the best; being of before nourished in an opinion that his life would be in danger in case these noblemen might be his masters; and now, having him and his servants in their power, they had used no rigour nor vengeance. His Majesty remembered also how frequently I had forewarned him of this and the like accidents, that I said would fall out upon the Earl of Arran's rash proceedings. He said that he had been an evil instrument, so that he should never have place nor credit again about him. He desired me to remain at court, and help to do all good offices betwixt him and his nobility; and to tell them the truth, who was to blame for their trouble, and that he had great hurt and no advantage thereby, as a prince that sought no man's life, lands or goods, but only the settling of his subjects among themselves, and his pastime, which certainly I might justly testify. His Majesty told me also how he had shown unto the noblemen my honest and friendly advices toward them, and that I opposed myself continually to the Earl of Arran's proceedings. He desired me also to help to satisfy the ministers, who were seeking also to be restored unto their former free assemblies, which had been forbidden in time of the Earl of Arran. So that I tarried a while beside His Majesty, till matters took some steadfast settling. Divers of the lords also requested me to stay, offering me great kindness; saying that His

* A raven messenger. An allusion to the raven sent out by Noah, and consequently a dilatory or unfaithful messenger.

Majesty had told them every man's part and behaviour towards their banishment and persecution, and that I was ever for a moderate course, desiring an act of oblivion to be made for all bygones during his minority. The said lords therefore caused me to propose some of their suits to His Majesty, whom in nothing they would press beyond his own pleasure.

But the council was of different opinions concerning the restoring of the ministers to their former privileges; where I was brought in to give my opinion. The most part thought fit to delay them for a time, chiefly such as had remained about His Majesty, and had said too much before to the contrary. My opinion was that His Majesty was not to be blamed that the noblemen were banished or the ministers' privileges taken from them, but all the insolencies were committed by evil instruments, who ruled over His Majesty's good mind and ear through the vehemency of their ambition; who now being fled and absent, why should not the ministers be restored to their former privileges, as well as the noblemen to their lands and honours; or else the blame will be laid upon His Majesty. The secretary for the time [Maitland] was against this opinion; for he had formerly spoken too much on the contrary. But the rest of the noblemen and the council thought my opinion best. But at that time it was not followed, nor granted at that parliament. Yet shortly afterwards the ministers obtained at His Majesty all their former privileges.

It is above mentioned that the master almoner was sent to Denmark. Shortly after Colonel Stewart took occasion to go thither about his own affairs; for he had a pension from the king of Denmark. He obtained also some writing, whereby he was commissioned to speak of the king's marriage with the King of Denmark's eldest daughter. And they both returned with so good and friendly answers that there was little more mention made of the restitution of the isles of Orkney. The King of Denmark was also put in hope by them that His Majesty would send the next summer an honourable ambassage to Denmark, to deal further in these matters.

I have shown already the dangerous practices of the English ambassador, Mr Wotton, and a part of their effects; but the principal is yet behind.

The council of England having concluded to take the life from the Queen's Majesty, his highness's mother, after she had been many years captive in England, thought first to get the king, her son, in their hands, and to put him in hope that he should obtain the crown of England, the rather that he was within their country; and, in the mean time, to be sure that he should not be able to revenge his mother's death, but might be as a pledge among them, in case his countrymen, or his foreign and French friends, would pretend to menace them or to make war for his liberty, or in revenge of her death: that they might threaten to cut him off, if for his cause they should be troubled. And however it were, through time it was suspected that they intended to take his life also, after that they had laid their plots how to make him odious to the people by false counterfeit letters, and alleged practices (as they had craftily and deceitfully alleged upon his mother) against the state. But finding this design of carrying him to England discovered by my brother's intelligence, the said ambassador fled, as said is. And for the next best, thought fit to see His Majesty put in the hands of the most part of his nobility who were banished for the time, and by wicked instruments so wrecked and offended that it was enough to have caused them to take his life, or else kept him in perpetual prison.

But the noblemen that had been banished and were sent home out of England for that intention on England's part used themselves so moderately and discreetly for their part that they sought nothing but their own native country and lands, and that they might have access to serve and obey their prince, without any further vengeance or rigour against their particular enemies; as all their actions and proceedings have sufficiently declared since to the great increase of their favour with His Majesty, and estimation of the whole country. It hath been seldom seen in any country that there have been so many great alterations, with so little bloodshed, as hath been in Scotland lately in this king's time.

Now those who were enemies to our queen and king's title to the right of the crown of England, seeing some of their fetches to fail them, entered in deliberation what way to proceed to take the queen's life. Sometimes they minded to give her an Italian posset, sometimes to slay her at the hunting in a park; but at length to convict her by way of an assize. In this way they were well helped by the device of Mr Archibald Douglas and some other Scotsmen, who made communication with her to acquire credit, so that writings and cyphers passed between her and them and between her and some Catholics of England that favoured her. So that soon letters were forged, and other men's handwriting counterfeited; and when she made some answers, concerning her prospects of gaining liberty, these tricks of their own devising were interpreted against her for treason. Then Her Majesty had a French secretary, called M. Nau, who was easily corrupted to discover all her communications and doings; he was richly rewarded through the agency of Lord Burghley and was in no other way tormented to tell the truth.

All these calumnies and false accusations being presented in writing to the Queen of England, her heart would not suffer her, as she alleged, to let any sentence be given forth against the queen, her dear sister and cousin, so near to her in blood; until the council, nobility and estates of England, at least such as were seduced to that effect, sat down upon their knees, humbly requesting Her Majesty to have compassion upon their unsure estate, albeit she cared not for her own, endangered by the practices of the Queen of Scotland. Whereby she was at length moved, for very pity of them, to give forth sentence of death upon the queen, with condition that it should rather serve to be a fear and terror unto her, to cause her to cease from making any more practices, than that she would see the blood of so noble a princess being shed. And in the mean time the written sentence was given to be kept to Mr Davison, one of her secretaries, not to be delivered without Her Majesty's command. Nevertheless the said Davison, being deceived by the council, afterwards delivered unto them the said written sentence of death.

Whereupon they gave the queen warning a night before, to prepare her for God. Which short warning she took very patiently, and lay not down that night to sleep, but wrote some letters unto the king, her son, the King of France, and to some other princes, her friends. And after she had made her testament, she put the gold she had in as many little purses as she had servants, more or less in every purse, conform to their qualities and deservings. The rest of the night she employed in prayer. And being in the morning conveyed out of her chamber to the great hall where the scaffold was prepared, she took her death patiently and constantly, courageously ending her life, being cruelly handled by the executioner with divers strokes of the axe.

Which execution was the boldlier performed because that some Scotsmen assured them that the king her son would soon forget it. Albeit His Majesty, when he understood this sorrowful news, took heavy displeasure, and convened a parliament, wherein, lamenting the mishandling of his mother by his enemies who were in England, he desired the assistance of his subjects to seek to be revenged. Where all the estates in one voice cried out in a great rage, to set forward; promising that they should all hazard their lives, and spend their goods and gear largely to the effect, to get amends for that unkindly and unlawful murder. Which put the council of England in great fear for a while; but some of our countrymen comforted them, and so did some English that haunted our court, alleging it would be soon forgot. Others said that the blood was already fallen from His Majesty's heart; and if it were not, they should cause the matter fall out so to their satisfaction.

First when the King's Majesty heard that they were about to accuse and convict his mother, he sent the Master of Gray and Sir Robert, my brother, to deal for Her Majesty. Where my brother spoke brave and stout language to the council of England; so that the queen herself threatened his life. And afterward he would have been retained captive, but for the credit his colleague had and the promises he had made; whereby they were both suffered to come home together.

Four months before, His Majesty caused write for me, to be sent to England to confirm a bond of alliance offensive and defensive with the queen and crown of England and to take the Queen of England's oath for observing the said bond. And Mr Randolph, who was here already, was to take the king's oath, and use the like ceremonies here.

Melville was unwilling to be an agent for the conclusion of an alliance with England, which he held to involve a breach of the traditional league with France. The king himself would take no excuse, but Randolph urged James to select another envoy, because the Melvilles had been too closely linked with Mary to be acceptable to Elizabeth, and preferred either the Master of Gray or Archibald Douglas. However, no envoy was sent at once, for Elizabeth was satisfied with a letter from James promising one when she thought it necessary. James's letter was sent to the English ambassador in France to demonstrate to the French court that James was seeking an alliance with England and to bring him into discredit with the French.

Likewise when the rumour was of the Spanish navy, in the year 1587, to come to these parts, I was ordained to be sent to Spain; which voyage I happily also eschewed.

Now to return again to Mr Archibald Douglas. He returned back to England, to remain ambassador there for His Majesty. By the which means he obtained the greater credit with the queen, His Majesty's mother. But my brother Sir Robert, when he was sent there to procure and to use sharp and threatening language to see if it might save the queen's life, discharged Mr Archibald of the office of ambassador. This is a parenthesis by the way, to show how far a good king has been abused, and by minions whom he liked well, to his great hurt and dishonour. In the mean time, for some disorder upon the west border betwixt the Maxwells and Johnstones, His Majesty went there to reform their disobedience. But some houses were kept, and would not render unto him. Whereupon, Mr John Maitland being made chancellor, the Master of Gray and other favourers of the English faction did counsel His Majesty to send to Berwick, because it was alleged to be nearest, to borrow cannons to besiege the said house. Which guns were gladly lent by the governor of Berwick. Which apparently he durst not have done without knowledge and consent of the queen and council, who thought thereby that His Majesty had forgot the great threat that was made at the forenamed parliament concerning the revenge of his mother's death. For after His Majesty had ripely considered the best and worst of that deed, he remembered himself of the many friends he had in England, who had no blame for his mother's ruin; and for a few who guided the queen and court, he would not trouble the state of the whole country, of which he was apparent heir. And also because the queen was of good years, and not able to live too long, he would abide his time to be revenged upon his enemies. As for the queen, his good sister, she had sworn and purged herself of the death of his mother, being deceived by her council and by the secretary, Davison, whom she committed to be warded in the tower of London. This was the convoy of that uncouth, unkindly murder.

Shortly after this, there was a great rumour of the Spanish navy, bound for landing in England, Scotland or Ireland. . . . How that the Spanish great navy was three years in making their preparation, and were sufficiently and substantially furnished with men, munition, and all sorts of necessaries, is now manifest to all Europe. What was their intent and purpose was so secret that the chieftains of the army knew no more but as they should understand by the opening of their stamped instructions at every appointed landing place. Many are of opinion that they were first disappointed by the Duke of Parma, governor of Flanders, who had behaved himself in his charge so circumspectly, in his promises so truly, in his enterprises so stoutly, that he won the hearts of his soldiers and the favour of his enemies, so that he was suspected by the King of Spain to entertain designs of usurping the estate of Flanders; and therefore he was minded to remove him out of that great and rich government. He being hereupon discontent, as was alleged, neither furnished the said army victuals, nor assisted them with ships and men, nor suffered them to land in his bounds. At last they were so suspicious of him that they landed not, but were lying at anchor, when Sir Francis Drake, by a stratagem subtly devised of a ship full of powder with a burning match, which kindled up the powder so soon as the English ship was driven by a direct vehement wind within the midst of the part where the Spanish ships lay, burning thereby several of their great ships and causing the rest to cut the cables of their anchors for haste, to eschew the fury of the fire. And in the mean time God sent such a strange* storm of wind, that the whole navy was blown and broken upon divers coasts of our isles and of Ireland; and their wreck was the greater, that they wanted their anchors.

It is before mentioned that Mr Peter Young, Master Almoner to his Majesty, and Colonel Stewart were returned from Denmark well rewarded, and contented with every thing that they had seen, and

* ? strang, i.e. strong.

chiefly with the fair young princesses; and also how they had put the King of Denmark in hope that the king should the next summer send thither an honourable ambassage, to deal further to the increase of a greater society and amity. And for this effect, the Bishop of St Andrews, the laird of Segie and I were named to be sent: but I was retired, and had no will to meddle, perceiving His Majesty's affairs so hindered by such as had greatest handling about him. Therefore the chancellor devised the laird of Barnbarroch and the said Mr Peter to be employed in this matter, with uncertain and irresolute instructions; always to propose marriage, and with divers fair allegations concerning His Majesty's sufficient right to the isles of Orkney; which the King of Denmark was minded to suit more sharply, but for the hope he was put in of the apparent marriage of the King's Majesty with his eldest daughter.

These ambassadors were not well embarked, when Monsieur Dubartas arrived here to visit the King's Majesty, who, he heard, had him in great esteem for his rare poesies set out in the French tongue. He would not say that he had a secret commission to propose the princess of Navarre to be married to His Majesty, but that the King of Navarre's secretary willed him, seeing he was to come this way, as of his own head to propose the said marriage. Monsieur Dubartas's qualities were so good, and his credit so great with His Majesty, that it appeared, if the ambassadors had not already made sail, that their voyage should have been stayed for that season. The chancellor assured Monsieur Dubartas, (as he showed me) that the marriage of Denmark should not take effect. For our ambassadors had indeed such strait injunctions, and so slender a commission, that it was enough to have caused the King of Denmark to start and to quarrel with our king, were it not that they dealt beyond their commission. Which kept that king in some temper, albeit they returned without fruit, full of displeasure, thinking themselves scorned, as they were indeed.

In the mean time that they were in Denmark, Monsieur Dubartas, being in Falkland with His Majesty, came to my house, to persuade me to take a commission in hand, which, he said, His Majesty would lay to my charge; which was, to be sent unto the King of Navarre and to be acquainted with madame the princess, his sister. And because His Majesty knew that I would be loath to go, he named also my Lord of Tongland, my brother,* who undertook the journey, and became well acquainted with the said princess, and was well treated and rewarded by the king her brother, now King of France, and brought with him the picture of the princess, with a good report of her rare qualities.

The laird of Barnbarroch and Mr Peter Young, being returned back

---

* William Melville had a gift of the property of the abbey of Tongland in 1588.

from Denmark, declared that the King of Denmark thought nothing of
their commission but ineffective dealing and driving of time and fair
language, without any power to conclude. I am uncertain whether he
got intelligence of His Majesty's sending my brother to the King of
Navarre: but the marrying of his eldest daughter so shortly after with
the Duke of Brunswick gave some appearance that he had got some
notice thereof from the court of England, who were well enough
informed of all our proceedings.

After this, Colonel Stewart, being willing to see the marriage with
the King of Denmark's daughter take effect, went thither on his own
expense divers times. And seeing the eldest daughter already married,
he excused the King's Majesty, and laid the blame upon those who had
the handling of his affairs. So that the King of Denmark promised yet
to give his second daughter unto the king, upon conditions that
ambassadors would be sent there the next year, before the first day of
May. In the mean time the King of Denmark took sickness and departed
this life, leaving the same commission with his council and such as were
appointed for regents of the realm.

Now the king being suited in marriage by sundry great princes, and
his ambassadors being come back both out of Denmark and Navarre,
with the pictures of the young princesses, His Majesty determined
first to seek counsel of God by earnest prayer, to direct him where it
would be meetest for the weal of himself and his country. So that after
fifteen days advisement and devout prayer, as said is, he called his
council together in his cabinet, and told them how he had been advising and praying to God the space of fifteen days to move his heart the
way that was meetest, and that he was resolved to marry in Denmark.

The council appeared all to be content with his resolution, requiring
meet instruments to be employed to conclude the marriage and to make
the contract. Then His Majesty said that he had already chosen me in
his mind for one, desiring the council to choose another; which they
did, to wit, the Lord of Altrie, uncle to the Earl Marischal. We two
being written for, and come to court, found not such earnestness with
the council as with the king; which my Lord of Altrie perceiving, he
drew home again, excusing himself upon his age and sickliness. His
Majesty used many persuasions and reasons to cause me to undertake
the voyage, declaring how he had many times sent for me to be employed in ambassages, and could not tell why I went not. I answered
that His Majesty would have done me that honour above my deserv-
ing, which he would not have done if he had known my inability and
insufficiency as well as I did myself. His Majesty said that this his
marriage was the greatest matter that ever he had to do, and that he
could take no refusal. I said that my Lord of Tongland, my brother,

DEN VIII february W̄
Stuart Schots Comi
Lyck Hebbende gefocht veel o
meef ter te maecken van
offe parlement Volcomely
Metren XIII.

THE EXECUTION OF MARY, QUEEN OF SCOTS

coning Marie van Schotlant

De onthalst Maria
ne s' stervende Roomsch Catho-
ten aen te richten haer selven
lant 't dvvelsck haer vanden raet
vverde vertoont. Anno 1587.
XIII. EN XIIII. v.

was far meeter than myself, being a good scholar, who could perfectly speak the High Dutch, the Latin, the Flemish and the French tongue. But His Majesty would still repose upon me in that errand; but was satisfied that my brother should pass in commission with me.

Then His Majesty said, 'Albeit the council will form your instructions, yet you shall receive mine out of my own mouth. Three heads in special:

'First, If the King of Denmark had at the pleasure of God been alive until this time,* he would not have stood to give a great portion with his daughter, wherein the regents and his council will be as sparing as they can. I doubt not therefore but you will draw from them as much as can be had; but at length stand not upon money to proceed with the conclusion of the marriage.

'Secondly, Know what friendship and assistance they will make me when it may please God to place me by right in the kingdom of England, by decease of this queen, in case any countryman or other would wrongously pretend to usurp and debar me from the same.

'Thirdly, Concerning the isles of Orkney, you must choose any man of law that you please; for that head must be answered and debated by form of law. Always if the marriage take effect, that purpose will not be over precisely suited nor handled. It may be that my council will give you straiter conditions; but this instruction of mine you shall follow forth, let them say what they please.'

I told His Majesty that I would take with me for a lawyer Mr John Skene. His Majesty thought then that there were many better lawyers. I said he was best acquainted with the conditions of the Germans and could make them long harangues in Latin; and was a good, true, stout man, like a Dutchman. Then His Majesty was content that he should go with me.

After that I tarried long at court, and could see no preparation for our despatch, neither money nor ship made ready; the appointed time wherein we should have been in Denmark was past, to wit, before the 1st of May: for it was so ordained by the King of Denmark ere he died, that in case that day was not kept they would think themselves but scoffed. This moved me the more to employ my friends at court to cause another be named in my place, seeing so many suiting to get the said commission. The chancellor gave me such terrous† as he could for his part.

Now the Earl Marischal had desired to supply the place of his uncle my Lord of Altrie; and His Majesty was content that he should be sent thither. Whereupon I took occasion to say to His Majesty that the

* Frederick II died in 1588 and his son, Christian IV, succeeded as a minor.

† ? tarrowis, i.e. delays, deferments.

said earl was very meet and would go the better contented if he might have in commission with him some of his own friends and acquaintance. His Majesty answered that it was his part to choose his own ambassadors; that the Earl Marischal should have the first place as a nobleman; but that he would repose the chief handling with the regents and council of Denmark upon me. Then I declared that the appointed time was past and that yet there was no appearance of any preparation of money or ship; whereat His Majesty was very angry. I named the laird of Barnbarroch or Mr Peter Young, who had been there before; but His Majesty would not, for the blame and responsibility was wrongously laid upon their insufficiency and mismanagement as the occasion that matters formerly took not the desired success.

Would not this kind of court-dealing scare any man from meddling in such weighty matters, where such men are preferred and the whole burden of the prince's affairs committed to their care and credit? They counselled His Majesty first to send to the Queen of England, and require her advice and consent to the said marriage with Denmark; who they knew would not only dissuade him from the said marriage but also stay him from any marriage, as she and her council had ever done and dealt, both with his mother and himself. When I understood of this new delay, I obtained licence to go home to my house and make me ready against the next warning. In the mean time, the season of the year was well spent. The Queen of England's answer was, not to marry with Denmark. She said that she had credit with the King and princess of Navarre, which would be far better. In the mean time she did write to the King of Navarre, to hold back the marriage of his sister for three years, for such frivolous respects as carried no reason. Upon this answer of England, our council was convened, and practised on and enticed to vote against the marriage of Denmark, as most of them did. Whereat His Majesty took such a despite that he caused one of his most familiar servants to deal secretly with some of the deacons of the craftsmen of Edinburgh to make a kind of mutiny against the chancellor and council, threatening to slay him in case the marriage with the King of Denmark's daughter were hindered or longer delayed. This boasting and fear caused a new resolution to be taken that the Earl Marischal should be despatched with diligence, with the constable of Dundee and the Lord Andrew Keith, whom the said earl requested His Majesty to send with him. Which His Majesty granted the more easily, because he found so many difficulties in the matter, and some of my friends had informed him that I would not be miscontent if he sent with the said earl such as he desired.

Now it was yet a long time before the Earl Marischal could be made ready and despatched. Then, as to his dealing with the council of

Denmark, his power to conclude was so limited and his commission so slender that he was compelled to send back again my Lord Dingwall, either for a licence to come home or for a sufficient power to conclude. Where it chanced that he found His Majesty at Aberdeen, and the chancellor and most part of the council absent. Which was a great furtherance to get a full power to conclude the contract and ceremony of the marriage by the Earl Marischal; who was incontinent despatched by the regent and council of Denmark, and the queen* sent home with him well accompanied. But the tempestuous winds drove them upon the coast of Norway, where they landed, and stayed a long time for fair winds and weather. Which storm of wind was alleged to have been raised by the witches of Denmark, as by sundry of them was acknowledged when they were for that cause burnt. That which moved them thereto was, as they said, a cuff or blow which the admiral of Denmark gave to one of the bailies of Copenhagen, whose wife, consulting with her associates in that art, raised the storm, to be revenged upon the said admiral.

His Majesty had heard that they were upon the sea, and left nothing undone to make all in a readiness to receive the queen and her company honourably; but in the mean time was very impatient and sorrowful for her long delay, laying the blame thereof upon the chancellor and such others of his council as had plainly voted against the said marriage, and thereby had delayed the despatch of the ambassadors so long, until the season of sailing upon the seas was near past. The storms were also so great here, that a boat perished betwixt Burntisland and Leith, wherein was a gentlewoman called Jean Kennedy, who had been long in England with the queen His Majesty's mother and was since married to Sir Andrew Melville of Garvock, my brother, master of Her Majesty's household.† Which gentlewoman, being discreet and grave, was sent for by His Majesty to be about the queen his bedfellow. She being willing to make diligence, would not by the storm be stopped from sailing on the ferry; where the vehement storm drove a ship forcibly upon the said boat, and drowned the gentlewoman and all the persons, except two. This the Scottish witches confessed to His Majesty to have done. In that boat I lost also two servants.

Now His Majesty remained quietly in the castle of Craigmillar, not content with the greatest part of his council, as said is. He could neither sleep nor rest. In the mean time, he directed Colonel Stewart to my brother Sir Robert and me, charging us to take care of his mishandled estate in time coming, lamenting that he was abused by such as he had too much trusted to, and that he had always found us faithful and

* Anne was married by proxy at Copenhagen on 20 August 1589.
† Sir Andrew had been master of Mary's household during part of her captivity.

careful of his welfare. He willed us to sit down and advise how he might best put remedy to things past and eschew such inconveniences in time coming, seeing he was determined hereafter to repose most upon our counsel. Our answer to His Majesty was that we had great cause to render His Majesty most humble thanks for the good opinion he had of us, which we should take pains at our power to deserve, and were very sorry for the displeasure His Majesty had taken; praying His Majesty to take patience, seeing that as he had always reposed upon God and not man, that the same God would mend his estate, as he had oft-times done before: presently our only care could be how to receive the queen honourably, who was upon the sea (we daily looking for her landing), and next, how to treat and reward the noblemen of Denmark, Her Majesty's convoy. That being done, and they returned back to their country, it would be best to take order with the affairs of the kingdom conform to His Majesty's desire, with the concurrence of so many of the council as His Majesty had found most faithful and least factious. But we did not think best to take upon us the whole burden, in respect that hath been always the chief cause of the wreck of Scots Kings, especially of all His Majesty's troubles, in laying the whole burden of his affairs upon any one or two, who most commonly for greediness and ambition abuse good princes; then few or none dare control them, for fear of their great authority and credit.

The chancellor, being advertised of His Majesty's discontent and displeasure, as said is, made preparation to go off the country, and caused it to come to His Majesty's ears that he would sail and bring the queen with him, and that they were all but snaffelers* who were with her. He forgot not to anoint the hands of some who were familiar with His Majesty, to interpret this his enterprise so favourably, that it put all other bygones in forgetfulness; and, by little and little, he informed His Majesty so well of the said voyage, and the great charges he had bestowed upon a fair and swift-sailing ship, that His Majesty was moved to take the voyage himself, and to sail in the same ship with the chancellor, with great secrecy and short preparation, making no man privy thereto but such as the chancellor pleased and such as formerly had been upon his faction. He had also heard an inkling of a word that His Majesty, in the time of his heavy displeasure, had sent to my brother and me to take the burden of his affairs; whereat he had a great hidden envy and despite, and was the cause why His Majesty made me not privy to his voyage into Denmark. He was very discontent when His Majesty had appointed my brother, Sir Robert, to be left vice-chancellor, to convene the council in His Majesty's absence, to hold hand with the Duke of Lennox, my Lord Hamilton,

* Snaffle = purloin.

Bothwell* and other noblemen, with the officers of the crown, to rule the country in His Majesty's absence.

Three other ships sailed with His Majesty, wherein was the justice-clerk, Carmichael the provost of Lincluden, William Keith, George Hume, James Sandilands, with his master almoner and all His Majesty's ordinary servants. The weather was rough enough; for it was in the beginning of winter. But the last day was so extreme stormy, that they were all in great hazard; but His Majesty landed that same night at [Oslo] in Norway, where the queen was awaiting a fair wind, and there he accomplished his marriage in person. But he could not be persuaded to return to Scotland that winter, by reason of the raging seas and storm he had sustained a little before.

The Queen and council of Denmark, being advertised that His Majesty was to abide all that winter at [Oslo], sent and requested him to come to Denmark; whither he went by land, with the queen, his new bride, and behaved himself honourably and liberally by the way and at the court of Denmark so long as he tarried there.

But the company who were with His Majesty held him in great trouble to agree their continual strife, pride and partialities. The Earl Marischal, by reason that he was an ancient earl, and had been [first] employed in this honourable commission, thought to have the first place next unto His Majesty so long as he was there. The chancellor, by reason of his office, would needs have the pre-eminence. There were also contentions betwixt him and the justice-clerk. The constable of Dundee and my Lord Dingwall contended for the first place. George Hume did quietly shoot out William Keith from his office of master of the wardrobe. At length they were all divided into two factions; the one for the Earl Marischal, the other for the chancellor, who was the stronger, because the king took his part. So that the chancellor triumphed, and, being yet in Denmark, devised many reformations to be made, and new forms and customs to be set forward at His Majesty's return; as, to have no privy council but the exchequer, and the nobility to be debarred from it; sundry of the lords of the session to be put out and others put in their rooms. He caused a proclamation to be penned which was sent home to be proclaimed before His Majesty's return, that none of the nobility should come to court not being sent for, and then to bring with them six persons and no more; likewise every baron to bring but four. He was also minded that no knights should be made at the queen's coronation but such as were of worthy estimation by honourable behaviour either in the wars or that had been employed as ambassadors to other princes. Likewise it was devised to put in ward such as had been unruly and disobedient during

---

* Francis Stewart, son-in-law of James Hepburn.

His Majesty's absence, as the Earl Bothwell, the Lord Hume and divers Borderers and Highlandmen.

The next spring, as said is, their Majesties came home, and landed at Leith, well accompanied with the admiral of Denmark and divers of the council and many other gentlemen. All whom His Majesty treated honourably; and after the queen's coronation they were rewarded in princely manner with more than twelve golden chains and many medals of gold with His Majesty's picture.

His Majesty, at his landing, had sent for me to bear them company; which I did until their parting, to His Majesty's great contentment. . . .

IX

The Earl of Bothwell and the Witches

AFTER the coronation of the Queen's Majesty and banqueting and rewarding the strangers, they returned home well contented. There was another convention appointed, for taking order with the affairs of the country, to which many noblemen and barons were written for; but very few obeyed the said letters, or would come near the court, because when they were first written for to the queen's coronation, they thought not themselves well used, for hall, chamber, and all doors were so straitly and indiscreetly kept* that they could get no entry. Therefore many of them returned discontent to their houses; there was no man appointed to welcome them, and to direct them, except so many as were made knights. Which was the cause that so few came again to court the next time they were written for. For they who had been lately in Denmark with His Majesty thought to retain him and the whole government in their hands, and had given His Majesty counsel not to be over familiar, nor of too easy access; none to enter his chamber but such as were gentlemen of his chamber, with the chancellor and some of the council. They were not content to have the only access and whole handling at all other times, but even also at these conventions they continually occupied His Majesty's ear in presence of the whole assembly, to let their great credit be seen, that they might be courted and bribed by such as had to do with the king.

None of them all had more occasion of occupying His Majesty's ear than I had at that time. Yet when it would please him to call upon me, to know how every stranger was treated and satisfied, I would give him a short answer, and with a great reverence retire and draw aside. Which was perceived by some of the nobility and barons who were come to the said convention; in the which sundry necessary reformations were intended, though nothing was performed; which was the more spoken of, because every man hoped to see a settled estate at His Majesty's homecoming, and with the greater assurance by reason of His Majesty's promise, made publicly in the High Kirk of Edinburgh, to be a new man and to take up another kind of care and doing in his

*Melville's meaning is that it was impolitic to exclude the nobility.

own person than ever had been seen or used before. Which certainly
His Majesty was very willing to put in execution. But alas he lacked
help and assistance, for such as he reposed most upon had no further
care of his affairs than as they might best serve their own particular
profit and advancement to such ambitious marks as they shot at;
making His Majesty in the mean time believe that all was well ruled
and ordered. The contrary being too manifest moved me to present
unto His Majesty at divers times some memorials and informations
concerning his estate and government; the most part whereof I had
set down in writing after that Colonel Stewart had brought commission from His Majesty to my brother Sir Robert and me, before His
Majesty's voyage to bring home the queen, during the time that he
was dolorous in Craigmillar and discontent with the chancellor and
such of the council as had been hinderers of his marriage. He had desired my said brother and me to sit down and advise upon some good
rules for the establishing of a good order in his country. . . .*

The officers of the exchequer continued a while to be the only
council; and the nobility, when they came, were kept at the door of
that council; of which number I being one took occasion to say to His
Majesty that it could do no harm to cause them come in, they being
great men, as my Lord Hamilton, my Lord Maxwell and others. But
His Majesty of his own motive and nature was not changeable from
the order laid down by them he liked and reposed upon. Yet I went
forth of the chamber and told the noblemen that His Majesty was upon
the ordering of his rents and daily expenses and that he was ashamed
they should see the sober estate thereof, which was the cause they
were suffered to stand without. This little excuse was somewhat satis-
factory to them. But that order was also soon altered.

Concerning the reducing of the Highlands and Isles: three of the
principals, as MacLean, MacDonald and Donald Gorm, were subtly
drawn to the court by the chancellor, who understood of the differences
among them, every one of them being by him put in hope to get his
hand above his enemy. But at their coming they were all three warded
in the castle of Edinburgh, to their great astonishment; for they had
committed such foul murders under trust that it would be horrible to
rehearse.† Being therefore apprehensive of their lives, they dealt
largely of their ill-won gold to those who had credit. Nevertheless,

* The document inserted by Melville at this point is printed as an Appendix
(p. 170).
† In 1586 the MacLean of Duart of the time had been murdered by his brother-
in-law, MacDonald of Dunivaig, and his men massacred. This inevitably led to a
blood-feud between MacLeans and MacDonalds. 'Donald Gorm' was MacDonald
of Sleat.

they were put to an assize, and convicted of treason and for many other
foul crimes; which caused them to redouble their gifts to the guiders,
but not to the king; in such sort that there was an agreement betwixt
His Majesty and them that they should give pledges that they should
pay yearly unto His Majesty 20,000 merks for the lands of the property
whereof they had no security; of the which they had of yearly rent,
as was given into the exchequer, 250,000 merks. This was all given
them for 20,000 merks. And whereas before they had no right nor
security, but a forcible possession, they obtained sure infeftments* by
charter, seisin and the great seal, and a remission of their foul crimes;
and, shortly after, their pledges, who were kept in the castle of Blackness, were released by giving 5000 merks to one of His Majesty's
chamber; and so the 20,000 merks were lost and never paid.

Here was a good prince ill-used and abused, and the half of his rents
robbed from him, and his God offended by sparing to do justice upon
such bloody tyrants, who acknowledged neither God nor the king.

I had advised His Majesty to go himself to the isles and build a fort
and to remain there two years, and promised to go with him; showing
His Majesty that the kings of Scotland were never rich since they left
the Highlands to dwell in the Lowlands, but have ever since diminished their rents, and increased their superfluous expenses in diet and
clothing, at the unevenly† example in following the customs of other
nations. Which His Majesty found to be most true; and His Majesty
was resolved to follow the said advice, but all was altered by the former
misrule. Matters thus proceeding, many began to lose hope of amendment or to see shortly such a reformation as was promised and expected, lamenting to see a good king so ill handled, and that himself
should oversee the same and suffer everything to pass at the pleasure
of those about him.

About this time His Majesty sent for me; and at my coming to
Falkland, where the court remained for the summer season, it pleased
His Majesty to tell me how that, at his coming out of Denmark, he had
promised to the queen and council there to place about the Queen's
Majesty, his bedfellow, good and discreet company; which he had left
too long undone, until at length, having advised with himself, he
thought me the fittest man to commit that charge to; desiring me not
to refuse the just calling of my prince, wherein I might serve as in a
lawful vocation; because they that suit for service at court, or for any
office, do it for their own profit; but they are more profitable for
princes that are sought after, and are chosen for their qualities. 'I
know', says he, 'that you would fain live at home in your own house,
with contentment of mind; but you know that a man is not born for

* Conveyances.   † Inequitable, ill-matched.

himself only, but also for the weal of his prince and country. And whereas your continual on-waiting will be chargeable and expensive to you, and hindersome to your own affairs at home, I shall ordain sufficient entertainment for your present relief; and recompense for this and your former faithful service.'

I answered that, as His Majesty's most humble servant and subject, I never refused to obey his commandment, and should by his direction do my utter diligence to satisfy his expectations. Then it pleased him to tell me that none of his council nor chamber nor no man was made privy to this design, but only one man; and that the queen had got word thereof, and supposed that I was to be put there to inform her rightly of the estate of the country, and concerning her behaviour to His Majesty and to every nobleman and lady, conform to their ranks and conditions, and to be her keeper.

Now His Majesty took occasion to enter in purpose with me, openly at the table, and showed unto the queen how that she and all her nation were obliged to me for the continual good will and report I had made of them, and also how I had seen many countries and had so great experience that both he and she might learn of me several things for the weal and standing of their estate; and that the queen his mother found herself much relieved by my conversation and service of importance, as well here at home as when I was employed by her abroad. Thus far His Majesty said above my deservings, to set me up and to cause Her Majesty to like me the better. Notwithstanding whereof, the queen did show me no great countenance, but took coldly with me, when after dinner it pleased His Majesty to present me unto her to be Her Highness's counsellor and gentleman of her chamber. Some days afterward Her Majesty asked me if I was ordained to be her keeper. I answered that Her Majesty was known to be descended of so noble and princely parents, and so well brought up, that she needed no keeper; albeit her dignity required to be honourably served with men and women, both young and old, in sundry occupations. She replied that I had been ill used; showing me that at first, when she was yet ignorant of every man's qualities, some indiscreet enviers would have put me in her displeasure. I answered that I was put in her service to instruct such indiscreet persons, and also to give them good example how to behave themselves dutifully and reverently unto Her Majesty, to hold them aback, and that way to keep her from their rashness and importunity. At length Her Majesty appeared to be well satisfied with my service, in which I spent [...] years, keeping sometimes the council-days, and sometime assisting upon the exchequer, when their Majesties were together; but when they were asunder, I waited only upon the queen.

About this time many witches were taken in Lothian, who deposed concerning some [design] of the Earl of Bothwell's, as they alleged, against His Majesty's person. Which coming to the said earl's ears, he entered in ward within the castle of Edinburgh, desiring to be tried; alleging that the devil, who was a liar from the beginning, ought not to be credited, nor yet his sworn witches. Especially a renowned midwife called Annie Sampsoun affirmed that she, in company with nine other witches, being convened in the night beside Prestonpans, the devil their master being present, standing in the midst of them, a body of wax, shapen and made by the said Annie Sampsoun, wrapped within a linen cloth, was first delivered to the devil; who, after he had pronounced his verdict, delivered the said picture to Annie Sampsoun, and she to her next neighbour, and so every one round about, saying, 'This is King James VI, ordained to be consumed at the instance of a nobleman, Francis, Earl Bothwell.'

Afterwards again at their meeting by night in the kirk of North Berwick, where the devil, clad in a black gown, with a black hat upon his head, preached unto a great number of them out of the pulpit, having like light candles round about him. The effect of his language was to know what hurt they had done, how many they had gained to their opinion since their last meeting, what success the melting of the picture had, and such vain toys. And because an old silly poor ploughman, called Gray Meill, chanced to say that nothing ailed the king yet, God be thanked, the Devil gave him a great blow. Then divers among them entered in reasoning, marvelling that all their devilry could do no harm to the king, as it had done to divers others. The devil answered, 'Il est un homme de Dieu.' Certainly he is a man of God, and does no wrong wittingly, but is inclined to all godliness, justice and virtue; therefore God hath preserved him in the midst of many dangers. Now after that the devil had ended his admonitions, he came down out of the pulpit, and caused all the company come kiss his arse: which they said was cold like ice; his body was hard like iron, as they thought who handled him; his face was terrible; his nose like the beak of an eagle; great burning eyes; his hands and his legs were hairy, with claws upon his hands and feet like the griffin; he spoke with a hollow voice.

The tricks and tragedy he played then among so many men and women in this country would hardly get credit by posterity, but Mr James Carmichael, minister of Haddington, has their history and whole depositions. Among other things, some of them did show that there was a westland man called Richie Graham, who had a familiar spirit, the which Richie they said could both do and tell many things, chiefly against the Earl of Bothwell. Whereupon the said Richie Graham was apprehended, and brought to Edinburgh; and, being examined before His Majesty, I being present, he granted that he had a familiar spirit, which showed him sundry things; but he denied that he was a witch, or had any frequentation with them. But when it was answered to him again how that Annie Sampsoun had declared that he caused the Earl of Bothwell address him to her, he granted that to be true, and that the Earl of Bothwell had knowledge of him by Effie Mackalloun and Barbara Napier, Edinburgh women. Whereupon he was sent for by the Earl Bothwell, who required his help to cause the King's Majesty his master to like well of him. And to that effect he gave the said earl some drug or herb, willing him at some convenient time to touch therewith His Majesty's face. Which being done by the said earl, and found him not the better, he dealt again with the said Richie to get His Majesty wrecked, as Richie alleged; who said that he could not do such things himself, but that a notable midwife who was a witch, called Annie Sampsoun, could bring any such purpose to pass. Thus far the said Richie Graham affirmed divers times before the council; nevertheless he was burnt, with the said Sampsoun and some other witches. This Richie alleged that it is certain [what is reported] of the fairy folk; and that spirits may take a form, and be seen, though not felt.

The Earl of Bothwell, as I said, was entered in ward within the castle of Edinburgh, His Majesty not willing to credit his devilish accusers; but the council thought meetest that for a while he should pass his time in other countries, upon some articles and conditions. But some of those who were appointed to deal with him endeavoured to make advantage of him to be his friends. Others, who were desirous to have the state troubled, made him false advertisements. Which caused him resolve to save himself out over the castle-wall, and retired himself to Caithness; where he was shortly after sent for by such as were malcontents; and others would have fished in troubled waters, alleging they had made him friends enough in court and that there was a fair enterprise devised to take the king and kill the chancellor. To this purpose, he was easily persuaded to come and make himself head of that enterprise.

He therefore, not long after, accompanied with James Douglas, sometime laird of Spott, the laird of Niddry, Mr John Colville and some others, entered into the king's palace, late, about supper-time, by the passage of an old stable, not without secret intelligence of some about His Majesty. So soon as they were all within the close of the palace, they cried, 'Justice, Justice; a Bothwell, a Bothwell'; and had been masters of the whole, were it not that James Douglas of Spott, after that he had taken the keys from the porters, entered within the porter's lodge to relieve some of his servants, who were kept there in prison and had been examined and booted* upon suspicion of the slaughter of his good-father,† the old laird of Spott; in which doing there was some resistance from the porters, the noise whereof did rise sooner than was the intention of the enterprisers. Which warned His Majesty, the chancellor and others to shut and fortify their chamber-doors and to make resistance till some relief came from the Canongate, conducted by my brother Sir Andrew Melville of Garvock, master of His Majesty's household, who knew a secret passage through the abbey church, and entered by the same in armour. Whereof the Earl of Bothwell and his company being advertised, they stole quietly through the galleries unto the part where they entered the palace, and fled, without doing any great harm, as God would have it. In his out-going he chanced to meet with John Shaw, master stabler to His Majesty, whom he slew, together with his brother, being in a rage that the enterprise had failed. But divers of his company were apprehended by my said brother and by others; who were all executed the next day.

Their manner of proceeding was: first, the laird of Spott with a company took the keys, and made themselves masters of the gates of the palace. Another company was directed to the chancellor, who was sitting at his supper, and my brother Sir Robert with him; and they had been taken, had it not been for the laird of Spott's earnestness to relieve his servants; the bruit whereof caused the chancellor to flee out of his hall to his chamber and shut the door after him, so that my said brother got no entry, but retired himself to another void house, whither none pursued him, neither was he in any fear for himself.

The Earl of Bothwell, accompanied with Mr John Colville and others, addressed themselves unto the queen's chamber-door, where he supposed the king would be found. But the door was defended well by Harry Lindsay of Kilfauns, master of her household. In the mean time, His Majesty was conveyed up to that tower above the said chamber, after the door of Her Majesty's chamber had been broken with sledge hammers in divers parts, and that Mr John Colville had caused bring fire to burn it. The door of the chancellor's chamber was manfully defended by himself. He caused his men to shoot out of the windows continually, and through doors; where Robert Scot, brother to the laird of Balweary, was shot through the thigh. And had not my brother, the master of the household, that was newly planted in the north side of the close, cried to the chancellor not to shoot towards that side, he would have been in danger also. But the chancellor took courage when he heard my brother's voice; and then the enterprisers fled, as said is.

At their first entry within the palace, I was sitting at the end of our
    * That is, tortured by 'the boot'.   † Father-in-law.

supper with my Lord Duke of Lennox, who incontinent took his sword
and pressed forth; but he had no company, and the place already was
full of enemies. We were compelled to fortify the doors and stairs, with
tables, forms and stools, and be spectators of that strange hurly burly
for the space of an hour, beholding with torchlight forth of the duke's
gallery their reeling, their rumbling with halberts, the clacking of their
culverins and pistols, the dunting★ of mells and sledge hammers, and
their crying for justice. Now there was a passage betwixt the chancellor's chamber and my lord duke's by a stair; and during this fray the
chancellor came up the said stair and desired entry into my lord duke's
chamber. My lord duke, by my advice, desired him to cause his men
debate at the nether-door so long as they might, and offered to receive
himself† within his chamber. Which the chancellor took in an evil part,
and suspected my lord duke; and so returned back again to his own
chamber, and debated the best he could, as said is. So soon as my lord
duke saw a company of friends within the close, he went forth to pursue
the Earl of Bothwell and his company; but the night was dark, and
they took them speedily to their horses, and escaped.

They being retired, we got entry to Her Majesty's chamber,
whither the king was for the time come down. Where His Majesty
discoursed with me a good space, concerning this terrible attempt, and
of his many hard fortunes. Where I left not to tell His Majesty some
of the special causes of the said enterprises, and how that many of them
might have been avoided and forestalled by a prudent and careful
government, as may be sufficiently marked and considered by the
many admonitions and former advertisements made unto His Majesty
before all the accidents that chanced unto him, and also in this. For
two days before this enterprise, my brother Sir Robert and I had got
intelligence that some such design was shortly to be put in execution
by the Earl of Bothwell and his complices, against His Majesty and the
guiders of court. Whereof His Majesty made no account, though
thereof advertised; but was the next day going to the hunts to take his
pastime; which coming to my brother's ears, he rose out of his bed in
his shirt, only in his night-gown; and came forth to the outer-close of
the Abbey, and took His Majesty's horse by the bridle (for he was
already upon horseback), using many persuasions to have stayed him,
though all in vain; for we were in doubt whether the enterprise would
be executed in the fields or in the palace.

After this attempt, His Majesty went up to the town of Edinburgh
for his greater security; where there were divers new enterprises made,
whereof my brother Sir Robert getting frequent advertisements,

★ Striking; 'mell' is almost synonymous with sledge hammer.
† i.e. receive the chancellor.

sometimes to keep his lodging such a night, sometimes to be well accompanied such a night, as being one who had done pleasures to many, and was not hated; nor would be in danger if he could but save himself from the first fury of the enterprisers.

This hath been the hard estate of this good king, for laying the burden of his affairs upon men hated and envied for their ambition, covetousness, partialities and vengeance, who, so soon as they had attained so weighty a charge, took only care how to make themselves soon rich, most commonly by the wreck of others, or their enemies; so blindly transported by ambition and greediness, that they neglected both king and commonwealth; satisfying the king with fair language, though displeasing the country by hurtful deeds; caring only how to discredit so many honest men as they knew would discover their mis-behaviour or who would oppose the same, which I may justly testify for my part.

Not long after this, a new enterprise was made, to make a great alteration in court, by some courtiers among themselves. When as the Master of Glamis was treasurer, Sir George Hume master of the ward-robe, my Lord of Spynie gentleman of the chamber, and young Logie, also Sir John Maitland, Lord Thirlestane, chancellor; Sir Robert my brother, treasurer-depute, had the principal handling of the office, by debursing and receiving; the provost of Lincluden collector and [David] Seton of Parbroath comptroller, Sir Richard Cockburn of Clerkington secretary; and I was one of the privy council, and gentle-man of Her Majesty's chamber. My Lord Duke of Lennox, my Lord Hume, and my Lord of Mar were drawn upon this course, to reform the abuses at court, as was alleged. There was no good liking between the Master of Glamis and my Lord of Spynie, chiefly for the feud between the houses of Crawford and Glamis.* At that time my Lord Spynie was in so great favour with His Majesty, and sometimes his bedfellow, that he was worthy to be envied, besides the foresaid feud. Then he was accused to have been a dealer with the Earl of Bothwell and was for a time decourted. Young Logie was also thought to have had much dealing with the said earl, and was accused, taken and warded for the same. But he escaped out of a window in Dalkeith, by the help of a Danish gentlewoman, whom he afterwards married.

There was great suspicion betwixt my lord duke and the chancellor, for, after the late enterprise in the abbey, the chancellor caused close

* Alexander Lindsay, Lord Spynie, was a son of the Earl of Crawford. Lord Chancellor Glamis, brother of the Master of Glamis, had been killed by Craw-ford's followers in 1578. The lands of Crawford and Glamis adjoined each other in Angus.

up the passage with stone and lime that was betwixt his lodgings and my lord duke's, whereby he gave the duke to understand that he suspected him; which was too rashly done by the said chancellor. For after that this new alteration was intended, and called 'the enterprise made at Dalkeith', my lord duke and my Lord Hume, riding from Dalkeith to Edinburgh, met the chancellor well accompanied riding to court, where the said lords made a mint* to set upon him to slay him; yet the matter was at that time helped by Alexander Hume of North-berwick and my brother Sir Robert, who were in company with the chancellor for the time. But shortly after that, the chancellor left the court, retiring himself to his house; and in his absence a great number of faults were charged upon him, and among the rest how he had so long hindered the king's marriage, whereby the Queen's Majesty was made his great enemy.

The Master of Glamis also would fain have had my brother out of his office to enjoy the whole office of treasurer alone. Therefore the laird of Carmichael, captain of the guard, was easily persuaded to cause a number of the guard, who stood with culverins at the gates of the house of Dalkeith, to threaten to slay my said brother divers times in his passing in and out of the same house; supposing that my brother should fear for his life and leave the court, as the chancellor had done. But my brother made no account of their threat; for he knew the duke was his friend, and that he had but few enemies. Therefore he fre-quented the court more frequently than formerly, but came always well accompanied; for they could get nothing to lay to his charge, but said to His Majesty that he was too lavish in his office to be a treasurer, over easy in his compositions,† and over gentle to such as were put to the horn.‡ The Queen's Majesty, according to her custom, whenever she understands that His Majesty by wrong information is stirred up against any honest servant or subject, she incontinent intercedes for them, and useth great diligence to get sure knowledge of the verity, that she may the boldlier speak in their favour. Therefore so soon as Her Majesty understood that they were dealing against Sir Robert my brother, it pleased her to speak far in his favour, declaring how that, at her first landing in this country, His Majesty had presented him to her, praising him as one who had been a true servant to the queen-regent, his grandmother, to the queen his mother, and to himself; willing her to look upon him as such, and to follow his good advice. Also many of the lords took my brother's part in such sort, as he still kept the court and his office.

When this alteration was made, I was absent, and at my coming

* Proposal.   † The sums paid in return for various gifts of revenues accuring to the crown.   ‡ Outlawed, as a stage in legal procedure.

KING JAMES VI AND ANNE OF DENMARK

again to court His Majesty told me of the chancellor's fearful retreat, and that he was in no danger in his company. I answered again that the prince's presence should be a safeguard, albeit it was not always so in Scotland. It appeared that His Majesty, by hard informations, was somewhat altered upon the chancellor, my Lord Spynie and my brother. For as the Master of Glamis would have had his office, so others misliked him because he haunted the chancellor's company and was looked upon as his great friend; so that His Majesty was moved to think and say that he was not meet for his office. I, being present, answered that I lamented to hear and see so good a prince always environed with evil company, causing him so oft without offence to cast off his most ancient and faithful servants; and that it would be seen, let men serve never so well, if they were misrepresented by such as had his ear, it availed nothing. To this His Majesty replied that he knew my brother to be a true servant, but too gentle, liberal, and easy in his compositions, and that he would never alter upon him nor me; so that he continued constant against the intentions of some who were about him.

Here it may be seen how necessary it is to have good friends about the prince, and how hurtful and dangerous it is for a courtier when such as have the prince's ear are his enemies. Otherwise, whatsoever he be that reposes upon good service, he is commonly upset and wrecked.

About this time the Earl of Arran, who had been absent ever since the Raid of Stirling, came to court and spoke with His Majesty, and pretended* to have obtained again his office of chancellor. His Majesty had still favour for him, and would have been content of his company; but others held him back, and, shortly after that, he was surprised and slain by James Douglas of Parkhead, in revenge of the death of the Earl of Morton, his uncle. Little diligence was made to revenge the same, many thinking strange that he was permitted so long to live, in respect of his insolent behaviour when he had the court. He had won many that were about His Majesty, and some ministers consented to his incoming again to the court.

Now the chancellor, who was decourted at the alteration made in Dalkeith, did what he could to procure His Majesty's favour; which he obtained, and was again introduced. But the queen would not see him nor have to do with him; yet at length by the means of Sir Robert Ker of Cessford, who had married his brother's daughter, his peace was made with Her Majesty also.

About this time there did arise great strife and disorder in the country between the Earls of Huntly and Moray; between the Earls of

* Claimed.

Caithness and Sutherland; between my Lords Hamilton and Angus:
for divers of them had made suits and obtained commissions with
ample privileges over others' lands, as well as over their own, which
engendered many discords; whereof I advertised His Majesty, that
order might be taken therewith. Whereupon, the council being convened, they ordained letters to be directed in His Majesty's name,
charging them all to desist from hostility and to compear* before the
privy council at prefixed days. First the Earls of Moray and Huntly
compeared, there being a gentleman of the name of Gordon killed with
a shot out of the house of Darnaway by the Earl of Moray, whom they
threatened at his own house.† Both the parties being come strong to
court, were commanded to keep their lodgings, for preventing of
trouble before their compearing. When His Majesty was advised by
the chancellor and some of his chamber what order should be meetest
to be taken between them, then His Majesty proposed the same to
the council himself: to wit, three points, either present agreement to
be made, or warding both the earls, or caution to be taken of both;
then to send home the one, and hold the other still at court for a while.

His Majesty, following forth this proposition, declared first that
the parties could not be presently agreed, because of the hot blood of
the laird of Cluny, Gordon's brother, lately slain. Concerning warding,
he alleged that the castle of Edinburgh had enough of prisoners already;
that the abbey was not a fit prison for noblemen; so that it would be
best to take caution‡ of them both, and to hold them sundry, to send
home the one, and retain the other at court for a season. The chancellor
was of that opinion, and sundry others who used commonly to please
them who had the chief handling. Then His Majesty commanded me
to tell my opinion; which was that I wished no delay, but present
agreement, supposing that the Earl of Huntly, for His Majesty's
pleasure and command, would not refuse nor think shame to obey his
prince by a present uptaking, seeing he was come so great a journey
with his lady and whole household, to remain all winter at court. At
this the chancellor checked me up tauntingly, saying that the Earl of
Huntly would tarry at court all that day till to-morrow, and would part
no sooner; for he had promised to the said earl that advantage over his
enemy, albeit the earl's intention was to tarry all winter at court. The
justice-clerk was of my opinion, but said that it appeared His Majesty
with the chancellor had already concluded to send Huntly home, and
let the other remain at court. So soon as Huntly was at home in the
north and wanting his competitor, he triumphed and took sundry

* Appear after being judicially summoned.
† Huntly was head of the Gordon family; Darnaway was Moray's residence.
‡ Judicial security.

advantages upon the Earl of Moray's lands, giving the earl just occasion of complaint; but getting no redress, he retired himself from the court, and became so malcontent that he took plain part with the Earl of Bothwell, who was still upon his enterprises.

The Earl of Huntly, being advertised that his adversary was an outlaw with the Earl of Bothwell, returned again to court, to get yet some advantage upon him. But in the mean time the Lord Ochiltree endeavoured to agree them by consent of His Majesty. He drew the Earl of Moray to Donibristle to be near hand, that conditions and articles might be added or pared at the pleasure of their friends. The Earl of Huntly, being also made privy to his coming to Donibristle, obtained incontinent a commission (appearing to do His Majesty acceptable service) to pursue by fire and sword the Earl of Bothwell and all his partakers. Little knew His Majesty that he was minded under this general commission to assail the Earl of Moray at his own house, on pretext of conferring with him, and to kill him, as he did, to the regret of many. But the Lord Ochiltree took such a despite that his friend was so slain under communing,* as he alleged, that he took plain part with the Earl of Bothwell, and so did divers others, encouraging the said earl to assail His Majesty within his palace of Falkland, having divers in court familiar enough with His Majesty upon the said conspiracy with him, whose counsel His Majesty followed most. So that they drew him into a hoise net† to abide still in Falkland, notwithstanding the many sure advertisements that had been made unto him. Such hath been His Majesty's hard fortune in many such strait times.

The few number who were faithful to, and careful of, His Majesty, counselled him, after the first advertisement, to pass to Cupar, and convene, with all possible diligence, the barons of Fife for his defence. But such as sought his wreck persuaded him to tarry and delay, alleging that they had sure advertisement that the Earl of Bothwell would not come out of Lothian till such a day; which would have been two days longer, and behind the day which he kept; and he came to Falkland two days sooner. This advice was given that His Majesty might be surprised before he could either enter within the tower of Falkland or be provided with any forces to defend him. And because they knew my brother and me to be careful for him, they advised His Majesty to send us home to our houses, that same night that we understood the Earl of Bothwell would be there, and had so told His Majesty; but he believed his abusers better. But we gave His Majesty counsel to ride quietly to Balmerino, and make no man privy thereto but one and let it appear that he was still in Falkland, secretly within the tower; then at their coming, missing His Majesty, they would be discouraged,

* When he was engaged in a conference.   † A small bag-shaped fishing net.

and if they came to pursue him in Balmerino he might take a boat and go over to Angus, where he would have leisure to convene the towns of Perth and Dundee and the country thereabouts. But this advice was also overthrown by those who were upon the contrary part.

Thus we being commanded by His Majesty to ride home and to warn the country in case he were besieged within the tower, we obeyed. My brother that same night, by the way, was advertised by one of the Earl of Bothwell's own company that he was already in Fife and would be in Falkland about supper-time. Upon which advertisement he sent one of his gentlemen, called Robert Auchinleck, back to acquaint His Majesty therewith, and to request him to enter within the tower in due time. When the said Robert declared the matter unto His Majesty, they all laughed him to scorn, calling him a fool. The said Robert riding back again, malcontent to be so mocked, met the Earl of Bothwell and his company upon the height of the Lomonds,* when it was already dark night, and turned incontinent, as if he had been one of their company. He used great diligence to be first at His Majesty. Entering within the palace of Falkland, he closed the gates himself, and cried continually to cause His Majesty enter within the tower; who at length believed him, and mocked him no more.

The Earl of Bothwell at his coming had petards to break up gates and doors. It was alleged that some of those who shot out of the tower for His Majesty's defence had charged their culverins only with paper, but some of His Majesty's household-officers shot out bullets, which gave the earl and his company a great scare; as also the king's entering within the tower before he was surprised. And supposing that the country would gather together, the said earl and his company retired and fled, none pursuing them; whereas a few might easily have overtaken and overthrown them. That same night I lay in my boots upon my bed, expecting word from Falkland, where there was one left to that effect. At whose back-coming, I with other friends and neighbours did ride to convene the country at Cupar, to have rescued His Majesty. Thither the king sent us advertisement that the earl and his company were fled; yet he desired the barons and towns to come forward to Falkland, as they did to the number of 3000 that afternoon. Thus God miraculously delivered His Majesty, as He had done divers times before.

About this time came to His Majesty an honest gentleman from Ireland, who made offers of consequence to His Majesty. Whereof the Queen of England was incontinent advertised to require the said gentleman to be delivered to her; which the most part of the council persuaded His Majesty to do. But the justice-clerk, my brother, and I,

* The Lomond hills in Fife, near Falkland.

were of the contrary opinion. Which deed did great harm to the weal of His Majesty's affairs in England and Ireland. This I speak with great regret, because it was so far against His Majesty's own mind; and yet he suffered it to be done, because the chief ring-leaders have been always won to the devotion of England.

Now the prince* being born at Stirling the [19 February 1594] His Majesty thought fit to send ambassadors to England, Denmark, France and Flanders, to require their ambassadors to be sent to the baptism of the prince his first-born son. The council were commanded to nominate such as were meetest to be sent on that message; as they did. Yet such as procured to be sent obtained the commission, although some of them were unmeet for that errand, as Sir William Keith; he could neither speak Latin, French nor Flemish. The laird of Easter Wemyss procured to carry the commission to France, and also to England, because he was to go thither about his own affairs, being the King of France's servant. But Mr Peter Young sped best, who was sent to Denmark, and to the Dukes of Mecklenburg and Brunswick; for he got three fair chains. But the King of France nor the Queen of England gave nothing; which their duty would have caused them to do, if ambassadors had been sent to them express. Neither sent the King [of France] any ambassador here at that time. The Queen of England was at first minded to do the same, till she was advertised by her ambassador in France that the king would send none. Then very late she sent the Earl of Sussex, to let us think that she would ever be a ready friend, when France would refuse and lie back. On the other part, the Dukes of Mecklenburg and Brunswick were discontent that they were so far slighted, as not to have a man sent express to each of them. A special day was appointed for solemnizing the said baptism. The ambassadors of Denmark and Dutchland arrived almost together. His Majesty had sent for me of before to be there at their landing, to receive them and to entertain them. But the ambassadors of Mecklenburg and Brunswick would not ride out of Leith in company with the Danish ambassador, when they were convoyed up to Edinburgh, but would have a convoy apart.

A few days after them arrived the ambassadors of the estates of the Low Countries, to wit, Monsieur de Brederod and Monsieur Folk, great treasurer of Holland and Zealand, who landed at Newhaven,† where I was well accompanied to receive them, having horse and foot-mantles in readiness to carry them up to Edinburgh to their lodgings.

A little before the landing of the said ambassadors, the day of the baptism was delayed, because there was no word of an ambassador from France or England, and the king's chapel in the castle of Stirling, which

* James's eldest son, Henry.   † About two miles from Edinburgh.

was cast down, to be built again in a better form, was not yet completed: so that the ambassadors were ordained to remain in Edinburgh till all might be put in good order. Therefore His Majesty appointed the master of his household, and my Lord Tongland, my brother, together with me, to entertain them upon His Highness's charges, and also to bear them company. After they had tarried long in Edinburgh (there being no appearance of any ambassadors from France or England), we were commanded with some others of the council to convoy them to Stirling; where His Majesty made his excuses that they were so long delayed at Edinburgh without any acquaintance, pleasure or comfort. But they alleged that they had great contentment in our company. Which His Majesty forgot not to declare before the whole council, giving me great thanks, alleging that I had done many good offices, and this among the rest, which he would never forget; and that he had three other of my brothers, all fit for such matters and for foreign affairs.

Now being in doubt of the English ambassador's coming, the ceremony was to be solemnized without longer delay. In the mean time, there came word that the Earl of Sussex was upon his journey toward Scotland, for the queen his mistress, on whom the action stayed. The day of the solemnity, there was great business for their honours and seats. That being agreed, there was an empty chair set before the rest for the King of France's ambassador. The order of the banquet and triumph I leave to others to set out.

When the ambassadors had audience of the Queen's Majesty, I was appointed to stand a little behind, and next unto Her Majesty. To the English, Danish and Dutch ambassadors, Her Majesty made answer herself. But though she could speak seemly French, yet she rounded in my ear to declare her answer to the ambassadors of the states of Holland. Then every one of them, by order, gave their presents for the god-bairn gift.★ The jewels of precious stones the queen received in her own hand and then delivered them unto me, to put them again in their cases, and lay them upon a table which was prepared in the midst of the chamber to set them upon. The Queen of England's had a great show, being a fair cupboard of silver overgilt, cunningly wrought, and some cups of massy gold. The ambassadors of the states presented a golden box, wherein was written on parchment, in letters of gold, 'A gift of a yearly pension to the prince of five thousand . . . by year', with great cups of massy gold, two especially which were enough for me to lift and set them down upon the said table. I leave it to others to set down their weight and value. But I say, these which were of gold, which should have been kept in store to posterity, were soon melted

★ A gift made to a godchild.

and spent; but then, those who advised to break them had wanted their part, as they had of the queen's dowry.

All these ambassadors being despatched and well rewarded, those of Denmark were advised, by John Lindsay of Menmuir, to cause with all diligence send new ambassadors, to require the contract of marriage made in Denmark to be fulfilled; alleging that the chancellor, who made it, had left out the rents of the abbey of Dunfermline that lay besouth* the water of Forth, fraudfully, and had taken in feu† to himself all the lordship of Musselburgh. For this end two ambassadors were sent from Denmark, to wit, Stean Bill and Doctor Craik, upon whom I was appointed to attend, to see them well used and entertained. As they were well instructed, so they happened upon a meet time; for the chancellor was for the time decourted, and my brother was ambassador for His Majesty in England. So the chancellor was caused to renounce his part. And because my brother Sir Robert was absent, young Sir Robert, his son, and I, obliged us that his part, which was thirteen chalders‡ of victual, should be also renounced at his return; which was accordingly done. Divers others, who had portions of these lands, were likewise compelled to renounce, either voluntarily, or by a new law made for that effect. His Majesty promised to send my brother as much heritage in another part, in respect that his gift was obtained long before the contract of marriage.§

These two ambassadors being well satisfied, and ready to return in Denmark, there fell out another foul attempt in the king's palace, by the Earl of Bothwell and his associates, by the convoy of some that were about His Majesty. The said earl, early in a morning, entered in at the back gate beside the kitchen, as the said gate was opened to let forth of the palace my Lady Atholl, passing that way to visit her mother the Lady Gowrie, that lodged hard without the palace. The said earl, with a few company at the first, entered within His Majesty's chamber, which was easily opened unto him. He had a drawn sword in his‖ . . . and Mr John Colville another. His Majesty's clothes were loose, and . . . his . . . of his hose not knit up; yet he was in no ways astonished, but by . . . calling them false traitors, bidding them strike if they durst.

But when they perceived that His Majesty would take no fear, Mr

* On the south side of.

† By a feu charter, a grant in perpetuity for a fixed duty.

‡ A large measure of capacity.

§ The meaning of this paragraph is that persons with claims on properties assigned to Queen Anne in her marriage settlement had to be brought in one way or another to renounce them.

‖ From this point the text is defective.

John Colville rounded in the earl's ear; who after that fell down upon his knees, humbly craving pardon, alleging that he had waited on long secretly in the town of Edinburgh, to have suited grace and mercy on the same manner upon the High Street, as divers others had done; and that his intention was discovered to such of his enemies as were about His Majesty, who had appointed men to shoot him; so that he was compelled to take this harder course for his latter refuge; requesting His Majesty either to pardon him or else to take his own sword and slay him. With this he laid his long hair under His Majesty's feet, and took his foot with his hand and set it upon his hair, in sign of greater humility. Which moved His Majesty to have pity and compassion upon him, and granted him pardon freely without compulsion; as His Majesty told me that same day, and the whole manner of his in-coming.

In the mean time that this was in doing, the alarm came up to the town. The common bell rang, and many ran down, and I among the rest, to see what help might be made. Being in the outer close, I cried up at the window of His Majesty's chamber, asking how His Majesty did. He came to the window and said all would be well enough; and said he had agreed with them upon certain conditions, 'which are presently to be put in writ. Therefore', said he, 'cause so many of the town as are come to my relief to stay in the abbey kirkyard till I send them further word, and return again within half an hour yourself.' Now after that I had told my commission to the few number of the town that were come, they tarried not long. So great was their miscon-tentment for the time, that many desired a change.

After this I passed to the two Danish ambassadors, that were lodged in the house of Kinloch; who were in a great displeasure for His Majesty's estate and willed me in their name to return and desire further knowledge of the welfare of both king and queen. His Majesty came again to the window, and brought the queen with him; and they both bade me tell the ambassadors that they were well, and that things were fully agreed. Then the said ambassadors directed me to the Earl Bothwell, to desire leave that they might come in afternoon to the court to see their Majesties. Which being granted, I passed with them to the queen's chamber; and leaving them there, passed forward to see His Majesty, who was glad to get any of his own that he might speak to, and declared unto me the whole manner; lamenting more the evil favoured form of doing of the most part of them that were about him, than he did the Earl Bothwell's proceeding upon so great necessity. I again, after that I had comforted him the best I could, said that it was lamentable that he, who had such a pregnant wit and so sincere an inclination, should cast himself continually in the company of wicked men, whom he loved for their pleasant language, albeit he had oft

THE DARNLEY MEMORIAL, c. 1567

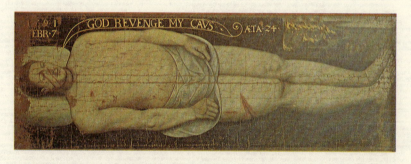

THE CORPSE OF THE BONNIE EARL OF MORAY, 1592

proof of their infidelity; and waived and did cast off such true honest men as had a continual care of his honour and surety, by showing him the verity in sure and unpleasant language. He said it was his chance to believe that men unto whom he had been very beneficial should love him. Where I remembered him of the saying of Plutarch unto Trajan, to think better of their counsel that loved him than of theirs that he loved.*

* The last five paragraphs printed here do not appear in Scott's edition. The Maitland Club edition has four further pages, but they represent a manuscript which is becoming increasingly defective and barely intelligible.

Appendix: Melville's Advice to King James*

SIR,

Your Majesty's happy return† hath greatly rejoiced your whole subjects. The expectation they have had of you ever since your birth hath been great both far and near. Your public promise to take upon you a more kingly care since your home-coming, through greater experience, hath augmented their good hope of a gracious government. Your religion pure and clean, your zeal to godliness and justice, your chaste and sincere life, your promptitude to suppress rebellions when they arise, ravisheth the hearts of most part of your subjects to love you and esteem you the best king that hath been these many years in this realm. And yet they all marvel with stupified minds to see your affairs so clumsily handled, complaining heavily that your country was never in greater disorder and distress, the Kirk so evil content, your house so evil at point, the nobility so divided, the barons in greater poverty, the commons more oppressed, nor never more taxations raised, mostly applied to the utility of private persons, more parliaments holden, more laws cast loose and broken, your proclamations and missives less obeyed, and murder and blood-shed more increased, than since your home-coming and public promise, than it was during your absence.

Therefore, Sir, as in a perilous storm upon the sea, or to quench sudden kindled fire on the land, every man's help is requisite and acceptable; so I hope Your Majesty's clemency will consider and give gentle audience, and your prudence will take in good part this my dutiful declaration and admonition, the boldlier enterprised under the warrant of your favourable allowance, following your familiar commandment before Your Majesty's going to Denmark that my brother and I should set down the causes of the evils and disorders that have been and are, with the meetest remedies for reforming and amending the misrule.

There be three chief causes of all these evils and disorders.

* This is clearly a composite document, written at various times between 1590 and 1597.   † From Denmark in 1590.

The First, concerning God's service.

The Second, concerning your own estate, and the provision of your house.

The Third, concerning the policy and common weal of the country.

As concerning the service of God, neglected by our sins and carelessness in setting forth His glory, it should be redressed and amended by humble repentance, amendment of life, and good example first in your own person, upon which every man's eye is fixed, as the head to rule the rest of the members, with religion, justice, prudence, temperance and fortitude.

Chiefly by religion and justice have all the best commonwealths been ruled; so that such countries as wanted the knowledge of true religion, seeing the great works that God brought to pass by his own peculiar people observing his religion, they invented religions, thinking to imitate the Jews, and fell into idolatry and superstition; yet they straitly observed their said invented religion, and caused punish with death such as despised or spoke against the same. Far more should Your Majesty be careful to advance the true religion, and to see the same reverenced and observed. And for that effect should devout and discreet ministers be chosen, whose Christian lives may preach as well as their doctrine: and such to be provided with sufficient local stipends, neither too much, to entice them to avarice, nor too little, to make them so indigent as to cry out in all their preachings of their poverty; in such sort as they may have no occasion yearly to leave their flocks to come and make suit for their living, with great pain and expenses, as they do presently.

Divers are the causes of the disorder in your court and house. Officers and servants are not chosen for their qualities, but at the instance of this or that friend or courtier. Then the number of all sorts of servants are not limited, by placing about Your Majesty so many as are needful, but an extraordinary number; whereas two in every office are enough. And then your prudence will be best known when you shall be seen to make good election of fit persons for every occupation; for the prince is ever esteemed to be like unto those sort of servants as he likes best to be about him. Much consists in this, to have in court discreet, modest courts and ungreedy courtiers. Nothing wins more the hearts of the people to the prince: for so long as they see about him such persons, they are out of fear of being unmeasurably burdened. When they see men who are not greedy, importune cravers, nor prodigal spenders of the prince's goods and their own, nor stirrers up of the prince to take men's lives for their lands, they are in hope that every man may live upon his own, and the prince also upon his proper patrimony. Therefore should the exchequer be also chosen of true restrick* men, by the foresight of the prince, who should be frequently present himself, and hear his own accounts; for few dare control, or find fault with, the wrong accounts of such officers as are great courtiers and in great favour. Which I have oft-times seen and found fault with, when upon the exchequer, to my great hurt and discredit.

The causes why the patrimony of the crown is so diminished, is because Your Majesty's predecessors disposed much to the church for devotion, and to noblemen and barons for good service. And sometimes when princes were careless to prevent rebellions, occasioned by their misgovernment, they were compelled to buy the assistance of a sort, by disposition of lands, to repress another number of unnatural subjects. Which their careful and provident government might have prevented and eschewed.

Your Majesty also, out of your noble and princely nature, disposed liberally unto divers greedy and importunate persons, during your minority, divers lands and rents, which would have stood in great stead to the entertainment of your house. And you always heaped gift upon gift to a sort of greedy cravers, and that by the persuasions of such as had your ear, and not to those who deserved best. Now the exchequer being well chosen, as said is, and the rent-masters and their officers who are accountable, to be true responsible mean men, neither too great men nor great courtiers, but such as men dare control and will not fear to offend. All vacant benefices and casualties should be retained in your own hands, till you see what you may spare.

Then the best part of the property lies in the Highlands, where neither God nor the king is served nor obeyed. Your rents may be redoubled, if the Highlands and the Islands were reduced, as was done by your grandfather King James V. For the kings of Scotland were never rich since they left the Highlands and the Isles to dwell in the Lowlands; for since that, their rents have been diminished, and their superfluous expenses increased at the unevenly† example of other neighbour nations.

Then Your Majesty's parks would be plenished and put to profit, which will be found a necessary help to the keeping of your house. The rest of your store-grounds, lying in the far south-parts, are in such hands as it is not fit to meddle with them yet; but some yearly number of wedders‡ will be easily granted by them who possess presently the said store-grounds.

Also the forbidden goods that go yearly out of Scotland, if they were stayed and taken according to acts of parliament, would be very profitable.

The best means to bring these good purposes to pass, is a princely,

* Strict, severe.   † Inequitable, ill-matched.   ‡ Wethers.

prudent and gracious government; which is easiest brought to pass when the prince corrects himself before he corrects his subjects; for they will be soon subdued to his will when they see the same made subject unto reason; for being subject unto reason, the prince hath conquered himself, the readiest means also to conquer the hearts of all his subjects; their hearts being conquered, the country is easily conquered; the country being conquered, the prince may plant and establish good order there at his pleasure.

Theopompus* being demanded what way a king might best conserve and rule his realm, answered, in giving liberty to those who love him to tell him the truth.

The senate of Rome, writing unto Trajan, excuseth princes to be negligent in many things, not so much for that they have no desire to foresee, as because few or none dare warn them of the truth; and says, moreover, that it belongs to good princes rather to have regard to the benefit of their country than to the delights of their person; and rather to follow exercises to increase their reputation rather than their pastime; they should be sparing in speech, and prodigal in deeds.

Plutarch saith to the same Trajan, 'If thy government answer not the expectation of thy people, thou must necessarily be subject to many dangers.' He said further that princes should rule well, if they be thankful to the great God, patient in chances of fortune and in travail, diligent in execution, careful of their affairs and in dangers, mild to the people, tractable to strangers, not covetous of riches nor lovers of their own opinions and desires; for then the burden of their office will be easy unto them. As God is the ruler and spirit of the world, so ought princes to rule and be the spirit of their country. The heaven, the earth, the sea, the planets and all the elements obey God's ordinance by the strength of his continual motion and providence; so should the prince, who is God's place-holder, by continual care, providence and motion, cause every lieutenant, minister, magistrate, judge, officer and sheriff to keep their due course in their vocation. For the which effect, it may please Your Majesty to consider the nature and wrong kind of Scottish government, by a continual long corrupted custom.

Scotland is indeed hereditary, and a monarchy; yet, among all other monarchical kingdoms, it is oftest out of tune, by the sloth and carelessness of princes, the unruliness and sturdiness of the subjects, the great rents of the nobility and their great number; also the many great cumbersome† clans, so ready to concur together and to rebel for the defence of any of their name or to revenge the just execution of some of them for murder, slaughter, theft, or such other crimes. Our kings, wanting the means of hired soldiers remaining in garrisons, as

* A Greek historian and orator.   † Troublesome.

other monarchs have, may not at all occasions punish and redress such wrongs and disorders; except so many of them as by wisdom and virtue had conquered their own passions, opinions and desires, and by the same means ravished the hearts of the most and best part of the subjects, to assist them with their heart and hand to suppress the rebels and to punish the offenders. Such kings again as command absolutely, not caring for the hearts of their subjects, their proclamations will be outwardly obeyed with their bodies, but their doings will stand the prince in no stead in time of need, save only to help to ruin him. There is nothing more dangerous for a Scots king that hath not the love of his subjects than when a great number are convened together; for at such times they use to take sudden consultations to put order to the prince and his most familiar minions. Of these two sorts of kings, the first is more than a monarch; and the last less than elective. Of the first, in Scotland too few have reigned, and of the last too many; which is the cause that the country is not wholly conquered to the lawful king. Which is also the cause that the corrupt customs and disorders have lasted so long, and are not able to be remedied until it please God to send three such kings as I have named of the best sort, granting them long life, each one to succeed after other. I pray God that Your Majesty may begin and continue to be the first of the three. But where it appears Your Majesty is advised by creating more noblemen to increase your forces, whereby it rather makes them the stronger; whereas divers other princes endeavoured to make them lower and fewer; by reason of the old emulation which hath lasted between the kings of Scotland and their nobility, the kings to command absolutely as sovereign monarchs, the nobles to withstand their absolute power, sometimes by secret and indirect means and oft-times by plain resistance and force. Then the wise, virtuous and potent kings, whereof there have been but few, were always sovereign monarchs and obtained the mastery; whereas the careless, slothful and simple princes, that were ruled by mean men, were commonly kept captives or slain. The good and worthy prince took upon him more or less absolute power and authority, as he found himself able by assistance, substance and alliance, or as he found his nobility feeble, foolish and divided.

England believes itself always to be in the better estate by shedding the blood of their nobility and debarring them from the council and handling of the prince's affairs; Scotland now contrariwise, by sparing the nobility and barons, and by making them partakers of honours and offices. For the away-taking the life of a nobleman or baron breeds an hundred enemies more or less, according to the greatness of the clan or surname; of which number some will lie at wait to be revenged, albeit long after, when they find their opportunity. For the

nobility being so numerous, by long evil custom they esteem themselves to be born counsellors; and yet will not remain at court nor
upon the council, unless it be at conventions or for some particular
profit. And if the prince pretend to rule without them, they use to
make sudden enterprises against him and his familiars, with the which
tragedies the chronicles are filled and defiled. Then after such a violent
alteration, they think themselves odious to the prince, so that they
commonly seek to be masters over him from that time forth, lest he
should, when he sees his time, take his revenge for their contempt.

It is not best then to debar your nobility from being upon your
council, but grant place to a number of the wisest of them, whereof
they will soon be weary, and retire when their purses begin to grow
empty. Thus your ordinance shall take effect of will, and they will
want occasion to grudge or rebel.

It is meet also to gain by good deeds part of the worthiest of your
nobility; which may be a means to keep the rest from rebellion, when
they see so many of their sort daily about you, and in your favour.

Princes are by Homer called Pastors; by the Romans, Fathers of the
country. None can be answerable to such honourable names without
extreme diligence and fatherly care to see every officer occupy his
vocation, and strait account to be taken how they discharge their duty,
rewarding well-doers and punishing offenders; reward and punishment
being the pillars whereupon the commonwealth stands. Especially
take care this first year of your marriage;* for the reputation obtained
the first year will last long afterward, whether it be good or evil.

Be earnest and liberal to get good intelligence as well of the estate of
neighbour countries as of your own; of the grievances of your subjects,
and their partialities and feuds; which will open your eyes to see
sundry outgates in matters of state.

Give familiar access to your nobility and barons, when they come;
chiefly to all such who are written for to your conventions. Give open
audience, once every week at least, to rich and poor, receiving their
supplications and complaints, with strict command to the council and
master of requests to give them answer with sudden despatch.

Cause reform the superfluity of clothing and banqueting, as well by
your own example as commandment.

Now, supposing Your Majesty to be ripe fruit, and no more green,
I hope your dear bought experience hath made you apt enough to
receive all profitable impressions presented to Your Majesty by your
faithful proved servants, and not to commit so easily again your
weighty charge to any one, two or three; whom you have seen to have
always shot at their own marks, and not yours, but to make themselves

* i.e. 1590.

great and rich, imperilling your estate to bring their own turns to pass; which kind of doing, by some careless princes, caused the poet Du Bellay to cry out

O trois et quatre fois malheureuse la terre
Dont le prince ne void que par les yeux d'autruy,
N'entend que par ceux qui respondent pour luy,
*Aveugle, sourd et muet, plus que n'est une pierre.**

No man will think it strange that, during your younger years, you have been pressed and persuaded to lay the burden of affairs off yourself upon others, who greedily courted that weighty charge above their capacity, wanting care, knowledge, credit and ability to bear it. But now every man will marvel if you should do it in your perfect age; thinking that your pregnant ability, excellent memory and hurtful experience must compel you to exercise the office of a king in your own person. For whence hath proceeded so many attempts, so many enterprises, so many takings of Your Majesty's person, so many alterations and changes of court, counsellors, servants and laws, but by committing the charge and keeping of your sheep and subjects to certain ambitious and ravenous wolves, who chose and bring into court, for their assistance, such as they knew to be of their own qualities, that they might concur together, first how to put out of your favour and debar from your ear all such honest true persons as would oppose their pernicious proceedings, that Your Majesty might neither see nor understand, but by their eyes and ears? Then all was well ruled and ordered, calm and fair weather, for a very few days. Your Majesty can well enough remember how oft for my part I have forewarned you of the storms which were to fall out through the misbehaviour of such insolent, such inconstant, such scornful and such partial persons, as have oftest possessed your ear and carried the vogue in your court. And what vantage I thereby gained to myself, Your Majesty knows. Yet I had this comfort, that Your Majesty confessed that I had shown you the verity; but the said confession was way behind the time, with over late repentance.

Here Your Majesty may reproach me of inconstant councils; because, a year after your returning from Denmark, I told you that your subjects were not satisfied of their expectation, nor of your public promises; praying Your Majesty yet to begin, and either rule as appertaineth a right king, only for a year, or else to submit the whole burden of your office to such a number as I should name, only for one

* O three and four times unhappy is the land whose prince sees only by the eyes of another and hears only by those who answer for him: blind, deaf and dumb, no better than a stone. (Du Bellay, *Regrets*, sonnet cxiv.)

year. In doing of any of these two, I said I should bind and oblige myself that your estate should be sufficiently settled at the year's end or else for my penalty to be put in prison or to be perpetually banished out of Scotland. Then it pleased Your Majesty to demand of me the manner that I would wish you to rule after? Whereunto I made answer that it did not become me, or any in Scotland, to show you the duty of a king, which you could do and declare better than any of your council if you pleased only for one year to take the pains to do your own office yourself. In so doing, I supposed that before the end of the year there should ensue such profitable effects, as you should think the government pleasant, and no more painful; by the which means Your Majesty should eschew the reproach of the poet, Paucŭŭe, in one of his verses, saying in French,

> *Je hay, dit il, entre les hommes ceux*
> *Qui sont esprits d'un vouloir paresseux*
> *Et tousjours semblent, s'on s'y fye*
> *Practiquer l'art de la philosophie.**

Italian
Chi non fa quel che deue, quel ch'aspetta non receue.†

Spanish
Si fueras regido por razon, a muchos regirías.‡

In four things a prince soonest wrecks himself: To be careless and slothful in his affairs; To forsake the sure counsel of his true servants; To give largely unto unthankful flatterers; and To spend above his rents.

To return again to the purpose: It pleased Your Majesty to enquire for the second point, viz. What might best settle your estate within the year? I said 'To submit the whole burden for a year to a number of such as I should name, joined to the best inclined of your own council.' To that Your Majesty agreed; but when I came more to particulars, Your Majesty thought it too much to be so far addicted and so entirely submitted. Then I requested Your Majesty to do the first, and do your own office.

Yet not long after,§ Your Majesty submitted yourself wholly and entirely to eight persons, called Octavians; and told me that you had

---

* 'I hate', said he, 'those men who are of a lazy disposition and always seem, if one believes them, to practice the art of philosophy.'

† He who does not do what he ought does not receive what he expects.

‡ If you were ruled by reason you would be ruler over many.

§ At the beginning of 1596.

followed my opinion therein, and had submitted simpliciter for your time to these eight persons. I replied that I spoke but for one year: and that I would have named some of the said number, but not all. They were wise men, learned and politic; but the unmeeter that they were choosers of themselves. Yet they began to do better than any had done before them; but they continued not, but divided among themselves, after they had divided the offices of the crown, to every man one: whereas at the first they had given forth that they should plant mean responsible men in the said offices, and they all to be only comptrollers of the said officers. So that many began to grudge against them, seeing them become so soon rich. And perceiving their great backs, the whole subjects and His Majesty's own domestics to follow and depend upon them, and His Majesty to pass through the streets with three or four, as forsaken; because none hoped any more for reward at his hands, but so much as might be had for serving and depending upon the said eight lords: they were also so hated and envied that there was a rebellion raised in Edinburgh against them, in His Majesty's presence,★ partly for the causes specified and also for suspicion of papistry, whereby they fled out of the town, and since would not take upon them the whole government, but were content to be joined with a number of noblemen and others of the council, to the number of twenty four. But the most part of the nobleman tarried not, but came when they were written for to the conventions, as formerly they used. So all this new device turned to the old *sicut antea*.†

★ This refers to a riot on 17 December 1596.   † As before.

Index

Pittarrow, laird of, 79, 86, 98–9
Pittenweem, 70n
— Priory, 83, 96
Prestonpans, 155

Queensferry, 123n

Randolph, 34–6, 40, 49, 75, 87–94 *passim*, 101, 106, 141
Riccio, David, 14, 43–5, 47–52, 58, 106
Ross, Bishop of, 55, 74, 79
Rothes, Earl of, 46, 53, 99, 110
Russell, Sir Francis, 132
Ruthven, Lord, 51, 54, 190n

St Andrews 110–11, 113
— Archbishop of, 108, 112; *see also* Hamilton, John
— castle, 132
— Commendator or Prior of, *see* Moray, Earl of
St Johnston, *see* Perth
St Quentin, 21
Sampsoun, Annie, 155–6
Sanda, Isle of, 19
Sandilands, James, 149
Scot, Robert, 157
Segie, laird of, 113, 116, 129, 132, 143
Seton, house of, 102
— Lord, 76, 122
— of Parbroath, 159
Sharp, John, 108
Shaw, 157
— William, 129
Shetland, 70
Sinclair, Oliver, 9
Sidney, Sir Henry, 39
Skene, John, 145
Smith, 126
Solway Moss, 9
Somerset, Duke of, 9
Spott, laird of, 156–7
Spynie, Lord, 159, 161
Stafford, Lady, 37, 39
Stewart, Colonel, 88, 110, 113, 116, 125, 132–47 *passim*, 152
— Esmé, *see* Lennox, Duke of
— Henry, *see* Darnley, Lord Henry
— Lord James, *see* Moray, Earl of
— James, *see* Arran, Earl of
— James (of Ochiltree), 104–6
— Sir James, 115

— Lady Arabella, 16
— Lord Robert, *see* Orkney, Earl of
— Robert, Bishop of Caithness and Earl of March, 16, 107, 110–11, 113, 132
— Sir William, 132
Stirling; Arran at, 117; James's birth and baptism, 56–64 *passim*; his coronation, 72; his upbringing, 103; his captivity, 109; his court at, 104–5; banished nobles' plan to capture, 124–5, 134; Prince Henry's birth and baptism, 125–6
Sussex, Earl of, 79, 86–7, 165–6
Sutherland, Earl of, 160–1

Tallo, Lord, 70
Tantallon, 83
Theophilus, Dr Nicholas, 129
Thirlestane, Lord, *see* Maitland, John
Throckmorton, Sir Nicholas, 33, 45, 49, 50, 55, 75
Tongland, Lord, 143–4, 166
Traquair, 53
Trent, 50
Tullibardine, laird of, 52, 68, 70, 73, 96, 135

Valence, Bishop of, 19, 20
Vendôme, Duke of, 101
— Marie de, 39
Viennois, 11
Villamonte, M. de, 50

Walsingham, Sir Francis, 18, 121–3, 126
Wauchton, laird of, 75
Wemyss, 45
— Easter, laird of, 165
Westminster, 15, 35
Westmorland, 79n
Whitelaw, laird of, 66, 75
Wood, John, 79–82
Wormiston, laird of, 86, 92
Wotton, 127–9, 132, 134, 138–9
— Doctor, 128

York, 15, 79, 80
Young, Peter, 103, 134, 138, 142–3, 146, 149, 165
Yvers (or Evers or Eure), Lord, 101n